AF531796

An Introduction to Vocational Development

An Introduction to Vocational Development

Govind Tandon

RANDOM PUBLICATIONS
NEW DELHI - 110 002 (INDIA)

An Introduction to Vocational Development

ISBN 978-93-51112-95-2

Published in 2014 in India by

Reprint 2020

RANDOM PUBLICATIONS

4376-A/4B, Gali Murari Lal, Ansari Road
New Delhi-110 002
Phone: +9111-43580356, 23289044
E-mail: randomexports@gmail.com; sales@randompublications.com; info@randompublications.com

Type Setting by: Friends Media, Delhi-110089
Printed at : Mehra Printers, Delhi-110092

Preface

National skills development policies and systems strive to meet labour market needs for skills and to improve productivity and competitiveness in all sectors in which human resources are critical for the integration of skills development into national employment and development strategies. Skills policies and systems encompass technical and vocational training (TVET), workplace learning, informal learning, learning opportunities in the informal and rural economies and education and training for lifelong learning. Skills development is a key factor in the employability of workers and the sustainability of enterprises. One of the objectives of skills development systems is therefore to ensure that the skills acquired match the skills valued in the workplace. Skills development systems must also help workers and enterprises adjust to change and handle new conditions. These may be triggered by climate change, globalization, demographic trends, technological progress or financial crisis. The development of career guidance and development into a global discipline requires a set of theoretical frameworks with universal validity and applications, as well as culture-specific models that could be used to explain career development issues and phenomenon at a local level. The focus of this book is on the five theories of career development that have guided career guidance and counselling practice and research in the past few decades in the USA as well as internationally. People will be more inclined to take on a task if they believe they can succeed. People generally avoid tasks where their self efficacy is low, but engage when it is high. Self efficacy significantly higher than ability can lead to psychological damage. Significantly low self efficacy leads to an inability to grow and expand skills. Optimum levels of self efficacy are a little above ability, which encourages people to tackle challenging tasks and gain valuable experience.

People with higher self efficacy in a task are likely to expend more effort and persist longer than with low efficacy. On the other hand, low self efficacy may provide an incentive to learn more and prepare better than a person with higher self efficacy. Low self efficacy can lead people to believe tasks are harder than they actually are. This leads to poor planning and stress. A person with higher self efficacy will attribute a failure to external factors, whereas a person with lower self efficacy will attribute it to low ability. Self-beliefs about abilities play a central role in the career decision-making process. People move toward those occupations requiring capabilities they think they either have or can develop. People move away from those occupations requiring capabilities they think they do not possess or they cannot develop. Personal goals also influence career behaviours in important ways. Personal goals relate to one's determination to engage in certain activities to produce a particular outcome. Goals help to organize and guide behaviour over long periods of time. Self-efficacy beliefs and outcome expectations in turn shape people's interests, goals, actions, and eventually their attainments.

It is hoped that the book will serve the purpose of students and scholars on the subject and can be useful to them in allied fields.

I thank all members of my team who have helped in the preparation of the book. My special thanks go to "Random Publications" who have published the book.

—Govind Tandon

Contents

1

Introduction

A vocation is an occupation to which a person is specially drawn or for which he or she is suited, trained, or qualified. Though now often used in non-religious contexts, the meanings of the term originated in Christianity. Since the establishment of Vocational Guidance in 1908 by the engineer Frank Parsons, the use of the term "vocation" has evolved, with emphasis shifting to an individual's development of talents and abilities in the choice and enjoyment of a career. This semantic expansion has meant some diminishment of reference to the term's religious meanings in everyday usage.

What is Career Development?

Career development is a lifelong process that is unique for every individual. There are many influences that contribute to your career such as:

Who You are as an Individual

This includes your self-concept, interests, skills, knowledge, personality, ethnicity, age, gender, ability, disability, health, beliefs and sexual orientation. For example, your choice of hobbies reflects your interests and abilities.

Role of Community

The community plays an important role in forming your identity, beliefs and attitudes. Members of your community can be your family, peers, friends or colleagues from your school or workplace, employers, the media, community groups and clubs. They can influence the lifestyle you want to aspire towards, the work you choose, the life roles you take on and what you value about yourself.

The Environment and Wider Society

This refers to the opportunities or constraints caused by factors such as the region or location you live in (ie rural or metropolitan), what is happening in the employment market (eg are there job vacancies in your career field), your socioeconomic status (eg do you have to consider financial commitments such as mortgages or children's education), historical trends (eg changes in women's participation in the workforce) and political decisions (eg government grants available for enterprise development).

Random and unpredictable events may also impact on your career. Different sets of influences will be dominant at different stages in your life as you grow and develop as a person.

For example, in childhood, ideas about life roles and work are expressed in play and are based on the adults with whom you identify strongly.

In adolescence, career exploration is based on identifying interests, abilities, capacities and values; learning about the world of work through observing adults at work; participating in the workforce; and accessing career resources and programmes.

As an adult, your career development becomes more intricate. If you are a mature age reassessing your career options can also help you on your career development path. It can help with the choices you've made regarding lifestyle, the life roles you take on, learning pathways, changing career direction, employment/unemployment, enterprise opportunities, and many other personal life events.

Companies often speak of career development opportunities. Although that sounds intriguing, it is a rather broad term. What exactly does it mean and what opportunities does it include? While career development is defined differently at every organization, there are common elements that should be investigated as you search for a new position or within your current company. As a recruiter at a rapidly growing business technology firm, my team discusses the following points with our potential candidates regarding career development.

- Always remember that YOU own your career - The employer does not own your career. An employer provides opportunities but you are responsible for taking the initiative to utilize the offerings. For example, if you are provided the opportunity to act as a mentor for a novice employee, take advantage of it!

Not only will you help a fellow employee grow within the field, but you too will expand your skill-set by learning how to manage and work with employees at all levels.

- Leadership Opportunities – Organizations offer a track to develop leadership skills. They provide employees seeking to gain leadership experience with opportunities to lead meaningful strategic projects for the company.
- Mentoring Programme – Does your organization offer a mentoring programme? If a programme is already established, ask what the qualifications are to become a mentor? Do you need to be employed for a certain amount of time? Do you need to have any prior managing experience, etc.? Stepping up to the plate and asking for additional responsibility will highlight your eagerness to become more deeply engaged with the organization.
- Defined Career Path - Does your organization provide a roadmap for career success and development? It is both reasonable and appropriate to ask for job expectations. This roadmap will outline what needs to be done in order to exceed your current job requirements while also stating the requirements for you to move to the next level.
- Training and Certification – Many organization offer additional training or compensate for the cost to retrieve required certifications. Proper training and certifications are a critical piece to the quality work we consistently deliver. Our consultants have access to a variety of training courses to encourage learning and development of skills to help them move forward with their career.
- Balanced Value - Companies typically look for a balanced value between the company, client, and employee. The goal of creating balance amongst the three stakeholders will result in a win-win-win model. The basic premise is that a healthy and sustainable relationship is attained by the trust and principled exchange of values between all three components in a balanced transfer of value. In short, this means that a company will strive to retain employees by providing opportunities for growth, recognition, and interesting work. The goal is to keep the employee happy so they deliver quality solutions for the client, which ultimately provides positive results for the company.

What do we Mean by Career Development?

Australian Blueprint for Career Development

Sometimes random and unexpected events can alter our plans. It is important to remember that the attitudes and skills needed to survive and flourish in times of change can be learnt. The Australian Blueprint for Career Development outlines eleven competencies that will help people to effectively negotiate and manage their careers in the dynamic environment of the 21st century. The main aim of the Blueprint is to guide the design of career development programmes in schools, universities and workplaces. However, it is useful for you, as a parent, to have an idea about what these competencies are, and to know that there are practical ways you can provide an environment for your child to learn and practice these skills from a very young age.

Personal Management Competencies

- build and maintain a positive self-image
- interact positively and effectively with others
- change and grow throughout life.

Learning and Work Exploration Competencies

- participate in life-long learning supportive of career goals
- locate and effectively use career information
- understand the relationship between work, society and the economy.

Career Building Competencies

With interest and support from family members, friends, teachers and career development practitioners, young people will learn how best to:

- secure/create and maintain work
- make career enhancing decisions
- maintain balanced life and work roles
- understand the changing nature of life and work roles
- understand, engage in and manage the career building process.

The Nature of Work

Work is a big part of people's lives. There's also a lot of social expectation that people will work. 'Work' is a hard word to define. One person's idea of work can be another person's idea of leisure. Something that you dislike doing at work, you might quite enjoy in a leisure setting. Most dictionary definitions of the word 'work' say that work activity is directed at a specific purpose, and involves mental or physical effort. Is work still work if you don't get paid for it? People work productively in all areas of life without being paid; unpaid work is estimated to be equal to approximately half of Australia's total gross domestic product (GDP). This unpaid work includes:

- housework in households, child care and shopping for the home
- volunteer and community work
- work done free of charge (favours for others).

Why Work?

When you ask people why they work, a lot of them will say they're 'only in it for the money'. When you work for money, you can be financially independent, and have some control over your life.

Sometimes money truly *is* the only reason a person works. But most people have more substantial reasons for working. For example:

- They like to spend their days doing something they're good at.
- They like being productive.
- Other people need their skills, and they feel obliged to supply them.

What if you didn't work and you had every day to yourself? You could choose to go to the beach, watch television, go to the movies, go shopping, read books, visit friends, visit places of interest, go out for meals, play sport...

This all sounds wonderful, but you'd need at least some money to do most of these things. Relaxing and doing what you please is great for a holiday, but after a while the pleasure can wear off and you can feel aimless and bored.

Your Way of Life Depends on Work

What would happen if no-one worked? How would we all survive? The goods and services we need to live and enjoy in our leisure time simply couldn't exist. For example, if you needed to catch a bus:

- Who would design and construct the bus?
- Who would supply the petrol for the bus?
- Who would drive the bus?

If you wanted to read a newspaper:

- Who would write the articles and take the pictures for it?
- Who would make the paper to print it on?
- Who would print it?
- Who would distribute it, and how?

Most Western societies are set up so that we buy essentials like water, food, clothing and shelter, rather than providing them for ourselves individually. We also need things like electricity and transport. Just to exist costs money, and to do any kind of activity will involve costs. Most of us work to meet those costs.

Work and Your Values

The benefits you get from paid and unpaid work are strongly linked to what your values are. When you know what your values are regarding work, you can:

- work out what you hope to achieve through working—what your overall ambitions are
- set meaningful goals for yourself
- choose jobs that will satisfy you in ways that are deeper than your 'hip pocket'
- understand why you feel dissatisfied in a job that doesn't fit with your values.

The two main reasons that people work are:

- to perform rewarding and meaningful activities
- for companionship.

'Rewarding' and 'meaningful' work is work that allows you to:

- fulfil most of your material needs
- meet your financial obligations
- feel as if you fit into and contribute to society
- feel a sense of well-being and accomplishment
- meet and interact with people of different backgrounds and cultures.

Conduct Your own Research About why you Work: 'Companionship' at work means having continued, shared interaction with other people, including sharing the rewards of a job well done, whether they be a sales bonus or a commendation from the managing director.

Job Satisfaction

Rewarding and meaningful work + companionship = job satisfaction

People get job satisfaction when their work:

- pays them enough to fulfil their most important needs
- pays them fairly for the work they do
- looks after them, providing a protective environment and ensuring their safety as they work.
- gives them a social life—they belong to a team and interact regularly with different people
- makes them feel good about themselves—they can see themselves gaining experience, expertise, status and acknowledgement by their colleagues and superiors
- fulfils them—it gives them a sense of personal achievement by presenting them with new challenges, helping them grow and be creative.

Why do you Work? What About your Friends and Family?

Conduct your own research about why people work.

- Think about the reasons why you work. Write down everything you can think of, as each reason occurs to you.
- When you can't think of any more, look at the list you've made and put the reasons in order from the most to the least important.

Interview five people you know and ask them why they work. Here are some questions you could ask them:

- What's the purpose of work, for you?
- Why is work important in your life?
- What would happen if your job didn't get done?
- How did you prepare for your career?
- Why are some people paid more?
- Do you dress in a particular way to go to work? Why?
- What tools do you use in your workplace?

The Course and Cycle of the Working Life

Career describes an individuals' journey through learning, work and other aspects of life. There are a number of ways to define a career and the term is used in a variety of ways.

Career is defined by the Oxford English Dictionary as a person's "course or progress through life (or a distinct portion of life)". In this definition career is understood to relate to a range of aspects of an individual's life, learning and work. Career is also frequently understood to relate only to the working aspects of an individuals life e.g. as in career woman. A third way in which the term career is used to describe an occupation or a profession that usually involves special training or formal education, and is considered to be a person's lifework. In this case "a career" is seen as a sequence of related jobs usually pursued within a single industry or sector e.g. "a career in law" or "a career in the building trade".

The etymology of the term comes from the m. French word carriere (16 c.) ("road, racecourse") which, in turn, comes from the Latin word "(via) cararia" (track for wheeled vehicles) which originated from the Latin word *carrus" which means "wagon".*

Historic Changes in Careers

For a Pre-modernist Notion of "Career", Compare Cursus Honorum: By the late 20th century, a wide range of choices (especially in the range of potential professions) and more widespread education had allowed it to become possible to plan (or design) a career: in this respect the careers of the career counsellor and of the career advisor have grown up.

It is also not uncommon for adults in the late 20th/early 21st centuries to have dual or multiple careers, either sequentially or concurrently. Thus, professional identities have become hyphenated or hybridized to reflect this shift in work ethic. Economist Richard Florida notes this trend generally and more specifically among the "creative class".

Career Management

Career management describes the active and purposeful management of a career by an individual. Ideas of what comprise "career management skills" are describe by the Blueprint model (in the United States, Canada, Australia, Scotland, and England) and the Seven C's of Digital Career Literacy (specifically relating to the Internet skills).

Key skills include the ability to reflect on one's current career, research the labour market, determine whether education is necessary, find openings, and make career changes.

Career Choice

According to Behling and others, an individual's decision to join a firm may depend on any of the three factors viz. objective factor, subjective factor and critical contact.

- Objective factor theory assumes that the applicants are rational. The choice, therefore, is exercised after an objective assessment of the tangible benefits of the job. Factors may include the salary, other benefits, location, opportunities for career advancement, etc.
- Subjective factor theory suggests that decision making is dominated by social and psychological factors. The status of the job, reputation of the organization and other similar factors plays an important role.
- Critical contact theory advances the idea that a candidate's observations while interacting with the organization plays a vital role in decision making. For example, how the recruiter keeps in touch with the candidate, the promptness of response and similar factors are important. This theory is more valid with experienced professionals.

These theories assume that candidates have a free choice of employers and careers. In reality the scarcity of jobs and strong competition for desirable jobs severely skews the decision making process. In many markets employees work particular careers simply because they were forced to accept whatever work was available to them.

Career (Occupation) Changing

Changing occupation is an important aspect of career and career management. Over a lifetime, both the individual and the labour market will change; it is to be expected that many people will change occupations during their lives. Data collected by the U.S. Bureau of Labour Statistics through the National Longitudinal Survey of Youth in 1979 showed that individuals between the ages of 18 and 38 will hold more than 10 jobs.

A survey conducted by Right Management suggests the following reasons for career changing.

- The downsizing or the restructuring of an organization (54%).
- New challenges or opportunities that arise (30%).
- Poor or ineffective leadership (25%).

- Having a poor relationship with a manager(s) (22%).
- For the improvement of work/life balance (21%).
- Contributions are not being recognized (21%).
- For better compensation and benefits (18%),
- For better alignment with personal and organizational values (17%).
- Personal strengths and capabilities are not a good fit with an organization (16%).
- The financial instability of an organization (13%).
- An organization relocated (12%).

According to an article on Time.com, one out of three people currently employed (as of 2008) spends about an hour per day searching for another position.

Career Support

There are a range of different educational, counselling and human resource management interventions that can support individuals to develop and manage their careers.

Career support is commonly offered while people are in education, when they are transitioning to the labour market, when they are changing career, during periods of unemployment, and during transition to retirement.

Support may be offered by career professionals, other professionals or by non-professionals such as family and friends. Professional career support is sometimes known as "career guidance" as in the OECD definition of career guidance:

The activities may take place on an individual or group basis, and may be face-to-face or at a distance (including helplines and web-based services).

They include career information provision (in print, ICT-based and other forms), assessment and self-assessment tools, counselling interviews, career education programmes (to help individuals develop their self-awareness, opportunity awareness, and career management skills), taster programmes (to sample options before choosing them), work search programmes, and transition services."

However this use of the term "career guidance" can be confusing as the term is also commonly used to describe the activities of career counsellors.

Provision of Career Support

Career support is offered by a range of different mechanisms. Much career support is informal and provided through personal networks or existing relationships such as management. There is a market for private career support however the bulk of career support that exists as a professionalised activity is provided by the public sector.

Types of Career Support

Key types of career support include:

- Career information describes information that supports career and learning choices. An important sub-set of career information is labour market information (LMI), such as salaries of various professions, employment rate in various professions, available training programmes, and current job openings and .
- Career assessments are tests that come in a variety of forms and rely on both quantitative and qualitative methodologies. Career assessments can help individuals identify and better articulate their unique interests, personality, values, and skills to determine how well they may match with a certain career. Some skills that career assessments could help determine are job-specific skills, transferable skills, and self-management skills. Career assessments can also provide a window of potential opportunities by helping individuals discover the tasks, experience, education and training that is needed for a career they would want to pursue. Career counselors, executive coaches, educational institutions, career development centres, and outplacement companies often administer career assessments to help individuals focus their search on careers that closely match their unique personal profile.
- Career counselling assesses people's interests, personality, values and skills, and helps them to explore career options and research graduate and professional schools. Career counselling provides one-on-one or group professional assistance in exploration and decision making tasks related to choosing a major/occupation, transitioning into the world of work or further professional training.
- Career education describes a process by which individuals come to learn about themselves, their careers and the world of work. There is a strong tradition of career education in

schools, however career education can also occur in a wider range of other contexts including further and higher education and the workplace. A commonly used framework for careers education is DOTS which stands for decision learning (D), opportunity awareness (O), transition learning (T), and self-awareness (S). Oftentimes, higher education is thought of as being too narrow or too researched based and lacking of a deeper understanding of the material to develop the skills necessary for a certain career.

Some research shows adding one year of schooling beyond high school creates an increase of wages 17.8 percent per worker. However, additional years of schooling, beyond 9 or 10 years, have little effect on worker's wages. In summary, better educated, bigger benefits. In 2010, 90% of the U.S. Workforce had a high school diploma, 64% had some college, and 34% had at least a bachelor's degree.

The common problem that people may encounter when trying to achieve an education for a career is the cost. The career that comes with the education must pay well enough to be able to pay off the schooling. The benefits of schooling can differ greatly depending on the degree (or certification) obtained, the programmes the school may offer, and the ranking of the school. Sometimes, colleges provide students more with just education to prepare for careers. It is not uncommon for colleges to provide pathways and support straight into the workforce the students may desire.

Daniel Levinson Theories of Life Stages and Human Development

Daniel Levinson graduated from Yale as a psychologist. He later developed a comprehensive theory of adult development. This theory is important because it is one of the only ones which suggests that development and growth happens well into the adult years.

At the centre of Levinson's theory is the life structure. This is an underlying pattern of an individual's life at any given point in time. A person's life structure is shaped mainly by their social and physical environment, and it primarily involves family and work. Other variables such as religion, race, and status are often important as well.

In his theory there are two key concepts:

1) *the Stable Period* - This is the time when a person makes crucial choices in life.

2) *the Transitional Period* - This is the end of a person's stage and the beginning of a new one. Life during these transitions can be either rocky or smooth, but the quality and significance of one's life commitments often change between the beginning and end of a period.

There are 6 stages of adulthood in Levinson's theory titled "Seasons of a Man's Life":

1) *Early adult transition (17-22)* - leave adolescence, make preliminary choices for adult life
2) *Entering the adult world (22-28)* - make initial choices in love, occupation, friendship, values, lifestyle
3) *Age 30 transition (28-33)* - changes occur in life structure, either a moderate change or, more often, a severe and stressful crisis
4) *Settling down (33-40)* - establish a niche in society, progress on a timetable, in both family and career accomplishments; are expected to think and behave like a parent so they are facing more demanding roles and expectations .
5) *Mid-life transition (40-45)* - life structure comes into question, usually a time of crisis in the meaning, direction, and value of each person's life. neglected parts of the self (talents, desires, aspirations) seek expression. Men are seen more as parents than as "brothers" to other men who are somewhat younger than them and this message comes as an irritation at first. Also at this time, men becoming increasingly aware of death and they are reminded of how short life really is. They become involved in trying to leave a legacy and this usually forms the core of the second half of his life.
6) *Entering middle adulthood (45-50)* - choices must be made, a new life structure formed. person must commit to new tasks.

* Some sources also stated that there was a *late adulthood* stage during which time a man spent time reflecting on past achievements and regrets, and making peace with one's self and others (including God).

** Daniel Levinson later went on to write a book titled "Seasons of a Woman's Life".

Problems with Levinson's theory: Daniel Levinson collected the data for his study many decades ago, shortly after the Great

Depression ended. Due to the time period, the men used for this study have 3 things in common:

1) they come from stable families
2) they had realistic goals for their life
3) became adults in an expanding economy

Men who have grown up in the last four or five decades , however, have had to deal with less stable families due to high divorce rates, and they tend to have goals which are much more difficult to achieve. They have also had to deal with a fluctuating economy, and because of these differences it is difficult to apply Levinson's studies to today's generation.

How Does this Theory Apply to School?

Since most most sources state that Levinson's theory begins at the age of 17 in the "Early Adult Transition", there isnt any reference to how one develops during the school years.

How Does This Theory Apply to Society?

"There are a number of attitudes expressed which would appear to have an affect on society. Firstly, many people are making the transition from youth to adulthood without any hope or optimism. This says that society as a whole throughout this age bracket is lacking enthusiasm and drive.

When men near the age of thirty, they have new expectations in society such as to provide for their children and aging parents. They are seen more as fathers than they were previously. The occurance of a culminating event in a man's life surfaces the midlife transition stage. When this happens, men usually become interested in acts of humanitarianism, and they are more cautious as they come to terms with the reality of death.

How Does This Theory Apply to the Workplace?

***In Levinson's Book he*:** Once men reach the age of thirty, or so, they are taking more senior positions in their jobs as their focus is to provide care for their children and their aging parents. Once a man reaches his forties, he begins questioning, "Is this all I am going to do for the rest of my life?". This often causes one to drastically change their field of work, an act that has come to be known as a "midlife crisis". By this age, men have often made the amount of money that they desire and so they begin looking into jobs that benefit others.

Adolescence as Exploration: Developing a Self Concept

Changes in adolescent physical and cognitive development are also accompanied by major changes in an adolescent's relationships with others, including family members and friends.

Family relationships are often reorganized with the onset of puberty, the desire for increased autonomy, and increased emotional distance between teens and their parents.

Adolescent attention often shifts to a more intense focus on social interactions and friendships expanding from same-sex friends to same-sex groups of friends to heterosexual groups of friends. Sexual maturity marks the need to reorganize friendships again to include an increased interest in dating and sexual relationships.

Developmental Changes in Relationship With Self

It is also during adolescence, with a focus on changing relationships with others, that a new understanding of one's self emerges. This may include changes in the following self-concepts:

- Independence. Independence is defined as making decisions for one's self and acting on the basis of one's own thought processes, judgement, and decision-making. Part of the developmental process for adolescents is to learn to work out one's own problems independently. With increasing cognitive and intuitive abilities, adolescents begin to face new responsibilities and to enjoy independent thoughts and actions. Adolescents begin to have thoughts and fantasies about their future and adult life (for example, college or job training, work, and marriage).
- Identity. Identity is defined as a sense of self or self-knowledge about one's characteristics, or personality. One of the fundamental tasks of adolescence is to achieve a sense of a personal identity and a secure sense of self. As an adolescent gains comfort with, and acceptance of, a more mature physical body, learns to use his or her own judgement, learns to make decisions independently, and addresses his or her own problems, he or she begins to develop a concept of himself or herself as an individual, and thus an identity. Difficulty in developing a clear concept of self or identity occurs when an adolescent is unable to resolve struggles about who he or she is as a physical, sexual, and independent person.

- Self-esteem. Self-esteem is defined as the feelings one has about one's self. Self-esteem is determined by answering the question "How much do I like myself?" With the onset of adolescence, a decrease in self-esteem is somewhat common—based on the many body changes occurring, new thoughts being developed, and new ways of thinking about things. During adolescence, teens become more thoughtful about who they are and who they want to be. They notice differences in the way they act and the way they think they should act. Once teens start thinking about their actions and characteristics, they are confronted with how they judge themselves. Many adolescents tend to place importance on attractiveness. When teens do not perceive themselves as attractive, it often causes poor self-esteem. Typically, self-esteem increases during late adolescence as teens develop a better sense of who they are.

Developmental Changes in Peer Relationships

The amount of time spent with friends increases during the course of adolescence. Most often, teenagers enjoy the time they spend with their friends more than other activities. They report feeling more understood and accepted by their friends. Less and less time is spent with parents and other family members.

Close friendships tend to develop between teens that are more similar in nature, interest, social class, and ethnic backgrounds, than younger age friendships. While childhood friendships tend to be based on common activities, adolescent friendships expand to include similarities in attitudes, values, as well as shared activities. Teen friendships also tend to be based on similarities in the level of involvement in academic and educational interest. Especially for girls, close, intimate, self-disclosing conversations with friends help to explore identities and define one's sense of self. Conversations within these important friendships also assist adolescents in exploring their sexuality and how they feel about it. The friendships of adolescent boys tend to be less intimate than those of girls. Boys are more prone to form an alliance with a group of friends who validate each other's worth through actions and deeds rather than interpersonal disclosure.

Developmental Changes in Male-female Relationships

The adolescent transition to male-female and sexual relationships is influenced by sexual interest and by social and cultural influences and expectations. Social and cultural expectations and behaviours in male-female or sexual relationships are learned from observations and practice. During adolescence, developmental tasks include struggles to gain control over sexual and aggressive urges, and discovering potential or actual love relationships. Sexual behaviours during adolescence may include impulsive behaviour, a wide range of experimental interactions of mutual exploring, and eventually intercourse. Biological differences, and differences in the socialization of males and females, set the stage for males and females to have different expectations of sexual and love relationships that may influence sexual experiences and may also have consequences for later sexual behaviour and partnerships. Ultimately, achievement of a mutually satisfying sexual partnership within a love relationship may be established.

Developmental Changes in Family Relationships

One of the developmental tasks of adolescence is to achieve separation from one's family as one emerges into an independent young adult. A part of this process is coming to terms with specific feelings about one's family. During adolescence, teens begin to realize that their parents and significant authority figures do not know everything or have solutions to all types of struggles.

Some teenage rebellion against parents is common and normal. With the onset of puberty, adolescent females tend to have more disagreements with their mothers. Adolescent males, especially those who mature early, also tend to have more disagreements with their mothers than with their fathers. While over time disagreements often decrease, adolescent relationships with mothers tend to change more than adolescent relationships with fathers. As adolescents become more independent from their parents, they are more likely to turn to their peers for advice.

Self Concept

One's self-concept (also called self-construction, self-identity or self-perspective) is a collection of beliefs about oneself that includes elements such as academic performance, gender roles and sexuality, racial identity, and many others. Generally, self-concept embodies the answer to "Who am I?"

Self-concept is distinguishable from self-awareness, which refers to the extent to which self-knowledge is clearly defined, consistent and currently applicable to one's attitudes and dispositions. Self-concept is made up of one's self-schemas. Additionally, self-concept interacts with self-esteem, self-knowledge, and social self to form the self. Self-esteem refers to the evaluation or comparison of one's self-concept and self-schemas to form one's overall self-worth.

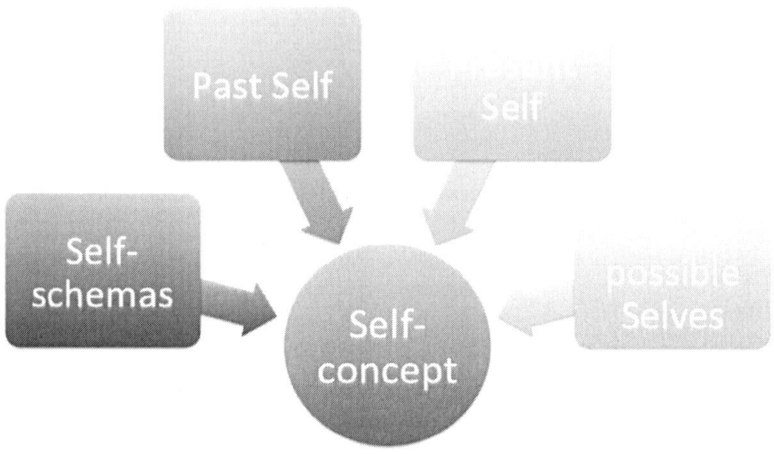

Figure: *One's self-concept is made up of self-schemas, their past, present and future selves.*

The self-concept includes past, present and future selves. Future or possible selves represent individuals' ideas of what they might become, what they would like to become, or what they are afraid of becoming. These different selves correspond to one's hopes, fears, standards, goals, and threats for their present selves.

Possible selves may function as incentives for future behaviour and also provide an evaluative and interpretive context for the current view of self that is used when one self-evaluates, contributing to one's self-esteem. Self-esteem and self-concept cannot be used interchangeably. Self-esteem focuses on an evaluative and opinionated aspect to one's self (e.g., I feel good about the fact that I am a fast runner), whereas self-concept is more of a cognitive or descriptive component to one's self (e.g., I am a fast runner). This distinction is important to note, as self-concept and self-esteem closely interact to form an overall view of the self.

The perception which people have about their past or future selves is related to the perception of their current self. The temporal self-appraisal theory argues that people have a tendency to maintain a positive evaluation of the current self by distancing their self-concepts from their negative selves and paying more attention to their positive selves. In addition, people have a tendency to perceive the past self less favourably (e.g., I'm better than I used to be) and the future self more positively (e.g., I will be better than I am now).

Psychologists Carl Rogers and Abraham Maslow paved the way for this concept. According to Rogers, everyone strives to become more like an "ideal self". The closer one is to their ideal self, the happier one will be. Rogers also claimed that one factor in a person's happiness is unconditional positive regard, or UPR, from others. UPR often occurs in close or familial relationships, and involves a consistent level of affection regardless of the recipient's actions. Rogers explained UPR as neither approving nor disapproving of someone based on their behaviours or characteristics but rather accepting them without judgement. From a therapy frame of reference, Rogers identified the significance of a client perceiving a therapist's UPR towards them, so that the client would not feel judged as they attempt to accurately express themselves. Evidence of UPR in self-concept research is apparent in studies by Benner and Mistry (2007) and Tiedemann (2000). Research has indicated that adolescents whose mothers and teachers had high expectations for their future educational attainment experienced more academic success than those whose adult influences had lower expectations. Adults' high expectations for children are also reported as being important buffers from the negative effects of other parties' low expectations by developing feelings of positive regard in adolescents. In research about parent stereotypes, the correlation between parents' beliefs about their early elementary age children's mathematics abilities and the children's actual abilities increased as children aged. This demonstrates the strong relationship between adults' beliefs about children and children's beliefs about themselves, indicating the importance of developing unconditional positive regard for students so they can develop it themselves.

An important theory related to self-concept is the self-categorization theory (SCT), which states that the self-concept consists of at least two "levels," a personal identity and a social identity. In other words, one's self-evaluation rely on both one's self-perceptions and how one fits in socially. The self-concept can alternate rapidly between the personal and social identity. Research by Trautwein et al.(2009) indicates that children and adolescents begin integrating social comparison information into their own self-concept in elementary school by assessing their position among their peers. Gest et al.'s (2008) research findings reveal that peer acceptance has a significant impact on one's self-concept by age 5, affecting children's behaviour and academic success. Both of these research examples demonstrate the social influences on a person's self-concept.

Model of Self-concept

The self-concept is an internal model that uses self-assessments in order to define one's self-schemas. Features such as personality, skills and abilities, occupation(s) and hobbies, physical characteristics, etc. are assessed and applied to self-schemas, which are ideas one has of oneself in a particular dimension (e.g., someone that considers themselves a geek will associate geek-like qualities and be an expert on those qualities). A collection of self-schemas make up one's overall self-concept. For example, the statement "I am lazy" is a self-assessment that contributes to the self-concept. It is important to note that statements such as "I am tired" would not be part of someone's self-concept, since being tired is a temporary emotional state and therefore cannot become a part of a self-schema. A person's self-concept may change with time as reassessment occurs, which in extreme cases can lead to identity crises.

Academic Self-concept

Academic Self-Concept (ASC) refers to the personal beliefs someone develops about their academic abilities or skills. A person's ASC develops and evolves as they age. Some research suggests that ASC begins developing in early childhood, from age 3 to 5, due to parental/ family and early educators' influences, While other research contends that ASC does not develop until age 7 or 8, when children begin evaluating their own academic abilities based on the feedback they receive from parents, teachers and their peers. By age 10 or 11, children view their academic abilities by comparing themselves to their peers. These social comparisons are also referred to as self-estimates. Self-estimates are frequently utilized to help one form an idea of oneself. Research shows that self-estimates of cognitive ability were most accurate when numerical ability was estimated. Furthermore, research shows that self-estimates were more likely to be poor in other areas of cognitive ability such as reasoning speed that are considered less frequently.

There are a variety of social factors that contribute to development of an ASC and developing a positive ASC has been related to people's behaviours and emotions in other domains of their life, influencing happiness, self-esteem, and anxiety levels to name a few. Due to the significant impact ASC has on a person's life, it has been argued that educational systems should foster positive self-concept development in children.

These research findings are important because they have practical implications for parents and teachers. Research indicates that parents and teachers need to provide children with specific feedback that focuses on their particular skills or expressed abilities in order to increase ASC. Other research suggests that learning opportunities should be conducted in a variety of mixed-ability and like-ability groupings that down-play social comparison because too much of either type of grouping can have adverse effects on children's ASC in the way they view themselves in relation to their peers.

Effects of Success and Failure

Various studies have examined the effects that success and failure can have on an individual's self-concept. Individuals often form their self-concept based on past experiences of success or failure, attributing the outcome to their own personal worth. By doing this, individuals can commit the fundamental attribution error. In this case, the error may arise when the person falsely believes that a specific aspect of who they are determined the positive or negative outcome. By attributing a negative outcome to oneself, self-concept can be unnecessarily harmed. However, attributing positive outcomes to oneself can increase self-concept. These attributions can even have an effect on self-perception, achievement behaviours in the future, and expectancies. Austin and Vispoel (1998) found strong links between where an individual attributed success or failure and, specifically, musical self-concept.

Changes in self-concept can be mediated and predicted by various factors. One important factor in academics is evaluation of performance by peers, or peer academic reputation (PAR). Gest, Rulison, Davidson, and Welsh (2008) found evidence for the predictive ability of PAR with regard to students' in upper grades academic self-concept. If a student has a reputation for success or failure in the academic setting, the student may develop a negative self-concept. This shows that it is may not only be the actual success or failure that has an effect, but may also be the secondary effects of poor academic reputation among peers that influence students' self-concept.

There are also effects that have been studying by looking at how self-concept can influence success or failure and attributions of success and failure. In a study of university undergraduate students, self-esteem was studied by examining students' attributions for their success or failure after being given a word association test. Dutton and Brown (1997) found that self-esteem could predict participants' attribution of their success or failure in the word test. Individuals with high self-esteem tended to make more self-serving attributions to outcomes than did individuals with low self-esteem.

Expectations, Conditioning, and Gauging

According to Kathleen Berger, author of *The Developing Person*, guilt plays a significant role in shaping a young child's self-concept. As an example, she describes a child that is coddled at home, and his/her socially unacceptable behaviour is never thwarted by the parent(s). When the child is denied whatever they want from another child, he/she strikes out towards other children, not understanding that there will be consequences and possible retaliation. If this kind of behaviour were to occur in a classroom environment, a teacher could use guilt in an attempt to shape the spoiled child's self-concept by reminding the student that hitting others is not acceptable in most social situations. In essence, guilt shapes behaviour. Berger goes on to explain that most children over the age of 5 have some sense of the rules and regulations that govern social behaviour that they learn from a guardian, thus shaping their self-concept without using guilt. In some cases, if maladaptive behaviour is left unchecked, the seeds of bullying could start to germinate.

Self-concept is linked directly to a person's level of anxiety, according to the humanistic psychologist Carl Rogers. According to Rogers, if a child feels highly valued and wanted, that person is more likely to grow up with a positive self-image, with the possibility of becoming self-actualized. Rogers describes this individual as a *fully functioning person* with a low level of anxiety, which he attributes to inconsistencies between self-perceptions and possible-self. Here again, expectations play a major role in shaping self-concept. Dr. Rogers hypothesizes that psychologically healthy people actively move away from roles created by others' expectations but instead look within themselves for validation.

"Neurotic and psychotic people, on the other hand, have self-concepts that do not match their experiences.. They are afraid to accept their own experiences as valid, so they distort them, either to protect themselves or to win approval from others." Children learn at an early age that certain conditions will be placed upon them in exchange for approval or love from the parents. For example, a parent may tell a child that he/she must love the new baby sister or brother, or else Mommy and Daddy won't love them. This kind of hostage mentality could harbor and suppress negative ill will towards the new baby which will eventually express itself later on in life.

To gauge a child's self-concept, Susan Harter developed the Self-Perception Profile for Adolescents. In it, domains such as scholastic competence, behaviour conduct, close friendships, social acceptance, athletic competence, romantic appeal, and physical appearance are rated using a number of indicators. Some of the positive indicators include whether the child or adolescent expresses their opinion, maintains eye contact during conversion, works cooperatively in a group, maintains a comfortable space between self and others, and uses proper voice levels for various situation. Negative indicators could include teasing, gossiping, using dramatic gesturing, engaging in inappropriate touching or avoiding physical contact, verbally putting down self or others, or bragging about achievements, skills, or appearance.

Cultural Differences

Worldviews about the self in relation to others differs across and within cultures. In Western cultures, an individualistic and independent approach is adopted where society places particular importance on becoming independent and to express one's own attributes. Relationships, memberships, groups, and their needs and goals, tend to be secondary to the self. Self-assessment of one's self-concept also includes social comparisons. The Social comparison theory states that people strive to accurately define themselves and therefore utilize social comparisons to accurately define the self during the self-evaluative process. Within these social comparisons, one will find upward (e.g., positive) and downward (e.g., negative) comparisons that can either enhance or threaten our self-concept and self-esteem. In such cases where we feel threatened, it is not uncommon to make explanations for why we are not performing to the same degree as others, thereby preserving our self-concept and self-esteem. In Asian cultures, an interdependent view of the self is more prevalent and these cultures often experience identity fusion more frequently. Interpersonal relationships are more central than one's individual accomplishments, as individuals experience a sense of oneness with the group. Great emphasis is placed on these relationships, and the self is seen primarily as an integral part of society. Research has shown that this identity fusion can have positive and negative consequences. The positive impact that identity fusion can have on people is that they feel that their existence is meaningful (e.g., Japanese nuclear plant workers expose themselves to radiation to help fix the plant after a tsunami) and this type of mindset is associated with a high quality of life. On the other hand, such strong interdependence can lead to catastrophic events (e.g., acts of terrorism).

A study published in the International Journal of Intercultural Relations gives another division of the independent and interdependent selves based on subcultures. A small study done in Israel shows the different characteristics most prevalent of mid-level merchants in an urban community versus those in a communal settlement, called the kibbutz. Similar to the Western v. non-Western perspectives, the collectivist members valued the interdependent self more that the urban members. Likewise, the urban samples held more value to independent traits than the kibbutz. Both answered with more independent traits than interdependent. The study divided the independent and interdependent traits into subcategories to further define what are the most valued by the two subcultures. On the independent scale, personal traits showed the greatest prevalence for the individualists, while hobbies and preferences were greater for the collectivists. Work and school were the most frequently described interdependent responses for the urban sector, while residence was most often referred to by the kibbutz. Overall, the study intensifies the knowledge that self-concept depends on inner attributes, abilities, and opinions from the community based on collective ideology. Further studies on other subcultures would be needed to create a generalization on a wider scale.

Gender Differences

Gender has also been shown to be an important factor in the formation of self-concept. Early research inspired by the differences in self-concept across culture suggested that men tend to be more independent while women tend to be more interdependent. Independent self-construct refers to the fact that representations of others are separate from the self. Interdependent self-construct refers to the fact that representations of others are considered as part of the self. However, more recent research has shown that, while men and women do not differ between independence and interdependence generally, they do differ in the distinction between relational and collective interdependence. Men utilize collective interdependence while women utilize relational interdependence. In other words, women identify more with dyadic (one-on-one) relationships or small cliques, whereas men define themselves more often within the context of larger groups. Research also shows that as gender roles become blurred in Western society (e.g., more men are staying at home and women are being empowered in the workplace), these differences may change.

Women have often been stereotyped as being more emotional than men. This area of gender differences is important to research, as self-concepts that encompass gender may also encompass the self-conscious emotions or tendencies associated with gender. Women, for example, allegedly show more guilt, shame and embarrassment whereas men show more pride. Research shows that women in fact do show more guilt, shame and embarrassment than men but that men and women show the same amount of pride. Furthermore, gender differences in self-conscious emotions are different between ethnicities and are greatest within white populations when compared to Black or African, Asian, and Latin American samples. More research in this area is needed to extrapolate the gender differences across different cultures and ethnicities, as most of the samples used in gender studies are White samples. This reliance on a specific sample can lead researchers to overestimate the magnitude of gender differences in terms of emotions of women in comparison to men.

The Developmental Perspective

Research by Tiedemann (2000) found that parents' and teachers' gender stereotypes about children's mathematical abilities influenced children's self-concepts about their mathematical ability prior to having extensive experience with math in school. Tiedemann's (2000) research findings also indicate that the correlation between adult's gendered stereotypes and children's beliefs about themselves increased as children aged throughout elementary school. Additional research by Benner and Mistry (2007) indicates that parent's initial expectations for their children, during early childhood, correlate with children's academic success. These findings highlight the influence of adult stereotypes and expectations on children's self-concept formation.

Research by Eleanor Maccoby (1990) found that boys and girls choose same-sex play partners by age 3 and maintain their preferences until late elementary school. Boys and girls become involved in different social interactions and relationships. Girls tend to prefer one-on-one dyadic interaction, while boys prefer group activities. Girls tend to share secrets and form tight, intimate bonds with one another. Furthermore, girls are more likely to wait their turn to speak, agree with others, and acknowledge the contributions of others. Boys, on the other hand, build larger group relationships based on shared interests and activities. Boys are more likely to threaten, boast, and call names, suggesting the importance of dominance and hierarchy in groups of male friends. Subsequently, the social characteristics of boys and girls tend to carry over later in life as they become men and women.

Researchers debate when self-concept development begins but agree on the importance of person's life. Tiedemann (2000) indicates that parents' gender stereotypes and expectations for their children impact children's understandings of themselves by approximately age 3. Others suggest that self-concept develops later, around age 7 or 8, as children are developmentally prepared to begin interpreting their own feelings, abilities, and interpretations of feedback they receive from parents, teachers, and peers about themselves. Despite differing opinions about the onset of self-concept development, researchers agree on the importance of one's self-concept, which influences people's behaviours and cognitive and emotional outcomes including (but not limited to) academic achievement, levels of happiness, anxiety, social integration, self-esteem, and life-satisfaction.

Empirical Evidence

In a 1999 study by Gabriel and Gardner, five separate experiments were conducted to demonstrate gender differences in self-concept: a 20 statement test evaluating self-construal ("I am..." statements), a series of surveys evaluating trait identification, an exercise evaluating selective memory for emotional events, a diary reading paradigm evaluating selective memory, and a survey concerning a situational dilemma evaluating behavioural intention and desire to behave. Each of these five studies showed in no significant difference between men and women in levels of independence. However, they were able to show a bias among women toward relational interdependence and a bias among men toward collective interdependence in affect, cognition, and behaviour. Other psychologists have postulated that men display an independent concept while women display an interdependent self-concept. One study exploring this aimed to discover whether gender stereotypes have an effect on this gender difference in self-construal. Participants read a list of traits and rated the extent to which the traits applied to a typical man, a typical woman, and the self. When rating men and women in general, both males and females displayed a stereotype for "relational" women (focused on their relationships with others) and "agentic" men (focused on themselves and their individual accomplishments). Self-ratings also corresponded to these stereotypes. The researchers then hypothesized that the stereotypes themselves contribute to the difference in self-construal, and found that this effect is more potent for women than for men. One possible explanation for this imbalance is that "relational" traits tend to be more positively viewed than "agentic" traits, and therefore participants are more likely to apply relational traits to themselves. This research supports the SCT, showing that one's self-concept is affected by the interplay of self-assessments and social roles (in this case, belonging to the larger group of males or females).

One study, focusing on the developmental perspective, aimed to discover girls' and boys' preferences for socialization. Thirty-three-month-old children were assigned to play in pairs. Some pairs were same-sex, others were mixed. Researchers measured both positive and negative social behaviours during play. Both boys and girls had higher levels of social behaviour when playing with the same sex than with the opposite sex. In addition, in the mixed-sex pairs, girls were more likely to passively watch a male partner play than vice versa. Boys were more likely to be unresponsive to what their female partners were saying than vice versa.

Another study observed performance in unisex and mixed-sex groups of children. 10-year-old children were placed in either all-male pairs, all-male groups, all-female pairs, or all-female groups. The children were given a task that was equally interesting to males and females. The results of the study found significant correlation between sex of the participants and social structure. Boys performed almost twice as well in groups than in pairs, whereas girls did not show a significant difference. The increased productivity of boys in groups was expected due to the greater number of participants, whereas girls did not benefit from more participants.

The Transition From School to Work: reality Testing

School-to-work transition is a phrase referring to on-the-job training, apprenticeships, cooperative education agreements or other programmes designed to prepare students to enter the job market. This education system is primarily employed in the United States, partially as a response to work training as it is done in Asia.

School to Work is a system to introduce the philosophy of school-based, work-based, and connecting activities as early as kindergarten to expose students to potential future careers. School to Work emphasizes lifelong learning.

School to Work is funded and sponsored at the federal level by the U.S. Department of Labour and U.S. Department of Education. At the state level in states like Arizona, the grant is administered by the Arizona Department of Commerce, School to Work Division. This grant was funded for a maximum of five years with decreasing funds years three through five;

An example of county level involvement is the Cochise County School to Work Consortia in Arizona. It is composed of more than fifty Cochise County public and private schools, kindergarten through four-year university level, local and community-based organizations, and more than one hundred supporting business partners.

STW is part of a comprehensive education reform movement which includes formulating new standards which emphasize higher order thinking skills, new standards based assessments, and graduation exams, such as the Certificate of Initial Mastery which insure that students are ready for job training or college prep by age 16. Reformers believe that it is important and egalitarian that all students graduate ready for jobs and ready for college, rather than tracking students one way or the other.

Critics

"Back to basics" traditionalists observe that in Europe, apprenticeships typically mean that the worker essentially ends their formal education after age 16, and works full-time at reduced pay in exchange for learning "job skills" such as assembling automobiles. Some believe that it was better to have students who were not bound for college concentrate on career schools, while academic students should spend class time learning core academic subjects such as history or science rather than job-shadowing at a hospital or auto dealer. A student in North Dakota would have little opportunity to learn to be an auto designer, while one in Alabama would have little opportunity to do job shadowing at a major software company if job training were allocated according to local human resource needs, as many programmes are structured. Local businesses also need to structure their operations to accommodate student workers, and transportation since typically schools are situated close to homes, and not businesses which are typically a car or transit commute away from homes.

The Michigan STW Initiative states "students work without pay for two to three hours each day" and "students are able to perform what might otherwise be hazardous order work." which would contradict child labour laws. Data would be shared with state STW partnership network and local labour market areas which might be an invasion of privacy.

The state would utilize the national industry-recognized skill certificates when developed, which would be the Certificate of Initial Mastery. Critics call this a government-controlled passport to work. Michigan Rep. Harold J. Voorhees expressed concern that, with full implementation, a child would not be employed without this Certificate.

2

Outcome-based Education

Methods of outcome-based education (OBE) are student-centred learning methods that focus on empirically measuring student performance (the "outcome"). OBE contrasts with traditional education, which primarily focuses on the resources that are available to the student, which are called *inputs*. While OBE implementations often incorporate a host of many progressive pedagogical models and ideas, such as reform mathematics, block scheduling, project-based learning and whole language reading, OBE in itself does not specify or require *any* particular style of teaching or learning. Instead, it requires the students to demonstrate what they have learned the required skills and content. However in practice, OBE generally promotes curricula and assessment based on constructivist methods and discourages traditional education approaches based on direct instruction of facts and standard methods.

Each independent education agency specifies its own outcomes and its own methods of measuring student achievement according to those outcomes. The results of these measurements can be used for different purposes. For example, one agency may use the information to determine how well the overall education system is performing, and another may use its assessments to determine whether an individual student has learned required material.

Outcome-based methods have been adopted for large numbers of students in several countries. In the United States, the Texas Assessment of Academic Skills started in 1991. In Australia, implementation of OBE in Western Australia was widely criticised by parents and teachers and was mostly dropped in January 2007. In

South Africa, OBE was dropped in mid-2010. On a smaller scale, some OBE practices, such as not passing a student who does not know the required material, have been used by individual teachers around the world for centuries.

OBE was a popular term in the United States during the 1980s and early 1990s. It is also called mastery education, performance-based education, and other names.

What is OBE?

The effort, often by a state or local education agency, to organize all the features of schooling (including aims, curriculum, instruction, and assessment) so as to produce specifically delineated results (often including noncognitive as well as cognitive results) and generally with the expectation that all students will demonstrate such results.

Outcome-based education is an effort of education that converges the traditional focus on what the school provides (Means + Ends) to students, in favour of making students demonstrate that they "know and are able to do" whatever the required outcomes (Final_cause) are.

OBE reforms emphasize setting clear standards for observable, measurable outcomes. A significant body of deductive sources at ERIC Database provide peer-reviewed research material about OBE requirements that enhance the adoption of specific outcomes. For example, many countries write their OBE standards so that they focus on mathematics, language, science, and history, without referring to attitudes, social skills, or moral values. Yet, a body of exceptions is gaining here: social skills for labour & job market, the reduction of youth unemployment is a moral value (International Labour Office ILO on Youth Employment Crisis).

The key features which may be used to judge if a system has implemented an outcomes-based education systems are:

- Creation of a curriculum framework that outlines specific, measurable outcomes. The standards included in the frameworks are usually chosen through the area's normal political process.
- A commitment not only to provide an opportunity of education, but to require learning outcomes for advancement. Promotion to the next grade, a diploma, or other reward is granted upon achievement of the standards, while extra classes, repeating the year, or other consequences entail upon those who do not meet the standards.

- Standards-based assessments that determines whether students have achieved the stated standard. Assessments may take *any* form, so long as the assessments actually measure whether the student knows the required information or can perform the required task.
- A commitment that all students of all groups will ultimately reach the same minimum standards. Schools may not "give up" on unsuccessful students.

Outcomes

The emphasis in an OBE education system is on measured outcomes rather than "inputs," such as how many hours students spend in class, or what textbooks are provided. Outcomes may include a range of skills and knowledge, reduction of youth unemployment, return-on-investment.

Generally, outcomes are expected to be concretely measurable, that is, "Student can run 50 metres in less than one minute" instead of "Student enjoys physical education class." A complete system of outcomes for a subject area normally includes everything from mere recitation of fact ("Students will name three tragedies written by Shakespeare") to complex analysis and interpretation ("Student will analyze the social context of a Shakespearean tragedy in an essay"). Writing appropriate and measurable outcomes can be very difficult, and the choice of specific outcomes is often a source of local controversies.

Each educational agency is responsible for setting its own outcomes. Under the OBE model, education agencies may specify any outcome (skills and knowledge), but not inputs (field trips, arrangement of the school day, teaching styles). Some popular models of outcomes include the National Science Education Standards and the NCTM's Principles and Standards for School Mathematics, as well as European Union's Rethinking Education.

Approaches to Grading, Reporting, and Promoting

An important by-product of this approach is that students are assessed against external, absolute objectives, instead of reporting the students' relative achievements. The traditional model of grading on a curve (top student gets the best grade, worst student always fails (even if they know all the material), everyone else is evenly distributed in the middle) is never accepted in OBE or standards-based education.

Instead, a student's performance is related in absolute terms: "Jane knows how to write the letters of the alphabet" or "Jane answered 80% of questions correctly" instead of "Jane answered more questions correctly than Mary."

Under OBE, teachers can use any objective grading system they choose, including letter grades. In fact, many schools adopt OBE methods and use the same grading systems that they have always used. However, for the purposes of graduation, advancement, and retention, a fully developed OBE system generally tracks and reports not just a single overall grade for a subject, but also give information about several specific outcomes within that subject. For example, rather than just getting a passing grade for mathematics, a student might be assessed as level 4 for number sense, level 5 for algebraic concepts, level 3 for measurement skills, etc. This approach is valuable to schools and parents by specifically identifying a student's strengths and weaknesses.

In one alternate grading approach, a student is awarded "levels" instead of letter grades. From Kindergarten to year 12, the student will receive either a Foundational level (which is pre-institutional) or be evidenced at levels 1 through to 8. In the simplest implementation, earning a "level" indicates that the teacher believes that a student has learned enough of the current material to be able to succeed in the next level of work. A student technically cannot flunk in this system: a student who needs to review the current material will simply not achieve the next level at the same time as most of his same-age peers. This acknowledges differential growth at different stages, and focuses the teacher on the individual needs of the students.

In this approach, students and their parents are better able to track progress from year to year, since the levels are based on criteria that remain constant for a student's whole time at school. However, this experience is perceived by some as a flaw in the system: While it is entirely normal for some students to work on the same level of outcomes for more than one year parents and students have been socialized into the expectation of a constant, steady progress through schoolwork. Parents and students therefore interpret the normal experience as failure.

This emphasis on recognizing positive achievements, and comparing the student to his own prior performance, has been accused by some of "dumbing down" education (and by others as making school much too hard), since it recognises achievement at different levels.

Even those who would not achieve a passing grade in a traditional age-based approach can be recognized for their concrete, positive, individual improvements.

OBE-oriented teachers think about the individual needs of each student and give opportunities for each student to achieve at a variety of levels. Thus, in theory, weaker students are given work within their grasp and exceptionally strong students are extended. In practice, managing independent study programmes for thirty or more individuals is difficult. Adjusting to students' abilities is something that good teachers have always done: OBE simply makes the approach explicit and reflects the approach in marking and reporting.

Differences with Traditional Education Methods

In a traditional education system and economy, students are given grades and rankings compared to each other. Content and performance expectations are based primarily on what was taught in the past to students of a given age.

The basic goal of traditional education was to present the knowledge and skills of the old generation to the new generation of students, and to provide students with an environment in which to learn, with little attention (beyond the classroom teacher) to whether or not any student ever learns any of the material. It was enough that the school presented an opportunity to learn. Actual achievement was neither measured nor required by the school system.

In fact, under the traditional model, student performance is expected to show a wide range of abilities. The failure of some students is accepted as a natural and unavoidable circumstance.

The highest-performing students are given the highest grades and test scores, and the lowest performing students are given low grades. (Local laws and traditions determine whether the lowest performing students were socially promoted or made to repeat the year.) Schools used norm-referenced tests, such as inexpensive, multiple-choice computer-scored questions with single correct answers, to quickly rank students on ability.

These tests do not give criterion-based judgements as to whether students have met a single standard of what every student is expected to know and do: they merely rank the students in comparison with each other. In this system, grade-level expectations are defined as the performance of the median student, a level at which half the students score better and half the students score worse. By this definition, in a normal population, half of students are expected to perform above grade level and half the students below grade level, no matter how much or how little the students have learned.

Claims in Favour of OBE

Proponents view OBE as a valuable replacement of the traditional model of relative ranking by ability and getting credit for merely sitting through class. OBE proponents support OBE because of its vision of high standards for all groups. OBE proponents endorse measuring outputs rather than inputs (such as money spent, number of hours of lecture given, new EU outcome requirements focus on reducing the youth unemployment rate) and requiring that student demonstrate learning rather than just showing up.

OBE proponents believe that all students can learn, regardless of ability, race, ethnicity, socioeconomic status, and gender. Furthermore, OBE recognizes that a complex organization is more likely to produce what it measures, and to downplay anything it considers unimportant. The adoption of measurable standards is seen as a means of ensuring that the content and skills covered by the standards will be a high priority in the education of students.

The standards-based education approach rejects social promotion and the inevitability of inferior performance by disadvantaged groups. While recognizing that some students will learn certain material faster than others, the standards movement rejects the idea that only a few can succeed. All students are capable of continuous improvement.

The opportunities that were previously afforded to those at the top of a bell curve are opened up to the diversity of all students, in a democratic vision, sometimes connected to social justice.

The approach presents the following positions and viewpoints on OBE:

- All students will complete rigorous academic coursework so that they leave high school prepared for college or technical training, without remedial courses.
- All students, including those who live in poverty, will meet district, state, and national standards.
- Staff will maintain high expectations and standards, believing all students will succeed if kept to high expectations
- Students should be measured against a fixed yardstick, a finish line, or "against the mountain" rather than against other students.

- Higher world class standards are required for 21st Century Skills.
- Students should demonstrate that they have met standards, not just put in seat time to advance to the next level.

We haven't taught many of them even up to middle school standards. It only punishes them more to give them an empty piece of paper we call a diploma when their high school experience hasn't prepared for any of the skills they'll need after high school. We give them a diploma that is a doorway to a street corner or unemployment line.

—(Russlynn Ali of Education Trust-West)

In essence, OBE seeks to reject a rank-ordered definition of success by essentially requiring that all students shall be required to cross the finish line, at least as well as the specified standards. In practice, OBE results in accountable spending, thus also enabling jobless-rate risk-prevention of students who were previously allowed to graduate while being functionally illiterate and innumerate. OBE's objective standards finally put a brake on useless & popgun grade inflation, clearly to the distress of students who prefer high, but meaningless, grades.

Deductive Evidence That OBE Actually Works

The ERIC Database provides a Thesaurus Descriptor "Outcome-based Education" with presently over 369 peer-reviewed hits. Meanwhile, OBE is a coherent bound collection of ideas, with uniformity in the way it is implemented from case to case. This enhances testability for OBE's effectiveness in a way that applies universally. The concreteness of OBE's conception of a "measurable outcome" is welcoming, both in implementing an OBE regime and in testing its effectiveness.

Criticism

Criticism of OBE falls into a few major groups:

- Opposition to standardized testing
- Criticism of inappropriate outcomes
- Extra burden on instructors and educational institutions
- Dislike of something that is not OBE

Though it is claimed the focus is not on "inputs", OBE is criticised for being used to justify increased funding requirements, increased graduation and testing requirements, and additional preparation, homework, and continuing education time spent by students, parents and teachers in supporting learning. It is also criticized for not being able to measure certain skills, much like IQ tests.

Opposition to Testing

Critics claim that existing tests do not adequately measure student mastery of the stated objectives.

Some parents also object to the use of standardized tests (all students take the same test under the same conditions) because they think it unfair for schools to require the same level of work or to use the achievement tests for impoverished or disadvantaged students as they do for more advantaged students.

The OBE philosophy insists that assessment models be carefully matched to the stated objectives. High-stakes tests are *not* required in an OBE system; norm-referenced tests are prohibited. Portfolios, daily assessments, teacher opinions, and other methods of assessment are perfectly compatible with OBE models. Furthermore, the OBE approach does not permit special, lower standards for students who have been badly served by public education in the past.

Inappropriate Outcomes

Many people oppose OBE reforms because they dislike the proposed outcomes. They may think that the standards are too easy, too hard, or wrongly conceived. Finally, some so-called OBE critics oppose non-OBE reforms that were presented as a part of a wide-ranging reform "package", rather than opposing OBE itself.

Standards can be set too low: Most fear that the focus on achievement by all students will result in "dumbing down" the definition of academic competence to a level that is achievable by even the weakest students. Critics are unhappy with having all students meet a minimum standard, instead of most students meeting a somewhat higher standard.

Some critics also question whether even such low goals are realistic or attainable, and whether success can only be framed in terms of high test scores and high incomes. The emphasis on higher reading standards and algebra for all appears to devalue vocational training and the achievement of those who do not get high test scores, but who are likely to become competent blue-collar workers. Standards can be set too high: Others object that the standards are too high. OBE models do not approve of social promotion, so non-disabled students who perform significantly below the stated standard may be held back or required to take additional instruction. Especially when the standards are relatively new, and the schools are just beginning to adjust to the new standards, a majority of students struggle with at least some of the requirements. Parents are understandably unhappy to learn that their children have not acquired the necessary skills, and occasionally respond by demanding that the standards be lowered until their children are declared to be passing.

Sometimes this demand that the standards be lowered is justified, because standards can be found developmentally inappropriate for all but the brightest students. The State of Washington found that some fourth grade WASL math problems were much more difficult than what is typically expected of nine-year-old students. A 2008 draft mathematics standard proposed that Kindergartners multiply to 30 by skip counting (also known as *counting by twos*: 2, 4, 6, 8...), and that second graders solve simple algebra story problems.

Committees often set standards without considering how many students are currently achieving at that level. For example, in the 1998 North Carolina Writing Assessment, less than 1 percent of fourth graders received the highest possible score for writing content. While a majority of students passed easily, parents were upset that so few were rated as being best.

Dislike of specific outcomes: Finally, many complaints are directed against the nature of certain standards. For example, a politician might propose that standards be included for education about sex or creationism. Opponents say that many educational agencies have adopted outcomes which focus too much on attitudes (e.g., "Students will enjoy physical education class") rather than academic content. Similarly, the "Who Controls Our Children" campaign in Pennsylvania claimed that an OBE reform effort was part of a federal programme that was "stressing values over academic content, and holding students accountable for goals that are so vague and fuzzy they can't be assessed at all." The Western Australian outcomes were criticised for being too vague.

Controversial standards are opposed because of their content, not simply because they are standards. OBE models always leave the choice of the exact standards to the educational authority, so that families can influence the choice of standards according to their community's preferences.

Extra Burden on Instructors and Educational Institutions

Critics sometimes oppose OBE because of the burden it imposes on instructors and educational institutions more broadly, a burden that they regard as unjustified by any evidence showing that OBE actually improves learning outcomes. Rather than issuing a single letter or number to summarize an entire term's achievements, an OBE system may require that the teacher track and report dozens of separate outcomes. It takes longer to report that a student can add, subtract, multiply, divide, solve story problems, and draw graphs than to report "passed mathematics class," but the burden imposed by OBE does not owe primarily to the *reporting* of more data. The burden is spread across the entire educational institution, in the form of (1) a new layer of assessment placed atop the old familiar one, (2) a new bureaucracy responsible for the institution-wide collection and presentation of data, and (3) the altering and curtailing of classroom instruction to make room for more intrusive testing. In view of the paucity of evidence showing that OBE actually works, many regard this extra burden as an unjustified drain on pedagogical resources.

Criticism of Educational Reforms Associated With OBE

Many criticisms of OBE are actually criticisms of other things that are introduced with an OBE system. Many people oppose OBE reforms because the OBE reforms are packaged with other reforms.

OBE reform is often packaged as part of a comprehensive school reform model which promotes constructivism, enquiry-based science, tax reform, teacher training, and more. Other educational reforms, including changes to the school calendar, the age of students that attend school in a certain building, or the way tax revenues are divided, may all be inappropriately labeled "OBE" reforms simply because they were proposed on the same day as an OBE programme. School to work may also be a component of these multi-faceted reform programmes. School-to-work programmes require students to spend time in an internship or other form of career training or experience.

OBE Programmes

Australia

One of the problems of OBE for students wishing to attend university is that it does not lend itself well to forming a competitive Tertiary Entrance Rank (TER). The suggested model for mapping levels to a TER has been attacked because it results in a score with more significant digits than the measures from which it is derived and so is charged with being mathematically unsound. William Spady promoted the OBE method as a way of getting beyond 'meaningless' percentages and marks, aiming for education for life beyond school, giving children and young adults a broader and more transformative education. Arguably inelegant implementation makes the future of OBE unclear, and at odds with the Australian Government in Canberra.

Western Australia

The current OBE controversy in Western Australia relates specifically to the introduction of OBE in upper school (year 11 and 12) classes. Many Western Australian schools have been using some form of OBE for K-10 students for several years. (OBE is only one part of the current changes to upper school education currently being implemented. Other aspects of the new courses of study that form the upper school review have received little public attention.)

As part of the debate over further introduction of OBE into the teaching practice of Western Australia, various groups of concerned citizens and those in the teaching profession formed various single-issue lobby and action groups to progress their viewpoints. One such group was *People Lobbying Against Teaching Outcomes* formed by Greg Williams. The core view of this group was their disagreement with the former Western Australian Minister for Education (Ljiljanna Ravlich) in respect to her commitment to implement OBE.

Another such group was Parents Against Outcomes Based Education, who took the position that the implementation of OBE would pose significant problems and potentially lead to the decreased knowledge and performance of school students. Their objection was not to OBE itself, but to the bundle of reforms, of which OBE was the most mentioned. The "Fuzzy Outcomes" criticism above applies.

In January 2007, the Western Australian Government responded to the massive opposition by teachers and parents to its implementation of an OBE system by stating that it would allow year 11 and 12 students to be graded traditionally.

South Africa

OBE was introduced to South Africa in the late 1990s by the post-apartheid government as part of its Curriculum 2005 programmeme [9], but it was widely viewed as a failure, and was eventually scrapped in 2010.

United States

In the early 1990s, several standards-based reform measures were passed in various states, creating the Texas Assessment of Academic Skills (1991), Washington Assessment of Student Learning (1993), the CLAS in California (1993), and the Massachusetts Comprehensive Assessment System (1993).

At the national level, Congress passed the Goals 2000 act in 1994. The best-known and most far-reaching standards-based education law in the U.S. is the No Child Left Behind Act, which mandated certain measurements as a condition of receiving federal education funds. States are free to set their own standards, but the federal law mandates public reporting of math and reading test scores for disadvantaged demographic subgroups, including racial minorities, low-income students, and special education students. Various consequences for schools that do not make "adequate yearly progress" are included in the law.

At the state level, exit examinations have proliferated, and now more than half of US high school students will be required to pass a high-stakes test to get a normal high school diploma. In some states, fewer than half of students and one-quarter of ethnic minorities have met these standards.

In some communities, such as Littleton, Colorado, organized opposition groups have forced educational agencies to rescind reforms. In Littleton, community members felt that vague, nonacademic outcomes were replacing content, and that technically unsound assessments would be used to determine something as important as high school graduation. They also objected to students being refused a high school diploma if they could not perform 36 separate mathematics skills, despite being given good grades in class.

OBE Diplomas

A certificate of initial mastery was a programme to provide students with an interim certification around the age of 16. The certificate was earned by taking and passing a written test, which had been designed to determine whether a student was performing at about the tenth grade level. A student who passed the 10th grade test would receive a Certificate of Initial Mastery.

The CIM concept was patterned after nations like Germany's hauptschule system, in which the students who are not going to elite universities end their school-based education around age 16 and start career-oriented training in fields like construction technology, allied health professions, and business. In a typical US proposal, a student who received a CIM would then take two more years of career-based training. A national standards board was proposed to create similar tests for eight career fields, with the hope that employers would prefer certificated employees. The CIM has been essentially abandoned; however, in its place, states frequently require passing the same exam as a condition of receiving a high school diploma. Oregon had proposed a CAM for "advanced mastery" at the 12th grade.

OBE's Relationship to College

One effect of high school exit examinations is that it may become more difficult to graduate from high school than enter college. There is no set passing level for college entry tests like the SAT, and such tests are often not required by the lowest-rated colleges. In the future, some states may require criterion-based standards either for admission to or graduation from public universities. States are attempting to align high school curricula with the minimum standards for beginning college in an effort to reduce college dropouts and the number of remedial classes being taught at universities.

European Union

In December 2012, the European Commission stated that it "present[ed a] new strategy in 22 languages: The youth unemployment rate is close to 23% across the European Union – yet at the same time there are more than 2 million vacancies that cannot be filled. Europe needs a radical rethink on how education and training systems can deliver the skills needed by the labour market. ... Rethinking Education calls for a fundamental shift in education, with more focus on 'learning outcomes' - the knowledge, skills and competences that students acquire. Merely having spent time in education is no longer sufficient."

Treaties

Washington Accord: The Washington Accord is an international accreditation agreement for professional engineering academic degrees, between the bodies responsible for accreditation in its signatory countries. The Washington Accord covers undergraduate engineering degrees under Outcome-based education approach.

Performance-based economy

Outcome-based methods are used in some businesses. For whole companies, outcome-based evaluations are the basis of stock exchange prices: Companies which produce higher profit growth are more valuable than companies which perform poorly. Employees who are paid for piecework or by commission are examples of traditional employment use of outcome-based pay. Alternatives include seniority systems (oldest worker gets highest pay).

Many private employers give standards-based tests to determine whether job applicants have necessary job skills (such as typing speed), and nearly all government employees have to take and pass a civil service examination. Furthermore, nearly all licensed professionals, from nurses to truck drivers to beauticians, already take such tests as a condition of entering their professions. Often these tests have disproportionate failure rates for disadvantaged subgroups, such as school dropouts and impoverished people.

The Floundering or Trial Process: Attempting to Implement a Self Concept.

One's self-concept (also called self-construction, self-identity or self-perspective) is a collection of beliefs about oneself that includes elements such as academic performance, gender roles and sexuality, racial identity, and many others. Generally, self-concept embodies the answer to "Who am I?"

Self-concept is distinguishable from self-awareness, which refers to the extent to which self-knowledge is clearly defined, consistent and currently applicable to one's attitudes and dispositions. Self-concept is made up of one's self-schemas. Additionally, self-concept interacts with self-esteem, self-knowledge, and social self to form the self. Self-esteem refers to the evaluation or comparison of one's self-concept and self-schemas to form one's overall self-worth.

The self-concept includes past, present and future selves. Future or possible selves represent individuals' ideas of what they might become, what they would like to become, or what they are afraid of becoming. These different selves correspond to one's hopes, fears, standards, goals, and threats for their present selves. Possible selves may function as incentives for future behaviour and also provide an evaluative and interpretive context for the current view of self that is used when one self-evaluates, contributing to one's self-esteem. Self-esteem and self-concept cannot be used interchangeably. Self-esteem focuses on an evaluative and opinionated aspect to one's self (e.g., I feel good about the fact that I am a fast runner), whereas self-concept is more of a cognitive or descriptive component to one's self (e.g., I am a fast runner). This distinction is important to note, as self-concept and self-esteem closely interact to form an overall view of the self.

The perception which people have about their past or future selves is related to the perception of their current self. The temporal self-appraisal theory argues that people have a tendency to maintain a positive evaluation of the current self by distancing their self-concepts from their negative selves and paying more attention to their positive selves. In addition, people have a tendency to perceive the past self less favourably (e.g., I'm better than I used to be) and the future self more positively (e.g., I will be better than I am now).

Psychologists Carl Rogers and Abraham Maslow paved the way for this concept. According to Rogers, everyone strives to become more like an "ideal self". The closer one is to their ideal self, the happier one will be. Rogers also claimed that one factor in a person's happiness is unconditional positive regard, or UPR, from others. UPR often occurs in close or familial relationships, and involves a consistent level of affection regardless of the recipient's actions. Rogers explained UPR as neither approving nor disapproving of someone based on their behaviours or characteristics but rather accepting them without judgement. From a therapy frame of reference, Rogers identified the significance of a client perceiving a therapist's UPR towards them, so that the client would not feel judged as they attempt to accurately express themselves. Evidence of UPR in self-concept research is apparent in studies by Benner and Mistry (2007) and Tiedemann (2000). Research has indicated that adolescents whose mothers and teachers had high expectations for their future educational attainment experienced more academic success than those whose adult influences had lower expectations. Adults' high expectations for children are also reported as being important buffers from the negative effects of other parties' low expectations by developing feelings of positive regard in adolescents. In research about parent stereotypes, the correlation between parents' beliefs about their early elementary age children's mathematics abilities and the children's actual abilities increased as children aged. This demonstrates the strong relationship between adults' beliefs about children and children's beliefs about themselves, indicating the importance of developing unconditional positive regard for students so they can develop it themselves.

An important theory related to self-concept is the self-categorization theory (SCT), which states that the self-concept consists of at least two "levels," a personal identity and a social identity. In other words, one's self-evaluation rely on both one's self-perceptions and how one fits in socially. The self-concept can alternate rapidly between the personal and social identity. Research by Trautwein et al.(2009) indicates that children and adolescents begin integrating social comparison information into their own self-concept in elementary school by assessing their position among their peers. Gest et al.'s (2008) research findings reveal that peer acceptance has a significant impact on one's self-concept by age 5, affecting children's behaviour and academic success. Both of these research examples demonstrate the social influences on a person's self-concept.

Model of Self-concept

The self-concept is an internal model that uses self-assessments in order to define one's self-schemas. Features such as personality, skills and abilities, occupation(s) and hobbies, physical characteristics, etc. are assessed and applied to self-schemas, which are ideas one has of oneself in a particular dimension (e.g., someone that considers themselves a geek will associate geek-like qualities and be an expert on those qualities). A collection of self-schemas make up one's overall self-concept. For example, the statement "I am lazy" is a self-assessment that contributes to the self-concept. It is important to note that statements such as "I am tired" would not be part of someone's self-concept, since being tired is a temporary emotional state and therefore cannot become a part of a self-schema. A person's self-concept may change with time as reassessment occurs, which in extreme cases can lead to identity crises.

Academic Self-concept

Academic Self-Concept (ASC) refers to the personal beliefs someone develops about their academic abilities or skills. A person's ASC develops and evolves as they age. Some research suggests that ASC begins developing in early childhood, from age 3 to 5, due to parental/ family and early educators' influences, While other research contends that ASC does not develop until age 7 or 8, when children begin evaluating their own academic abilities based on the feedback they receive from parents, teachers and their peers. By age 10 or 11, children view their academic abilities by comparing themselves to their peers. These social comparisons are also referred to as self-estimates. Self-estimates are frequently utilized to help one form an idea of oneself. Research shows that self-estimates of cognitive ability were most accurate when numerical ability was estimated. Furthermore, research shows that self-estimates were more likely to be poor in other areas of cognitive ability such as reasoning speed that are considered less frequently.

There are a variety of social factors that contribute to development of an ASC and developing a positive ASC has been related to people's behaviours and emotions in other domains of their life, influencing happiness, self-esteem, and anxiety levels to name a few. Due to the significant impact ASC has on a person's life, it has been argued that educational systems should foster positive self-concept development in children.

These research findings are important because they have practical implications for parents and teachers. Research indicates that parents and teachers need to provide children with specific feedback that focuses on their particular skills or expressed abilities in order to increase ASC. Other research suggests that learning opportunities should be conducted in a variety of mixed-ability and like-ability groupings that down-play social comparison because too much of either type of grouping can have adverse effects on children's ASC in the way they view themselves in relation to their peers.

Effects of Success and Failure

Various studies have examined the effects that success and failure can have on an individual's self-concept. Individuals often form their self-concept based on past experiences of success or failure, attributing the outcome to their own personal worth. By doing this, individuals can commit the fundamental attribution error. In this case, the error may arise when the person falsely believes that a specific aspect of who they are determined the positive or negative outcome. By attributing a negative outcome to oneself, self-concept can be unnecessarily harmed. However, attributing positive outcomes to oneself can increase self-concept. These attributions can even have an effect on self-perception, achievement behaviours in the future, and expectancies. Austin and Vispoel (1998) found strong links between where an individual attributed success or failure and, specifically, musical self-concept.

Changes in self-concept can be mediated and predicted by various factors. One important factor in academics is evaluation of performance by peers, or peer academic reputation (PAR). Gest, Rulison, Davidson, and Welsh (2008) found evidence for the predictive ability of PAR with regard to students' in upper grades academic self-concept. If a student has a reputation for success or failure in the academic setting, the student may develop a negative self-concept. This shows that it is may not only be the actual success or failure that has an effect, but may also be the secondary effects of poor academic reputation among peers that influence students' self-concept.

There are also effects that have been studying by looking at how self-concept can influence success or failure and attributions of success and failure. In a study of university undergraduate students, self-esteem was studied by examining students' attributions for their success or failure after being given a word association test. Dutton and Brown (1997) found that self-esteem could predict participants' attribution of their success or failure in the word test. Individuals with high self-esteem tended to make more self-serving attributions to outcomes than did individuals with low self-esteem.

Expectations, Conditioning, and Gauging

According to Kathleen Berger, author of *The Developing Person*, guilt plays a significant role in shaping a young child's self-concept. As an example, she describes a child that is coddled at home, and his/her socially unacceptable behaviour is never thwarted by the parent(s). When the child is denied whatever they want from another child, he/she strikes out towards other children, not understanding that there will be consequences and possible retaliation. If this kind of behaviour were to occur in a classroom environment, a teacher could use guilt in an attempt to shape the spoiled child's self-concept by reminding the student that hitting others is not acceptable in most social situations. In essence, guilt shapes behaviour. Berger goes on to explain that most children over the age of 5 have some sense of the rules and regulations that govern social behaviour that they learn from a guardian, thus shaping their self-concept without using guilt. In some cases, if maladaptive behaviour is left unchecked, the seeds of bullying could start to germinate.

Self-concept is linked directly to a person's level of anxiety, according to the humanistic psychologist Carl Rogers. According to Rogers, if a child feels highly valued and wanted, that person is more likely to grow up with a positive self-image, with the possibility of becoming self-actualized. Rogers describes this individual as a *fully functioning person* with a low level of anxiety, which he attributes to inconsistencies between self-perceptions and possible-self. Here again, expectations play a major role in shaping self-concept. Dr. Rogers hypothesizes that psychologically healthy people actively move away from roles created by others' expectations but instead look within themselves for validation.

"Neurotic and psychotic people, on the other hand, have self-concepts that do not match their experiences.. They are afraid to accept their own experiences as valid, so they distort them, either to protect themselves or to win approval from others."

Children learn at an early age that certain conditions will be placed upon them in exchange for approval or love from the parents. For example, a parent may tell a child that he/she must love the new baby sister or brother, or else Mommy and Daddy won't love them. This kind of hostage mentality could harbor and suppress negative ill will towards the new baby which will eventually express itself later on in life.

To gauge a child's self-concept, Susan Harter developed the Self-Perception Profile for Adolescents. In it, domains such as scholastic competence, behaviour conduct, close friendships, social acceptance, athletic competence, romantic appeal, and physical appearance are rated using a number of indicators. Some of the positive indicators include whether the child or adolescent expresses their opinion, maintains eye contact during conversion, works cooperatively in a group, maintains a comfortable space between self and others, and uses proper voice levels for various situation. Negative indicators could include teasing, gossiping, using dramatic gesturing, engaging in inappropriate touching or avoiding physical contact, verbally putting down self or others, or bragging about achievements, skills, or appearance.

Cultural Differences

Worldviews about the self in relation to others differs across and within cultures. In Western cultures, an individualistic and independent approach is adopted where society places particular importance on becoming independent and to express one's own attributes. Relationships, memberships, groups, and their needs and goals, tend to be secondary to the self. Self-assessment of one's self-concept also includes social comparisons. The Social comparison theory states that people strive to accurately define themselves and therefore utilize social comparisons to accurately define the self during the self-evaluative process. Within these social comparisons, one will find upward (e.g., positive) and downward (e.g., negative) comparisons that can either enhance or threaten our self-concept and self-esteem. In such cases where we feel threatened, it is not uncommon to make explanations for why we are not performing to the same degree as others, thereby preserving our self-concept and self-esteem. In Asian cultures, an interdependent view of the self is more prevalent and these cultures often experience identity fusion more frequently. Interpersonal relationships are more central than one's individual accomplishments, as individuals experience a sense of oneness with the group. Great emphasis is placed on these relationships, and the self is seen primarily as an integral part of society.

Research has shown that this identity fusion can have positive and negative consequences. The positive impact that identity fusion can have on people is that they feel that their existence is meaningful (e.g., Japanese nuclear plant workers expose themselves to radiation to help fix the plant after a tsunami) and this type of mindset is associated with a high quality of life. On the other hand, such strong interdependence can lead to catastrophic events (e.g., acts of terrorism).

A study published in the International Journal of Intercultural Relations gives another division of the independent and interdependent selves based on subcultures.

A small study done in Israel shows the different characteristics most prevalent of mid-level merchants in an urban community versus those in a communal settlement, called the kibbutz. Similar to the Western v. non-Western perspectives, the collectivist members valued the interdependent self more that the urban members. Likewise, the urban samples held more value to independent traits than the kibbutz.

Both answered with more independent traits than interdependent. The study divided the independent and interdependent traits into subcategories to further define what are the most valued by the two subcultures. On the independent scale, personal traits showed the greatest prevalence for the individualists, while hobbies and preferences were greater for the collectivists. Work and school were the most frequently described interdependent responses for the urban sector, while residence was most often referred to by the kibbutz. Overall, the study intensifies the knowledge that self-concept depends on inner attributes, abilities, and opinions from the community based on collective ideology. Further studies on other subcultures would be needed to create a generalization on a wider scale.

Gender Differences

Gender has also been shown to be an important factor in the formation of self-concept. Early research inspired by the differences in self-concept across culture suggested that men tend to be more independent while women tend to be more interdependent. Independent self-construct refers to the fact that representations of others are separate from the self. Interdependent self-construct refers to the fact that representations of others are considered as part of the self. However, more recent research has shown that, while men and women do not differ between independence and interdependence generally, they do differ in the distinction between relational and collective interdependence. Men utilize collective interdependence while women utilize relational interdependence. In other words, women identify more with dyadic (one-on-one) relationships or small cliques, whereas men define themselves more often within the context of larger groups. Research also shows that as gender roles become blurred in Western society (e.g., more men are staying at home and women are being empowered in the workplace), these differences may change.

Women have often been stereotyped as being more emotional than men. This area of gender differences is important to research, as self-concepts that encompass gender may also encompass the self-conscious emotions or tendencies associated with gender. Women, for example, allegedly show more guilt, shame and embarrassment whereas men show more pride. Research shows that women in fact do show more guilt, shame and embarrassment than men but that men and women show the same amount of pride. Furthermore, gender differences in self-conscious emotions are different between ethnicities and are greatest within white populations when compared to Black or African, Asian, and Latin American samples. More research in this area is needed to extrapolate the gender differences across different cultures and ethnicities, as most of the samples used in gender studies are White samples. This reliance on a specific sample can lead researchers to overestimate the magnitude of gender differences in terms of emotions of women in comparison to men.

The Developmental Perspective

Research by Tiedemann (2000) found that parents' and teachers' gender stereotypes about children's mathematical abilities influenced children's self-concepts about their mathematical ability prior to having extensive experience with math in school. Tiedemann's (2000) research findings also indicate that the correlation between adult's gendered stereotypes and children's beliefs about themselves increased as children aged throughout elementary school. Additional research by Benner and Mistry (2007) indicates that parent's initial expectations for their children, during early childhood, correlate with children's academic success. These findings highlight the influence of adult stereotypes and expectations on children's self-concept formation.

Research by Eleanor Maccoby (1990) found that boys and girls choose same-sex play partners by age 3 and maintain their preferences until late elementary school. Boys and girls become involved in different social interactions and relationships. Girls tend to prefer one-on-one dyadic interaction, while boys prefer group activities. Girls tend to share secrets and form tight, intimate bonds with one another. Furthermore, girls are more likely to wait their turn to speak, agree with others, and acknowledge the contributions of others. Boys, on the other hand, build larger group relationships based on shared interests and activities. Boys are more likely to threaten, boast, and call names, suggesting the importance of dominance and hierarchy in groups of male friends. Subsequently, the social characteristics of boys and girls tend to carry over later in life as they become men and women.

Researchers debate when self-concept development begins but agree on the importance of person's life. Tiedemann (2000) indicates that parents' gender stereotypes and expectations for their children impact children's understandings of themselves by approximately age 3. Others suggest that self-concept develops later, around age 7 or 8, as children are developmentally prepared to begin interpreting their own feelings, abilities, and interpretations of feedback they receive from parents, teachers, and peers about themselves. Despite differing opinions about the onset of self-concept development, researchers agree on the importance of one's self-concept, which influences people's behaviours and cognitive and emotional outcomes including (but not limited to) academic achievement, levels of happiness, anxiety, social integration, self-esteem, and life-satisfaction.

Empirical Evidence

In a 1999 study by Gabriel and Gardner, five separate experiments were conducted to demonstrate gender differences in self-concept: a 20 statement test evaluating self-construal ("I am..." statements), a series of surveys evaluating trait identification, an exercise evaluating selective memory for emotional events, a diary reading paradigm evaluating selective memory, and a survey concerning a situational dilemma evaluating behavioural intention and desire to behave. Each of these five studies showed in no significant difference between men and women in levels of independence. However, they were able to show a bias among women toward relational interdependence and a bias among men toward collective interdependence in affect, cognition, and behaviour.

Other psychologists have postulated that men display an independent concept while women display an interdependent self-concept. One study exploring this aimed to discover whether gender stereotypes have an effect on this gender difference in self-construal. Participants read a list of traits and rated the extent to which the traits applied to a typical man, a typical woman, and the self. When rating men and women in general, both males and females displayed a stereotype for "relational" women (focused on their relationships with others) and "agentic" men (focused on themselves and their individual accomplishments). Self-ratings also corresponded to these stereotypes. The researchers then hypothesized that the stereotypes themselves contribute to the difference in self-construal, and found that this effect is more potent for women than for men. One possible explanation for this imbalance is that "relational" traits tend to be more positively viewed than "agentic" traits, and therefore participants are more likely to apply relational traits to themselves. This research supports the SCT, showing that one's self-concept is affected by the interplay of self-assessments and social roles (in this case, belonging to the larger group of males or females).

One study, focusing on the developmental perspective, aimed to discover girls' and boys' preferences for socialization. Thirty-three-month-old children were assigned to play in pairs. Some pairs were same-sex, others were mixed. Researchers measured both positive and negative social behaviours during play. Both boys and girls had higher levels of social behaviour when playing with the same sex than with the opposite sex. In addition, in the mixed-sex pairs, girls were more likely to passively watch a male partner play than vice versa. Boys were more likely to be unresponsive to what their female partners were saying than vice versa.

Another study observed performance in unisex and mixed-sex groups of children. 10-year-old children were placed in either all-male pairs, all-male groups, all-female pairs, or all-female groups. The children were given a task that was equally interesting to males and females. The results of the study found significant correlation between sex of the participants and social structure. Boys performed almost twice as well in groups than in pairs, whereas girls did not show a significant difference. The increased productivity of boys in groups was expected due to the greater number of participants, whereas girls did not benefit from more participants.

Self-image

Not to be confused with Self-awareness, Self-concept, Self-consciousness, or Self-perception.

A person's self-image is the mental picture, generally of a kind that is quite resistant to change, that depicts not only details that are potentially available to objective investigation by others (height, weight, hair colour, gender, I.Q. score, etc.), but also items that have been learned by that person about himself or herself, either from personal experiences or by internalizing the judgements of others. A simple definition of a person's self-image is their answer to the question "What do you believe people think about you?".

Self-image may consist of three types:

1. Self-image resulting from how the individual sees himself or herself.
2. Self-image resulting from how others see the individual.
3. Self-image resulting from how the individual perceives others see him or her.

These three types may or may not be an accurate representation of the person. All, some or none of them may be true.

A more technical term for self-image that is commonly used by social and cognitive psychologists is self-schema. Like any schema, self-schemas store information and influence the way we think and remember. For example, research indicates that information which refers to the self is preferentially encoded and recalled in memory tests, a phenomenon known as "Self-referential encoding". Self-schemas are also considered the traits people use to define themselves, they draw information about the self into a coherent scheme.

Poor Self-image

Poor self-image may be the result of accumulated criticisms that the person collected as a child which have led to damaging their own view of themselves. Children in particular are vulnerable to accepting negative judgements from authority figures because they have yet to develop competency in evaluating such reports. Also, adolescents are highly targeted to suffer from poor body image issues. Individuals that already exhibit a low-sense of self-worth may be vulnerable to develop social disorders.

Negative self-images can arise from a variety of factors. A prominent factor, however, is personality type. Perfectionists, high achievers, and those with "type A" personalities seem to be prone to having negative self-images. This is because such people constantly set the standard for success high above a reasonable, attainable level. Thus, they are constantly disappointed in this "failure."

Self-image Maintenance

When people are in the position of evaluating others, self-image maintenance processes can lead to a more negative evaluation depending on the self-image of the evaluator. That is to say stereotyping and prejudice may be the way individuals maintain their self-image. When individuals evaluate a member of a stereotyped group, they are less likely to evaluate that person negatively if their self-images had been bolstered through a self-affirmation procedure, and they are more likely to evaluate that person stereotypically if their self-images have been threatened by negative feedback. Individuals may restore their self-esteem by derogating the member of a stereotyped group.

Fein and Spencer (1997) conducted an intriguing study on Self-image Maintenance and Discriminatory Behaviour. This study showed evidence that increased prejudice can result from a person's need to redeem a threatened positive perception of the self. The aim of the study was to test whether a particular threat to the self would instigate increased stereotyping and lead to actual discriminatory behaviour or tendencies towards a member of a *"negatively"* stereotyped group. The study began when Fein and Spencer gave participants an ostensible test of intelligence. Some of them received negative feedback, and others, positive and supportive feedback. In the second half of the experiment, the participants were asked to evaluate another person who either belonged to a *negatively stereotyped group*, or one who did not. The results of the experiment proved that the participants who had previously received unfavourable comments on their test, evaluated the target of the *negatively stereotyped group* in a more antagonistic or opposing way, than the participants who were given excellent reports on their intelligence test. They concluded that the negative feedback on the test threatened the participants' self-image and they evaluated the target in a more negative manner, all in efforts to restore their own self-esteem. A present study extends the studies of Fein and Spencer in which the principal behaviour examined was avoidance behaviour. In the study, Macrae et al. (2004) found that participants that had a salient negative stereotype of "skinheads" attached, physically placed themselves further from a skinhead target compared to those in which the stereotype was not as apparent. Therefore, greater salience of a negative stereotype led participants to show more stereotype-consistent behaviour towards the target.

Residual Self-image

Residual self-image is the concept that individuals tend to think of themselves as projecting a certain physical appearance, or certain position of social entitlement, or lack thereof. The term was used at least as early as 1968, but was popularized in fiction by the *Matrix* series, where persons who existed in a digitally created world would subconsciously maintain the physical appearance that they had become accustomed to projecting.

Self-image of Victimization

Victims of abuse and manipulation often get trapped into a self-image of victimisation. The psychological profile of victimisation includes a pervasive sense of helplessness, passivity, loss of control, pessimism, negative thinking, strong feelings of guilt, shame, self-blame and depression. This way of thinking can lead to hopelessness and despair.

Children's Self-image Disparity

Self-image disparity was found to be positively related to chronological age (CA) and intelligence, two factors thought to increase concomitantly with maturity: Capacity for guilt and ability for cognitive differentiation. However, males had larger self-image disparities than females, whites had larger disparities and higher ideal self images than blacks, and SES (socioeconomic status) affected self-images differentially for the 2nd and 5th graders.

Self-image Strengtheners

A child's self-awareness of who they are differentiates into 3 categories around the age of 5: their social self, academic persona, and physical attributes. Several ways to strengthen a child's self-image include communication, reassurance, support of hobbies, and finding role models.

Evolved Awareness of Self-image in Mirror

When does a child become aware that the image in a mirror is his own? Research was done on 88 children between 3 and 24 months. Their behaviours were observed before a mirror. The results indicated that children's awareness of self-image followed three major age-related sequences:

- From about 6 through 12 months of age, the first prolonged and repeated reaction of an infant to his mirror image is that of a sociable "playmate".
- In the second year of life, wariness and withdrawal appeared; self-admiring and embarrassed behaviour accompanied those avoidance behaviours starting at 14 months, and was shown by 75% of the subjects after 20 months of age.
- During the last part of the second year of life, from 20 to 24 months of age, 65% of the subjects demonstrated recognition of their mirror images.

Physical Activity and Self-image

Regular practice of endurance exercise was related to a more favourable self-image. There was a strong association between participation in sports and the type of personality that tends to be resistant to drug and alcohol addiction. Physical exercise was further significantly related to scores for physical and psychological well-being. Adolescents who engaged regularly in physical activity were characterised by lower anxiety-depression scores, and displayed much less social behavioural inhibition than their less active counterparts.

It is likely that discussion of recreational or exercise involvement may provide a useful point of entry for facilitating dialogue among adolescents about concerns relating to body image and self-esteem. In terms of psychotherapeutic applications, physical activity has many additional rewards for adolescents. It is probable that by promoting physical fitness, increased physical performance, lessening body mass and promoting a more favourable body shape and structure, exercise will provide more positive social feedback and recognition from peer groups, and this will subsequently lead to improvement in an individual's self-image.

Automatic Activation of Stereotypes and Self-image Threat

Does self-image threatening feedback make perceivers more likely to activate stereotypes when confronted by members of a minority group? Participants in Study 1 saw an Asian American or European American woman for several minutes, and participants in Studies 2 and 3 were exposed to drawings of an African American or European American male face for fractions of a second. These experiments found no evidence of automatic stereotype activation when perceivers were cognitively busy and when they had not received negative feedback. When perceivers had received negative feedback, however, evidence of stereotype activation emerged even when perceivers were cognitively busy.

Built-in Self-test

A built-in self-test (BIST) or built-in test (BIT) is a mechanism that permits a machine to test itself. Engineers design BISTs to meet requirements such as:

- high reliability
- lower repair cycle times

or constraints such as:

- limited technician accessibility
- cost of testing during manufacture

The main purpose of BIST is to reduce the complexity, and thereby decrease the cost and reduce reliance upon external (pattern-programmed) test equipment. BIST reduces cost in two ways:

1. reduces test-cycle duration
2. reduces the complexity of the test/probe setup, by reducing the number of I/O signals that must be driven/examined under tester control.

Both lead to a reduction in hourly charges for automated test equipment (ATE) service.

Naming

The BIST name and concept originated with the idea of including a pseudorandom number generator (PRNG) and cyclic redundancy check (CRC) on the IC. If all the registers that hold state in an IC are on one or more internal scan chains, then the function of the registers and the combinational logic between them will generate a unique CRC signature over a large enough sample of random inputs. So all an IC need do is store the expected CRC signature and test for it after a large enough sample set from the PRNG. The CRC comparison with expected signature or the actual resultant CRC signature is typically accessed via the JTAG IEEE 1149.1 standard.

Applications

BIST is commonplace in weapons, avionics, medical devices, automotive electronics, complex machinery of all types, unattended machinery of all types, and integrated circuits.

Automotive

Automotive tests itself to enhance safety and reliability. For example, most vehicles with antilock brakes test them once per safety interval. If the antilock brake system has a broken wire or other fault, the brake system reverts to operating as a normal brake system. Most automotive engine controllers incorporate a "limp mode" for each sensor, so that the engine will continue to operate if the sensor or its wiring fails. Another, more trivial example of a limp mode is that some cars test door switches, and automatically turn lights on using seat-belt occupancy sensors if the door switches fail.

Aviation

Almost all avionics now incorporate BIST. In avionics, the purpose is to isolate failing line-replaceable units, which are then removed and repaired elsewhere, usually in depots or at the manufacturer. Commercial aircraft only make money when they fly, so they use BIST to minimize the time on the ground needed for repair and to increase the level of safety of the system which contains BIST. Similar arguments apply to military aircraft. When BIST is used in flight, a fault causes the system to switch to an alternative mode or equipment that still operates. Critical flight equipment is normally duplicated, or redundant. Less critical flight equipment, such as entertainment systems, might have a "limp mode" that provides some functions.

Electronics

Integrated Circuit Manufacturing

BIST is used to make faster, less-expensive integrated circuit manufacturing tests. The IC has a function that verifies all or a portion of the internal functionality of the IC. In some cases, this is valuable to customers, as well. For example, a BIST mechanism is provided in advanced fieldbus systems to verify functionality. At a high level this can be viewed similar to the PC BIOS's power-on self-test (POST) that performs a self-test of the RAM and buses on power-up.

Computers

The typical personal computer tests itself at start-up (called POST) because it's a very complex piece of machinery. Since it includes a computer, a computerized self-test was an obvious, inexpensive feature. Most modern computers, including embedded systems, have self-tests of their computer, memory and software.

Unattended Machinery

Unattended machinery performs self-tests to discover whether it needs maintenance or repair. Typical tests are for temperature, humidity, bad communications, burglars, or a bad power supply. For example, power systems or batteries are often under stress, and can easily overheat or fail. So, they are often tested.

Often the communication test is a critical item in a remote system. One of the most common, and unsung unattended system is the humble telephone concentrator box. This contains complex electronics to accumulate telephone lines or data and route it to a central switch. Telephone concentrators test for communications continuously, by verifying the presence of periodic data patterns called frames. Frames repeat about 8,000 times per second.

Remote systems often have tests to loop-back the communications locally, to test transmitter and receiver, and remotely, to test the communication link without using the computer or software at the remote unit. Where electronic loop-backs are absent, the software usually provides the facility. For example, IP defines a local address which is a software loopback (IP-Address 127.0.0.1, usually locally mapped to name "localhost").

Many remote systems have automatic reset features to restart their remote computers. These can be triggered by lack of communications, improper software operation or other critical events. Satellites have automatic reset, and add automatic restart systems for power and attitude control, as well.

Medicine

Medical devices test themselves to assure their continued safety. Normally there are two tests. A power-on self-test (POST) will perform a comprehensive test. Then, a periodic test will assure that the device has not become unsafe since the power-on self test. Safety-critical devices normally define a "safety interval", a period of time too short for injury to occur. The self test of the most critical functions normally is completed at least once per safety interval. The periodic test is normally a subset of the power-on self test.

Military

One of the first computer-controlled BIST systems was in the U.S.'s Minuteman Missile. Using an internal computer to control the testing reduced the weight of cables and connectors for testing. The Minuteman was one of the first major weapons systems to field a permanently installed computer-controlled self-test.

Specializations

There are several specialized versions of BIST which are differentiated according to what they do or how they are implemented:

- Programmable built-in self-test (pBIST)

A built-in self-test (BIST) or built-in test (BIT) is a mechanism that permits a machine to test itself. Engineers design BISTs to meet requirements such as:

- high reliability
- lower repair cycle times

or constraints such as:

- limited technician accessibility
- cost of testing during manufacture

The main purpose of BIST is to reduce the complexity, and thereby decrease the cost and reduce reliance upon external (pattern-programmed) test equipment. BIST reduces cost in two ways:

1. reduces test-cycle duration
2. reduces the complexity of the test/probe setup, by reducing the number of I/O signals that must be driven/examined under tester control.

Both lead to a reduction in hourly charges for automated test equipment (ATE) service.

Naming

The BIST name and concept originated with the idea of including a pseudorandom number generator (PRNG) and cyclic redundancy check (CRC) on the IC. If all the registers that hold state in an IC are on one or more internal scan chains, then the function of the registers and the combinational logic between them will generate a unique CRC signature over a large enough sample of random inputs. So all an IC need do is store the expected CRC signature and test for it after a large enough sample set from the PRNG. The CRC comparison with expected signature or the actual resultant CRC signature is typically accessed via the JTAG IEEE 1149.1 standard.

Applications

BIST is commonplace in weapons, avionics, medical devices, automotive electronics, complex machinery of all types, unattended machinery of all types, and integrated circuits.

Automotive

Automotive tests itself to enhance safety and reliability. For example, most vehicles with antilock brakes test them once per safety interval. If the antilock brake system has a broken wire or other fault, the brake system reverts to operating as a normal brake system. Most automotive engine controllers incorporate a "limp mode" for each sensor, so that the engine will continue to operate if the sensor or its wiring fails. Another, more trivial example of a limp mode is that some cars test door switches, and automatically turn lights on using seat-belt occupancy sensors if the door switches fail.

Aviation

Almost all avionics now incorporate BIST. In avionics, the purpose is to isolate failing line-replaceable units, which are then removed and repaired elsewhere, usually in depots or at the manufacturer. Commercial aircraft only make money when they fly, so they use BIST to minimize the time on the ground needed for repair and to increase the level of safety of the system which contains BIST. Similar arguments apply to military aircraft. When BIST is used in flight, a fault causes the system to switch to an alternative mode or equipment that still operates. Critical flight equipment is normally duplicated, or redundant. Less critical flight equipment, such as entertainment systems, might have a "limp mode" that provides some functions.

Electronics

Integrated Circuit Manufacturing

BIST is used to make faster, less-expensive integrated circuit manufacturing tests. The IC has a function that verifies all or a portion of the internal functionality of the IC. In some cases, this is valuable to customers, as well. For example, a BIST mechanism is provided in advanced fieldbus systems to verify functionality. At a high level this can be viewed similar to the PC BIOS's power-on self-test (POST) that performs a self-test of the RAM and buses on power-up.

Computers

The typical personal computer tests itself at start-up (called POST) because it's a very complex piece of machinery. Since it includes a computer, a computerized self-test was an obvious, inexpensive feature. Most modern computers, including embedded systems, have self-tests of their computer, memory and software.

Unattended Machinery

Unattended machinery performs self-tests to discover whether it needs maintenance or repair. Typical tests are for temperature, humidity, bad communications, burglars, or a bad power supply. For example, power systems or batteries are often under stress, and can easily overheat or fail. So, they are often tested.

Often the communication test is a critical item in a remote system. One of the most common, and unsung unattended system is the humble telephone concentrator box.

This contains complex electronics to accumulate telephone lines or data and route it to a central switch. Telephone concentrators test for communications continuously, by verifying the presence of periodic data patterns called frames. Frames repeat about 8,000 times per second.

Remote systems often have tests to loop-back the communications locally, to test transmitter and receiver, and remotely, to test the communication link without using the computer or software at the remote unit. Where electronic loop-backs are absent, the software usually provides the facility. For example, IP defines a local address which is a software loopback (IP-Address 127.0.0.1, usually locally mapped to name "localhost").

Many remote systems have automatic reset features to restart their remote computers. These can be triggered by lack of communications, improper software operation or other critical events. Satellites have automatic reset, and add automatic restart systems for power and attitude control, as well.

Medicine

Medical devices test themselves to assure their continued safety. Normally there are two tests. A power-on self-test (POST) will perform a comprehensive test. Then, a periodic test will assure that the device has not become unsafe since the power-on self test. Safety-critical devices normally define a "safety interval", a period of time too short for injury to occur. The self test of the most critical functions normally is completed at least once per safety interval. The periodic test is normally a subset of the power-on self test.

Military

One of the first computer-controlled BIST systems was in the U.S.'s Minuteman Missile. Using an internal computer to control the testing reduced the weight of cables and connectors for testing. The Minuteman was one of the first major weapons systems to field a permanently installed computer-controlled self-test.

Specializations

There are several specialized versions of BIST which are differentiated according to what they do or how they are implemented:

- Programmable built-in self-test (pBIST)
- Memory built-in self-test (mBIST) - e.g. with the Marinescu algorithm
- Logic built-in self-test
- Analog and mixed-signal built-in self-test (AMBIST)
- Continuous built-in self-test (CBIST)
- Periodic built-in self-test
- Interrupt-driven built-in self-test (IBIST) or user-initiated built-in self-test
- Power-up built-in self-test (PupBIST)
- Automatic built-in self-test (ABIST)

Memory Built-in Self-test (mBIST) - e.g. with the Marinescu Algorithm

A built-in self-test (BIST) mechanism within an integrated circuit (IC) is a function that verifies all or a portion of the internal functionality of the IC. For example, a BIST mechanism is provided in advanced fieldbus systems to verify functionality. At a high level this can be viewed similar to the PC BIOS's Power-On Self-Test (POST) that performs a self-test of the RAM and buses on power-up.Alternative definition can be Built-in Self Test, or BIST, is the technique of designing additional hardware and software features into integrated circuits to allow them to perform self-testing, i.e., testing of their own operation (functionally, parametrically, or both) using their own circuits, thereby reducing dependence on an external automated test equipment (ATE).

Manufacturing test, as post-production chip testing is called, comprises a growing fraction of a modern IC device's total cost. Because of this, Design For Test (DFT) has shifted from an afterthought to a distinct design activity of a chip development cycle.

The main purpose of BIST is to reduce the complexity, and thereby decrease the cost and reduce reliance upon external (pattern-programmed) test equipment. BIST reduces cost in two ways: (1) reduces test-cycle duration; and (2) reduces the complexity of the test/probe setup, by reducing the number of I/O signals that must be driven/examined under tester control. Both lead to a reduction in hourly charges for automated test equipment (ATE) service.

Outside of manufacturing test, BIST can be designed to perform field-diagnostics of individual devices or entire systems. For example, at power-up, nearly all modern computer peripherals (printers, monitors, PCs) perform a limited self-diagnostic. Failure of the diagnostic is reported to the user. Sometimes these diagnostics will utilize BIST in the hardware to verify that buses, I/O's and major registers are operating.

The BIST name and concept originated with the idea of including a pseudo-random (PSR) number generator and CRC on the IC. If all the registers that hold state in an IC are on one or more internal scan chains, then the function of the registers and the combinatorial logic between them will generate a unique CRC signature over a large enough sample of random inputs. So all an IC need do is store the expected CRC signature and test for it after a large enough sample set from the PSR. The internal scan chain concept is formalized in the JTAG IEEE 1149.1 standard.

There are several specialized versions of BIST which are differentiated according to what they do or how they are implemented:

- Programmable Built-In Self-Test (pBIST)
- Memory Built-In Self-Test (mBIST) - e.g. with the Marinescu algorithm

- Logic Built-In Self-Test (LBIST)
- Analog and Mixed-Signal Built-In Self-Test (AMBIST)

Logic Built-in Self-test

Logic built-in self-test (or LBIST) is a form of built-in self-test (BIST) in which hardware and/or software is built into integrated circuits allowing them to test their own operation, as opposed to reliance on external automated test equipment.

Advantages

The main advantage of LBIST is the ability to test internal circuits having no direct connections to external pins, and thus unreachable by external automated test equipment. Another advantage is the ability to trigger the LBIST of an integrated circuit while running a built-in self test or power-on self test of the finished product.

Disadvantages

LBIST that requires additional circuitry (or read-only memory) increases the cost of the integrated circuit. LBIST that only requires temporary changes to programmemable logic or rewritable memory avoids this extra cost, but requires more time to first programme in the BIST and then to remove it and programme in the final configuration. Another disadvantage of LBIST is the possibility that the on-chip testing hardware itself can fail; external automated test equipment tests the integrated circuit with known-good test circuitry.

Related Technologies

Other, related technologies are MBIST (a BIST optimized for testing internal memory) and ABIST (either a BIST optimized for testing arrays or a BIST that is optimized for testing analog circuitry). The two uses may be distinguished by considering whether the integrated circuit being tested has an internal array or analog functions.

- Analog and mixed-signal built-in self-test (AMBIST)
- Continuous built-in self-test (CBIST)
- Periodic built-in self-test
- Interrupt-driven built-in self-test (IBIST) or user-initiated built-in self-test
- Power-up built-in self-test (PupBIST)
- Automatic built-in self-test (ABIST)

The Period of Establishment: the Self Concept Modified and Implemented.

An individual's self-concept is conceived as that individual's *summary formulation of his or her status.* This conception differs significantly from traditional ones in which the self-concept is universally considered to be a kind of organized informational summary of perceived facts about oneself, including such things as one's traits, values, social roles, interests, physical characteristics, and personal history.

A helpful means for making the transition from thinking in informational summary terms to thinking in status terms is to consider what we might naturally say to a child if we were teaching her the game of chess. Suppose that we have a board set up, the pieces arrayed in a midgame situation, and we are explaining what a "knight" is. In doing so, it is highly unlikely that we would use an informational summary approach, which would include telling her such things as that our knights were made of onyx, weighed 2 ounces, were forty years old, and were made in Mexico. Rather, we would provide her with information that has to do with the knight's *place* or *position* in the total scheme of things.

Thus, we would describe what a knight is by informing her of its relationships to the other pieces in the game (e.g., its ability to capture them, to block their movements, to move vis-a-vis them only in a certain distinctive fashion, etc.). Further, looking at any given knight's position relative to other pieces in the game situation displayed, we would help her to understand its current strategic importance. The crucial point here is that our thinking about the knight, indeed our thinking about *what it is to be a knight*, is quintessentially relational or positional in nature. When we have completed our description, what we have given our child is a summary formulation of the knight's *status*—its *overall place in the scheme of things*—not an informational summary of many different kinds of facts about knights.

Returning from chess pieces to persons, the status dynamic view maintains that the self-concept is most usefully identified, not with an organized summary of myriad perceived facts about oneself, but with *one's summary formulation of one's status.* That is to say, it is one's overall conception of one's place or position in relation to all of the elements in one's world, including oneself. In a simple and humorous, yet illuminating, illustration of this notion, cartoon character

Charlie Brown once lamented that he was unable to initiate a relationship with a little girl on the playground because "I'm a nothing and she's a something." He then went on to relate that, if he were a "something," or she a "nothing," he could pursue her, but that, since "nothings" cannot hope to succeed with "somethings," he could not act. In this example, Charlie provides us with a simplified illustration of the self-concept as a summary formulation of one's status ("nothing" existing in a world comprised of "somethings" and "nothings"); and illustrates how what is fundamental about self-concepts is not that they are informational summaries of myriad facts about oneself, but that they *place one somewhere in the scheme of things.*

Self-concept Delimits One's Behavioural Possibilities

A person's self-concept, by virtue of it being a summary formulation of his or her status, is in the bargain a summary formulation of his or her perceived behavioural possibilities, and of the limits on these. To pursue our chess analogy, when we have given a summary formulation of the status of a given knight by virtue both of its being a knight and its location vis-a-vis other pieces in an actual game, we have simultaneously formulated everything that this piece *can do and cannot do* at this point in the game. When Charlie Brown makes a summary appraisal of his own status as that of a "nothing in a world of somethings," we see that he has simultaneously appraised his behavioural possibilities and the limits on these.

One's self-concept sets limits on one's behavioural possibilities in several ways. The first of these, as captured in Charlie Brown's lament, is that, by virtue of one's self-assigned-status, one may appraise oneself as *ineligible* for many forms of valued life participation. When one considers certain commonly encountered, global, self-assigned statuses such as "unlovable," "irrational," "inadequate," "incompetent," "worthless," or "inferior," one can easily see that, by virtue of their ascription, persons have declared themselves ineligible for various forms of participation in life. To believe oneself "unlovable," for example, is to appraise oneself as ineligible for the love of another person. To believe oneself "irrational" is to appraise oneself as ineligible to render logical, well-grounded judgements and decisions, a perceived ineligibility that is vast in its behavioural implications.

A second limitation imposed by a person's self-concept is captured well in the expression: "I could never do that and still be me." Here, individuals are bound by self-concept in such a way that, being who they take themselves to be, the action in question is unthinkable as something they would or could do. In their minds, it would so violate who they are that, should they do it, they could no longer take themselves to be the same person, but would be forced to see themselves as a different (and usually distinctly lesser) person . In general, this constraint serves as a force for social good insofar as for most people antisocial acts such as child abuse or murder are "unthinkable" or "something I just could never do." However, at other times, this constraint proves debilitating in people's lives because crucially needed actions have become for them such unthinkables (e.g., leaving a destructive relationship, or defending their rights in an assertive and forceful manner).

A third and final type of limitation imposed by the self-concept is on what a person will take to be the case about the world. Essentially, persons will "read" the world in ways that are in keeping with their self-concepts. For them, this will be "just the way the world is." For example, one client, when urged to look at some positive things about himself, told his therapist that "You don't seem to understand; the deep-down bedrock truth about me is that I am a complete and utter a—hole." From the point of view of this client, given who he was, the therapist's favourable comments could only be read as a case of misunderstanding. For this same client, minor criticisms from his wife simply "were" emotional abandonments, and praise from his employees simply "was" ill-motivated, deceitful flattery. To have a self-concept is, in the end, not just to have a certain appraisal of oneself—it is to live in a certain world.

Self-concept Influences How It is Deemed Appropriate to Act

In addition to restricting the behavioural possibilities of persons, the self-concept has important positive implications for how such persons will deem it appropriate to act. An old expression in the American culture is that of persons "knowing their place." Often used with reference to individuals in disadvantageous social positions, the expression indicates that the person in question understands his or her position vis-a-vis others and what it calls for in terms of behaviour towards them, and acts accordingly. The expression, "knowing one's place," captures well certain behavioural implications of the self-concept when viewed as one's summary formulation of one's place or status. Clinically, we observe that persons whose self-concept is that of "lowly nothing" will often express this interpersonally by behaving in ways that are self-effacing, deferential, nonassertive, and even servile. In contrast, others, whose conception of themselves is that they are "special persons", will frequently express this with behaviour that is arrogant, demanding, presumptuous, condescending, and heedless of the desires and rights of these others.

An important special case of the self-concept determining how it is appropriate to act concerns the matter of how persons treat themselves. Depending on the status one assigns to oneself, one may judge it appropriate to do such things as continually criticize oneself for one's many failings, disregard oneself, doubt the soundness of one's own judgements, engage in continual efforts to transform oneself from an unacceptable human being into an acceptable one, or even in extreme cases to execute oneself.

Self-concept Resists Empirical Disconfirmation

An empirically well-documented fact about the self-concept is that it possesses a curious resistance to change in the face of apparently disconfirming facts. A man continues to believe himself to be inferior despite what others view as compelling evidence to the contrary, and does so even when this evidence consists of facts that he himself admits are veridical. A woman believes herself selfish despite the many factual counterinstances posed by her reassuring friends. World renowned musicians and actors, despite years of glowing reviews from critics, continue to believe that they will surely fail and disgrace themselves the next time they go on stage.

On the status dynamic view, the self-concepts' imperviousness to seemingly contradictory factual input is explained by the hypothesis that the self-concept does not function as an *informational* entity, but as a *positional* one, and by noting the way that positional conceptions function vis-a-vis factual input. Essentially, so long as the ascription or assignment of a status (position) to something does not change, there is no way for any new fact to be disconfirming of that status. Indeed, in such a situation, *there are no disconfirming facts.*

Further Barriers to Self-concept Change

In most cases involving problems of self-concept, the origins of the problem lie in the statuses that clients were assigned when they were very young by their families, peers, school personnel, and others. Parents, for example, may have assigned them statuses as various as "bad through and through," "mommy and daddy's perfect angel," or "our emotionally disturbed child," which statuses may have varied greatly in the degree to which they miscast the child. Each of these statuses carried with it certain ways that the child was to be regarded and treated, as well as a place or a part in the family drama that the child was to carry out·

For the most part, children tend to unreflectively accept the statuses that they have been assigned by important others. Unfortunately, by the time they have acquired the sorts of observational and critical powers that might enable them to evaluate and question these statuses, they already have well-established self-concepts.

Thus, for a considerable period of time, they have been operating from within a formulation of self-in-relation-to-world, which formulation has long been an unquestioned given powerfully determining how they saw themselves and their worlds, how they acted, how they restricted themselves, how they viewed events, and more. Furthermore, they have with some frequency incorporated certain attributes into their self-concepts (e.g., "irrational," "stupid," "crazy") that are such that they have disqualified themselves as persons who are competent to rethink and redecide their status. Finally, in many cases, they may find themselves unable to negotiate their status with important others (e.g., to effectively dispute the family's or the spouse's view of them as "irrationally emotional") (Kirsch, 1982). For all of these reasons, the effects of parents and others assigning negative statuses to children can be both devastating and permanent.

Despite this rather discouraging picture, clients nonetheless occupy a position of power, greater or lesser depending on the individual, from which to reconsider and to change their self-concepts. The critical fact here is that, in the last analysis, the self-concept is by definition *self-assigned*—is *one's own* conception of oneself. While individuals may in most cases have had little say in its formation, they are now in every case persons who are accepting the statuses assigned by others, and assigning them to themselves. As implied in Eleanor Roosevelt's assertion that "no one can make you feel inferior without your consent, they retain the critical power, at times precious small, to effectively dissent from and to revise the debilitating statuses that have been assigned to them by others.

Advantages of the Present Formulation

The present conception of the self-concept conveys a number of important advantages over traditional informational summary accounts. Foremost among these are the following.

Parsimonious account of resistance to change. As noted previously, abundant empirical evidence supports the contention that the self-concept is resistant to change in the face of seemingly disconfirming empirical evidence. If the self-concept is conceived as an organized summary of perceived facts about oneself, it becomes difficult to see how new information that is recognized by the person, and that is inconsistent with his or her current conception of self, does not result in self-concept change. Traditionally, the way out of dilemmas involving inconsistent factual information has been to posit ego-defensive mechanisms and biases that result in persons either failing to register negative evidence about themselves at all, or distorting such evidence so as to render it non-injurious to self. However, such accounts encounter several serious problems.

First of all, some of them entail positing unobservable and highly questionable censoring mechanisms that somehow review all facts, decide if their level of threat to the self is tolerable, and if not repress or distort them. Second, all such accounts have difficulty accomodating the frequent, highly clinically significant, cases where the disconfirming facts in question are positive, fully recognized, and acknowledged as veridical by the individual. Third, all such accounts require a commitment to a view of persons as inherently irrational (i.e., as creatures ineluctably caused to deny or distort reality in light of their needs), a position that is enormously undermining to the whole enterprise of science as a rational enterprise since presumably scientists, as persons, are not exempt from such reality-distorting inevitabilities. The formulation of self-concept as summary formulation of one's status, as demonstrated above, explains the phenomenon of resistance to change more parsimoniously, does so without mysterious mental mechanisms, easily accomodates the case where such resistance occurs in the face of positive and fully recognized information, and accomplishes all of this without any commitment to a view of persons as inherently irrational.

Ties together a wide range of phenomena. The present account of the self-concept ties together a wide variety of observed empirical phenomena. As documented above, it explains restrictions on individuals' behavioural possibilities, held conceptions of how it is appropriate to act, ways of viewing the world, the binding effects of the self-concept on changes in itself, and the resistance of self-concepts to change in the face of what would seem disconfirming evidence. From a pragmatic clinical standpoint, these many linkages bring home an important point for the efficient and powerful conduct of psychotherapy: the self-concept is a "linchpin" factor, i.e., a single causal/explanatory source lying at the heart of a wide array of factors crucial to the quality of clients' lives. Changes in it may therefore be expected to result in changes in these many factors and thus to have a profound impact on the overall quality of these lives. With this in mind, let us turn to a presentation of some core therapeutic interventions that are heuristically suggested by the present account, and that have been employed by the authors and their colleagues to good effect for many years.

Psychotherapy: Changing Self-Concepts

In the status dynamic approach to helping persons alter their self-concepts, change is fundamentally about enabling clients to move out of the limiting, self-assigned statuses that are the source of their problems, and assigning themselves new statuses that convey far more behaviour potential. To accomplish this objective, the fundamental general strategy of status dynamic therapists is to create a two-person community with their clients, assign certain statuses to them, and treat them with the utmost consistency as persons who have those statuses. In essence, while they might employ traditional means such as cognitive restructuring, insight conveyance, or behaviour rehearsal, their primary means of achieving change is that of *actually placing clients in relational positions that are incompatible with the ones articulated in their self-concepts* .

Since this conception of psychotherapy is a relatively novel one, the following examples, two fictional and one real, will hopefully serve to orient the reader to it. First, in the film classic "It's a Wonderful Life," the protagonist, George Bailey, holds a conception of himself as a "complete failure in life." George's "therapist" (and guardian angel), Clarence, has a rather different view. Appraising George as an invaluable positive contributor to his family, friends, and community, Clarence sets out to bring about a change in his self-concept. He does so, not by conventional therapeutic means, but by magically *placing George in a new relational position*, that of visitor to his small town community as it would have been had he never been born—an infinitely poorer place where people's lives are far more wretched. In essence, he places George in a position where he could not have been the failure that he takes himself to be and have made the kind of difference that in fact he has made. By this means, George comes to a new and far more positive conception of himself, his place in the world, and the significance of his entire life. Second, in the stage musical classic "Man of La Mancha," the hero Don Quixote brings about fundamental changes in the self-concept and in the life of the prostitute Aldonza when he assigns her the status of his "Dulcinea" (i.e., the elevated "lady" in whose service his knightly quests are undertaken) and steadfastly treats her accordingly. Finally, bringing this matter out of the fictional and into the real world realm of psychotherapy, the central element in the person-centreed therapy of Carl Rogers was his assignment to all clients of the status "unconditionally acceptable person" and his subsequent, highly persistent treatment of them as such.

We will relate some of the ways in which this core idea of therapeutic status assignment may be carried out by therapists in helping their clients to alter their self-concepts. First, we will discuss the essentially a priori application of this idea in the therapeutic relationship. Second, we will discuss other, more empirically-based applications. Throughout, it may be noted that the utilization of these ideas can be undertaken in concert with other, more traditional therapeutic interventions.

The Therapeutic Relationship: Assigning A Priori Statuses

Above, we briefly considered the therapeutic work of Carl Rogers. Expanding upon this, if we view his work, not through his own person-centred lenses, but through status dynamic ones, we see Rogers as someone who assigned to all of his clients the status "unconditionally acceptable human being," not on the basis of observation, but *a priori*. The central element in person-centred therapy, and indeed the element cited by its practitioners as necessary and sufficient by itself to achieve therapeutic change, consisted in providing a relationship in which clients, independently of the facts about their lives and persons, were genuinely regarded and treated as acceptable persons.

Where Rogers assigned one status a priori, the status dynamic approach to the therapeutic relationship advocates that therapists assign a large number of statuses on this basis. In status dynamic therapy, the client is regarded and treated, a priori, as a person (1) who is acceptable; (2) who makes sense; (3) whose best interests come first in the therapeutic relationship; (4) who is important and significant to the therapist; (5) who already possesses enabling strengths, knowledge, and other resources for solving problems; (6) who, given a choice between equally realistic but differentially degrading appraisals of him or her, is to be given the benefit of the doubt; and

(7) who is an agent (i.e., an individual capable of entertaining behavioural options and selecting from among them, as opposed to a helpless victim of genetic, historical, environmental, or other forces).

The therapeutic policy becomes one of assigning all of these statuses a priori, and treating the client with the utmost consistency as one who has them. Thus, in this two-person community, the therapist sees to it, to the limits of his or her ability, that the client *is* accepted, *does* make sense, *is* significant; *is* given the benefit of the doubt, and so forth.

Most people who come to therapy with negative self-concepts view themselves as not being acceptable, not being someone whose interests really matter to others, not being someone with significant personal power, and so forth. Thus, to be genuinely regarded and treated in the above ways is already to have been moved to a new and more accredited position, and is a critically important part of the effort to alter the client's self-concept.

Assessment, Reformulation, and Therapeutic Status Assignment

In the status dynamic approach, the fundamental task of assessment is to determine the nature of the individual's presenting difficulty and, when the facts so indicate, the problematic formulation self-in-relation-to-world that is at the root of it (Bergner, 1999). To return once again to our Charlie Brown heuristic, we would assess Charlie's presenting concerns of depression and behavioural paralysis, and establish how these are rooted in his conception of himself as an ineligible "nothing" existing in a world of worthy "somethings."

Having assessed these matters, the next task of the therapist is that of *reformulating* who the client is—of reformulating the client's status within his or her world. In the optimum case, this reformulation would possess the following characteristics. First, and most fundamentally, it would *expand the client's behaviour potential*. That is, it would take a form such that, should the client accept it, previous limitations would be diminished and new possibilities and alternatives would be opened up for him or her. Second, the reformulation would be *realistic*. It would be, as it was in the case of George Bailey, consistent with the facts regarding the client's actual position in the scheme of things. It would not be some implausible view that the client would find incredible or, should he or she accept it, find impossible to carry off in the real social world. Third, it would *alter the significance of the client's whole life*. In the optimum (if not always realized) case, the new status assignment would be one that would change the significance of the client's behaviour, and even of his or her whole life, without the client doing anything different. In the case of George Bailey once again, as soon as he had accepted Clarence's status assignment, the significance of what he had been doing all along, and indeed of his entire personal history, was transformed ex post facto: he already was and had long been an invaluable contributor to his family and community. The contrast here is to therapeutic approaches that would require clients to change their behaviour and/or cognitions first before success could be attributed: "Well, you are quite unassertive now, but with some assertiveness training I believe you can someday do much better." From a status dynamic point of view, it is better to provide clients with empowering actualities than it is to give them only hope for better possibilities.

The foregoing considerations apply straightforwardly to cases where the therapist, like Clarence above, assesses the situation and sees the client in very status-enhancing ways. However, as we will see in one of our cases below, there are times when the therapist surveys the situation and finds that the client's position in the scheme of things is a far less salutary one. To illustrate our point once again with a familiar fictional example, one has only to think of the three ghosts who placed Ebenezer Scrooge in a position to see the not very flattering picture of who he had become. In such cases, the therapist, like the three ghosts, may need to assign a less socially desirable status, but nonetheless one calculated to make an immediate difference in the client's behaviour potential. Such a status assignment, further, would hopefully prove transitional and would help the individual to a new and better position in the world and a corresponding conception of self.

Finally, having arrived at a reformulation of the client's status, the fundamental strategy of the status dynamic therapist is to assign the client this status, and to steadfastly treat him or her accordingly. The therapist, often in concert with traditional interventions such as imparting insight, altering maladaptive cognitions, and encouraging new behaviour, engages in the powerful tactic of putting the client in a new position, and treating him or her as an occupant of that position with the utmost consistency possible. Expressed verbally, it is as if the therapist is saying to the client: "This is who you are, and I will treat you as such." Obviously, as with any approach, it is critically important for therapists to be watchful for any reactions or further information from the client that would indicate that their assessments and/or interventions have been misguided, and to make appropriate modifications if needed.

In order to convey how the status dynamic approach to modifying self-concept is implemented in actual cases, we have given the following two case examples.

Case #1. Sandy, a young college woman, had long appraised herself as "intellectually dull." She had acquired this view of herself in the context of being the youngest child in a family composed of rather accomplished individuals. Since the family placed a great premium on the importance of being intelligent, being "slow" was a core, and very painful, element in her self-concept, and one that had caused her to set her sights in life rather low. Growing up in her family, Sandy was always a bit behind everyone else since she was two years younger than her next youngest sibling. The family treated her as the cute, amusing, but slightly dim "baby of the family," and she came in this way to adopt such a view of herself. Sandy, however, had completed grade school with virtually all A's, and matriculated from a very competitive high school with a 3.5 grade point average. When she entered therapy, she was carrying the identical 3.5 average while taking a rather demanding curriculum at a large state university.

In the course of therapy, Sandy was asked how she squared all of the evidence from her scholastic career with her view of herself as "intellectually dull." How could she continue to look at the countless "A" and "B" grades from teachers in demanding courses and still regard herself as unintelligent? In teasing out the answer to this question, Sandy revealed many ways in which she preserved this status in the face of what would seem contradictory evidence. Confronted with an "A" grade, for example, her primary explanation was along the lines of the old saying about genius being more a matter of perspiration than of inspiration: "Isn't it amazing what an unintelligent person like me can do if I work hard enough!" On other occasions, she would explain away her success on grounds that she had been lucky, that the professor was not very demanding, that she had fortunately studied just the right things, and/or that it was her roommate's help that got her through. Finally, when Sandy occasionally did receive a bad evaluation, she viewed this simply as confirmation of her lack of intelligence. The net result of all of this was that her self-assigned status, "unintelligent person," had remained remarkably intact despite massive evidence to the contrary.

In Sandy's case, the therapist brought about change in this central aspect of her self-concept in the following manner. First, having personally assigned her the status of "intelligent individual," he helped her to see how "unintelligent" was essentially a *place* that she had been assigned in her family of origin, and that the facts strongly suggested that this place was assigned more on the basis of her necessarily lagging position in the family than on anything factual about her intellectual abilities. Second, in collaboration with Sandy, he teased out the picture described in the preceding paragraph of how she unwittingly preserved her status, "unintelligent," by holding fast to it as an unquestioned given, while interpreting all events in light of it. Third, in order to place her squarely in a position of power that she already occupied but didn't realize, the therapist assigned her the following homework. Having written down on an index card all of the specific ways in which she preserved her self-concept in the face of seemingly disconfirming evidence, he instructed her to go out that week and, every time she did something that seemed to require significant intelligence, she was to take the card out and say to herself: "I am an unintelligent person; this seeming discrepancy can be explained away in the following manner..." and then to check off one or more of the discounting explanations listed on the card. In implementing this exercise, Sandy was in effect consciously occupying a position that she had unconsciously occupied all along, that of one who preserved a negative status by systematically discounting a great deal of evidence. Operating from this position, she found herself increasingly unable to continue to do so and, in the end, was able to assign to herself a new status: "intelligent person."

In this case, it should be underscored, the basic intervention was not the classical cognitive one of evaluating a self-schema in light of empirical evidence. Rather, it was the status dynamic one of placing the client in a new position, that of intelligent person who was actively (if unwittingly) discounting her own achievements, and of exploiting this new position to bring about fundamental change in her self-concept.

Case #2. TJ, a man in his late forties, requested therapy initially because he had been having multiple affairs during most of his 30 year marriage, despised himself for this, but did not think he could stop. In addition to this primary concern, TJ reported others. In his job, he was in trouble much of the time because he repeatedly informed his superiors that he was completing work when in fact he was not.

He was constantly in debt because he acted the role of "big spender" and "man of means" with others, when in fact he was often on the verge of bankruptcy. He had a long history of alcohol abuse, but had been sober for several years when he entered therapy. Basically, TJ lived his life with smoke and mirrors and was always just a few steps away from one crisis or another, all of his own making.

At the time of intake, TJ's basic conception of himself was that he was a "nobody masquerading as a somebody." Beneath his public displays of bravura, he saw himself as a weak man who in his countless affairs, pretenses at being a man of means, lies to his superiors, financial crises, and abuse of alcohol, had failed at everything in his life.

A man of relatively small stature who grew up in a tough neighbourhood, TJ had always yearned to be a big man on the street. In his neighbourhood, the model of a big man was the "made man" or professional criminal who played by his own rules, cared about little, and was afraid of nothing. While TJ did not have the size and strength to make it as a physical tough, he was able to achieve status in his neighbourhood by becoming a consummate con man—someone who could talk people into doing what he wanted, who could get women to feel sorry for him and lure them to his bed, who could always get around doing what he was supposed to do, and who was very good at getting out of any trouble he might create, often by having his parents, and later his wife, clean up any messes that he made.

In the past, other therapists had tended to tell TJ what was wrong with what he did, but TJ seldom went back for more than 2 or 3 sessions. Not wanting to repeat this unsuccessful strategy, the status dynamic therapist elected to assign TJ a new status, one that both fit the central facts of TJ's life and that cast him, in certain important respects, as both successful and powerful. However, given the largely unsavory details of TJ's life, the status assigned was less like the highly positive one assigned by Clarence to George Bailey, and more like the rather negative one assigned by the three ghosts to Ebenezer Scrooge. Like the latter, further, the hope in this case was that the new status would spur positive changes in TJ and thus prove a transitional one.

The therapist's basic message to TJ was: "The way I see it, you have succeeded very well in becoming exactly who you always wanted to be: a successful con man who can deceive others into giving him what he wants, who can get all the women he wants, who derives enormous satisfactions from presenting himself as a big man and a big spender, who doesn't have to play by the rules like everyone else, who can successfully avoid the tedious, day-to-day stuff that ordinary people have to put up with—and who at the end of the day can always get away with it. You've been very successful at becoming exactly who you wanted to be, so why give it up unless you find something even better."

TJ readily accepted this status assignment—this portrayal of who he was. However, since the portrayal spoke to and satisfied only one side of his ambivalence (i.e. the part of him that had always wanted to be a successful criminal; but not the part that had destroyed his marriage, family, and career, and that experienced emptiness, self-hatred, and worthlessness), it did not take him long to become dissatisfied with the status quo. TJ soon began to ask questions like, "Well, if it makes so much sense for me to do all these things, how come I don't enjoy them anymore?" and "How come nothing and nobody means anything to me?" The therapist then began to show TJ that the most he could ever accomplish if he pursued his lifelong agenda was to become a better con man, and no matter how good a con man he became, he was likely to find it provided limited satisfaction and little significance once he proved he could get away with it. Having given TJ the status of "successful con man," the therapist in essence turned the tables on him by having him experience the emptiness of his place in the world.

If TJ wanted enjoyment and significance in his life, the answer was conceptually simple: give up being a con man and be authentic; i.e., give up *impersonating* someone with something to offer and *be* someone with something genuine to offer. At this point, the therapist, noting certain motivations and other qualities in TJ, assigned him a second and more accrediting status: that of someone who did have something genuine and valuable to offer others. Not surprisingly, getting TJ to a place where he could see that he actually had something of value to offer others, and that he had more behaviour potential through being authentic than through being a con man, took a good deal of time. While the details of this effort are beyond the space limitations of the present article, two examples may serve to convey the nature of this final phase of the therapy.

TJ knew a good deal about computers and was something of a graphics expert. In the course of therapy, the therapist made it a point to ask for TJ's advice about a number of computer problems. In doing so, his objective was to assign TJ the status of "computer expert and consultant," and to treat him in this respect as someone who had a genuine, high quality contribution to make. TJ responded to this by offering his help freely and was obviously quite pleased that he was able to be helpful to the therapist. The therapist then focussed on what it was like for TJ to be in a relationship in which people could and would depend on him. This led to a series of discussions on what it would take for the therapist to trust TJ if they had met outside of therapy.

A second significant interaction had to do with the fact that TJ often ended up in situations in which he had to lie to his family or his employer. The therapist one day simply said to him, "You usually don't have to cover things up if you have clean hands." This became a motto for TJ in many of his subsequent dealings with the world. While he struggled with it, it became an important part of his formulation of who he was becoming: a person who played it straight and did not have to lie because he kept his hands clean.

Over several years time, TJ came to develop a radically different self-concept, that of someone who had something genuine and valuable to offer others, and who therefore could succeed without being a con man. As this conception developed, he began to venture into a wide range of new positions in the world.

He obtained a new job that put him in a place in which he had to produce at a high level on a regular basis. He decided to try to develop a love relationship with his wife even though that meant dealing with the results of many years of betrayal and mistrust. He was able to regain the respect of his children. At last report, he and his wife are making significant strides in their relationship. He has performed exceptionally well in his job. Recently, his difficulty in managing financial responsibilities resulted in a fairly significant crisis, but he took full responsiblity for the crisis and managed to find a way to deal with it on his own.

The Maintenance Stage: Preserving or Being Nagged by the Self Concept.

Self-verification Theory

Self-verification is a social psychological theory that asserts people want to be known and understood by others according to their firmly held beliefs and feelings about themselves, that is *self-views* (including self-concepts and self-esteem). A competing theory to self-verification is *self-enhancement* or the drive for positive evaluations.

Because chronic self-concepts and self-esteem play an important role in understanding the world, providing a sense of coherence, and guiding action, people become motivated to maintain them through self-verification. Such strivings provide stability to people's lives, making their experiences more coherent, orderly, and comprehensible than they would be otherwise. Self-verification processes are also adaptive for groups, groups of diverse backgrounds and the larger society, in that they make people predictable to one another thus serve to facilitate social interaction. To this end, people engage in a variety of activities that are designed to obtain self-verifying information.

Developed by William Swann (1983), the theory grew out of earlier writings which held that people form self-views so that they can understand and predict the responses of others and know how to act toward them.

Difference Between Positive and Negative Self-views

There are individual differences in people's views of themselves. Among people with *positive self-views*, the desire for self-verification works together with another important motive, the desire for positive evaluations or "self enhancement". For example, those who view themselves as "insightful" will find that their motives for both self-verification and self-enhancement encourage them to seek evidence that other people recognize their insightfulness.

In contrast, people with *negative self-views* will find that the desire for self-verification and self-enhancement are competing. Consider people who see themselves as disorganized. Whereas their desire for self-enhancement will compel them to seek evidence that others perceive them as organized, their desire for self-verification will compel such individuals to seek evidence that others perceive them as disorganized. Self verification strivings tend to prevail over self-enhancement strivings when people are certain of the self-concept and when they have extremely depressive self-views.

Self-verification strivings may have undesirable consequences for people with negative self-views (depressed people and those who suffer from low self-esteem). For example, self-verification strivings may cause people with negative self-views to gravitate toward partners who mistreat them, undermine their feelings of self-worth, or even abuse them. And if people with negative self-views seek therapy, returning home to a self-verifying partner may undo the progress that was made there. Finally, in the workplace, the feelings of worthlessness that plague people with low self-esteem may foster feelings of ambivalence about receiving fair treatment, feelings that may undercut their propensity to insist that they get what they deserve from their employers.

These findings and related ones point to the importance of efforts to improve the self-views of those who suffer from low self-esteem and depression.

Effects on Behaviour

In one series of studies, researchers asked participants with positive and negative self-views whether they would prefer to interact with evaluators who had favourable or unfavourable impressions of them. The results showed that those with positive self-views preferred favourable partners and those with negative self-views preferred unfavourable partners. The latter finding revealed that self-verification strivings may sometimes trump positivity strivings.

Self-verification motives operate for different dimensions of the self-concept and in many different situations. Men and women are equally inclined to display this tendency, and it does not matter whether the self-views refer to characteristics that are relatively *immutable* (e.g., intelligence) or *changeable* (e.g., diligence), or whether the self-views happen to be *highly specific* (e.g., athletic) or *global* (e.g., low self-esteem, worthlessness). Furthermore, when people chose negative partners over positive ones, it is not merely in an effort to avoid interacting with positive evaluators (that is, out of a concern that they might disappoint such positive evaluators). Rather, people chose self-verifying, negative partners even when the alternative is participating in a different experiment. Finally, recent work has shown that people work to verify self-views associated with group memberships. For example, women seek evaluations that confirm their belief that they possess qualities associated with being a woman.

Self-verification theory suggests that people may begin to shape others' evaluations of them before they even begin interacting with them. They may, for example, display identity cues. The most effective identity cues enable people to signal who they are to potential interaction partners.

- Physical appearance, such as clothes, body posture, demeanor. For example, the low self-esteem person who evokes reactions that confirm her negative self-views by slumping her shoulders and keeping her eyes fixed on the ground.
- Other cues, such as the car someone buys, the house they live in, the way they decorate their living environment. For example, an SUV evokes reactions that confirm a person's positive self-view.

Self-verification strivings may also influence the social contexts that people enter into and remain in. People reject those who provide social feedback that does not confirm their self-views, such as married people with negative self-views who reject spouses who see them positively and vice-versa. College room mates behave in a similar manner. People are more inclined to divorce partners who perceived them too favourably. In each of these instances, people gravitated toward relationships that provided them with evaluations that confirmed their self-views and fled from those that did not.

When people fail to gain self-verifying reactions through the display of identity cue or through choosing self-verifying social environments, they may still acquire such evaluations by systematically evoking confirming reactions. For example, depressed people behave in negative ways toward their room mates, thus causing these room mates to reject them.

Self-verification theory predicts that when people interact with others, there is a general tendency for them to bring others to see them as they see themselves. This tendency if especially pronounced when they start out believing that the other person has misconstrued them, apparently because people compensate by working especially hard to bring others to confirm their self-views. People will even stop working on tasks to which they have been assigned if they sense that their performance is eliciting non-verifying feedback.

3

Impression Management

In sociology and social psychology, impression management is a goal-directed conscious or unconscious process in which people attempt to influence the perceptions of other people about a person, object or event; they do so by regulating and controlling information in social interaction. It is usually used synonymously with self-presentation, in which a person tries to influence the perception of their image. The notion of impression management also refers to practices in professional communication and public relations, where the term is used to describe the process of formation of a company's or organization's public image.

Self-presentation

While impression management and self-presentation are often used interchangeably, some authors have argued that they are not the same. In particular, Schlenker (1980) believed that self-presentation should be used to describe attempts to control 'self-relevant' (pp. 6) images projected in "real or imagined social interactions'. This is because people may manage impressions of entities other than themselves such as businesses, cities and other individuals (Leary & Kowalski 1990).

Motives and Strategies

Self-presentation is expressive. We construct an image of ourselves to claim personal identity, and present ourselves in a manner that is consistent with that image. If we feel like this is restricted, we exhibit reactance/be defiant. We try to assert our freedom against those who would seek to curtail our self-presentation expressiveness. A classic example is the idea of the "preacher's daughter", whose suppressed personal identity and emotions cause an eventual backlash at her family and community.

People adopt many different impression management strategies. One of them is ingratiation, where we use flattery or praise to increase our social attractiveness by highlighting our better characteristics so that others will like us (Schlenker 1980, pp. 169).

Another strategy is intimidation, which is aggressively showing anger to get others to hear and obey us.

A strategy that has garnered a great amount of research attention is self-handicapping. In this case people create 'obstacles' and 'excuses' (Aronson et al. 2009, pp. 174) for themselves so that they can avoid self-blame when they do poorly. People who self-handicap choose to blame their failures on obstacles such as drugs and alcohol rather than their own lack of ability. Other individuals devise excuses such as shyness, anxiety, negative mood or physical symptoms as reasons for their failure.

Concerning the strategies followed to establish a certain impression, the main distinction is between defensive and assertive strategies. Whereas defensive strategies include behaviours like avoidance of threatening situations or means of self-handicapping, assertive strategies refer to more active behaviour like the verbal idealisation of the self, the use of status symbols or similar practices.

These strategies play important roles in one's maintenance of self-esteem. One's self-esteem is affected by his evaluation of his own performance and his perception of how others react to his performance. As a result, people actively portray impressions that will elicit self-esteem enhancing reactions from others.

Theory

Impression management (IM) theory states that any individual or organization must establish and maintain impressions that are congruent with the perceptions they want to convey to their publics. From both a communications and public relations viewpoint, the theory of impression management encompasses the vital ways in which one establishes and communicates this congruence between personal or organizational goals and their intended actions which create public perception.

The idea that perception is reality is the basis for this sociological and social psychology theory, which is framed around the presumption that the other's perceptions of you or your organization become the reality from which they form ideas and the basis for intended behaviours.

Basic Factors

A range of factors that govern impression management can be identified. It can be stated that impression management becomes necessary whenever there exists a kind of social situation, whether real or imaginary. Logically, the awareness of being a potential subject of monitoring is also crucial. Furthermore, the characteristics of a given social situation are important.

Specifically, the surrounding cultural norms determine the appropriateness of particular nonverbal behaviours. The actions have to be appropriate to the targets, and within that culture, so that the kind of audience as well as the relation to the audience influences the way impression management is realized. A person's goals are another factor governing the ways and strategies of impression management. This refers to the content of an assertion, which also leads to distinct ways of presentation of aspects of the self. The degree of self-efficacy describes whether a person is convinced that it is possible to convey the intended impression.

A new study finds that, all other things being equal, people are more likely to pay attention to faces that have been associated with negative gossip than those with neutral or positive associations. The study contributes to a body of work showing that far from being objective, our perceptions are shaped by unconscious brain processes that determine what we "choose" to see or ignore — even before we become aware of it. The findings also add to the idea that the brain evolved to be particularly sensitive to "bad guys" or cheaters — fellow humans who undermine social life by deception, theft or other non-cooperative behaviour.

Erving Goffman

Strategic interpersonal behaviour to shape or influence impressions formed by an audience is not a new field. Plato spoke of the "stage of human life" and Shakespeare crafted the famous sentence "All the world's a stage, and all the men and women merely players". In the 20th century, Erving Goffman also followed a dramaturgical analogy in his seminal book The Presentation of Self in Everyday Life, in which he said, "All the world is not, of course, a stage, but the crucial ways in which it isn't are not easy to specify."

Goffman presented impression management dramaturgically, explaining the motivations behind complex human performances within a social setting based on a play metaphor. Goffman's work incorporates aspects of a symbolic interactionist perspective, emphasizing a qualitative analysis of the interactive nature of the communication process.

The actor, shaped by the environment and target audience, sees interaction as a performance. The objective of the performance is to provide the audience with an impression consistent with the desired goals of the actor. Thus, impression management is also highly dependent on the situation. In addition to these goals, individuals differ in responses from the interactional environment, some may be irresponsive to audience's reactions while others actively respond to audience reactions in order to elicit positive results. These differences in response towards the environment and target audience are called self-monitoring. Another factor in impression management is self-verification, the act of conforming the audience to the person's self-concept.

The audience can be real or imaginary. IM style norms, part of the mental programming received through socialization, are so fundamental that we usually do not notice our expectations of them. While an actor (speaker) tries to project a desired image, an audience (listener) might attribute a resonant or discordant image. An example is provided by situations in which embarrassment occurs and threatens the image of a participant.

Social Psychology

The social psychologist, Edward E. Jones, brought the study of impression management to the field of psychology during the 1960s and extended it to include people's attempts to control others' impression of their personal characteristics. His work sparked an increased attention towards impression management as a fundamental interpersonal process.

Self, Social Identity and Social Interaction

The concept of self is important to the theory of impression management as the images people have of themselves shape and are shaped by social interactions. Our self-concept develops from social experience early in life. Schlenker (1980) further suggests that children anticipate the effect of their behaviours will have on others and how others will evaluate them, they control the impressions they might form on others and in doing so they control the outcomes they obtain from social interactions.

Social identity refers to how people are defined and regarded in social interactions. Individuals use impression management strategies to influence the social identity they project to others. The identity that people establish influences their behaviour in front of others, others' treatment of them and the outcomes they receive. Therefore, in their attempts to influence the impressions others form of themselves, a person plays an important role in affecting his social outcomes.

The Media

The medium of communication influences the actions taken in impression management. Self-efficacy can differ according to the fact whether the trial to convince somebody is made through face-to-face-interaction or by means of an e-mail. Communication via devices like telephone, e-mail or chat is governed by technical restrictions, so that the way people express personal features etc. can be changed. This often shows how far people will go.

Significance in Empirical Research and Economy

Impression management can distort the results of empirical research that relies on interviews and surveys, a phenomenon commonly referred to as "social desirability bias". Impression management Theory nevertheless constitutes a field of research on its own. When it comes to practical questions concerning public relations and the way organizations should handle their public image, the assumptions provided by impression management theory can also provide a framework.

An examination of different impression management strategies acted out by individuals who were facing criminal trials where the trial outcomes could range from a death sentence, life in prison or acquittal has been reported in the forensic literature. The Perri and Lichtenwald article examined female psychopathic killers, whom as a group were highly motivated to manage the impression that attorneys, judges, mental health professions and ultimately, a jury had of the murderers and the murder they committed. It provides legal case illustrations of the murderers combining and/or switching from one impression management strategy such as ingratiation or supplication to another as they worked towards their goal of diminishing or eliminating any accountability for the murders they committed.

Since the 1990s, researchers in the area of sport and exercise psychology have studied self-presentation. Concern about how one is perceived has been found to be relevant to the study of athletic performance. For example, anxiety may be produced when an athlete is in the presence of spectators. Self-presentational concerns have also been found to be relevant to exercise. For example, the concerns may elicit motivation to exercise. More recent research investigating the effects of impression management on social behaviour showed that social behaviours (e.g. eating) can serve to convey a desired impression to others and enhance one's self-image. Research on eating has shown that people tend to eat less when they believe that they are being observed by others.

Confirmation Bias

Confirmation bias (also called confirmatory bias or myside bias) is a tendency of people to favour information that confirms their beliefs or hypotheses. People display this bias when they gather or remember information selectively, or when they interpret it in a biased way. The effect is stronger for emotionally charged issues and for deeply entrenched beliefs. They also tend to interpret ambiguous evidence as supporting their existing position. Biased search, interpretation and memory have been invoked to explain attitude polarization (when a disagreement becomes more extreme even though the different parties are exposed to the same evidence), belief perseverance (when beliefs persist after the evidence for them is shown to be false), the irrational primacy effect (a greater reliance on information encountered early in a series) and illusory correlation (when people falsely perceive an association between two events or situations). A series of experiments in the 1960s suggested that people are biased toward confirming their existing beliefs. Later work re-interpreted these results as a tendency to test ideas in a one-sided way, focusing on one possibility and ignoring alternatives. In certain situations, this tendency can bias people's conclusions. Explanations for the observed biases include wishful thinking and the limited human capacity to process information. Another explanation is that people show confirmation bias because they are weighing up the costs of being wrong, rather than investigating in a neutral, scientific way.

Confirmation biases contribute to overconfidence in personal beliefs and can maintain or strengthen beliefs in the face of contrary evidence. Poor decisions due to these biases have been found in political and organizational contexts.

Types

Confirmation biases are effects in information processing, distinct from the *behavioural confirmation effect*, also called "self-fulfilling prophecy", in which people's expectations affect their behaviour to make the expectations come true. Some psychologists use "confirmation bias" to refer to any way in which people avoid rejecting a belief, whether in searching for evidence, interpreting it, or recalling it from memory. Others restrict the term to selective collection of evidence.

Biased Search for Information

Experiments have repeatedly found that people tend to test hypotheses in a one-sided way, by searching for evidence consistent with the hypothesis they hold at a given time. Rather than searching through all the relevant evidence, they ask questions that are phrased so that an affirmative answer supports their hypothesis. They look for the consequences that they would expect if their hypothesis were true, rather than what would happen if it were false. For example, someone who is trying to identify a number using yes/no questions and suspects that the number is 3 might ask, "Is it an odd number?" People prefer this sort of question, called a "positive test", even when a negative test such as "Is it an even number?" would yield exactly the same information. However, this does not mean that people seek tests that are guaranteed to give a positive answer. In studies where subjects could select either such pseudo-tests or genuinely diagnostic ones, they favoured the genuinely diagnostic.

The preference for positive tests is not itself a bias, since positive tests can be highly informative. However, in conjunction with other effects, this strategy can confirm existing beliefs or assumptions, independently of whether they are true. In real-world situations, evidence is often complex and mixed. For example, various contradictory ideas about someone could each be supported by concentrating on one aspect of his or her behaviour. Thus any search for evidence in favour of a hypothesis is likely to succeed. One illustration of this is the way the phrasing of a question can significantly change the answer. For example, people who are asked, "Are you happy with your social life?" Report greater satisfaction than those asked, "Are you *un*happy with your social life?"

Even a small change in the wording of a question can affect how people search through available information, and hence the conclusions they reach. This was shown using a fictional child custody case.

Subjects read that Parent A was moderately suitable to be the guardian in multiple ways. Parent B had a mix of salient positive and negative qualities: a close relationship with the child but a job that would take him or her away for long periods. When asked, "Which parent should have custody of the child?" The subjects looked for positive attributes and a majority chose Parent B. However, when the question was, "Which parent should be denied custody of the child?" They looked for negative attributes, but again a majority answered Parent B, implying that Parent A should have custody.

Similar studies have demonstrated how people engage in biased search for information, but also that this phenomenon may be limited by a preference for genuine diagnostic tests, where they are available. In an initial experiment, subjects had to rate another person on the introversion–extroversion personality dimension on the basis of an interview. They chose the interview questions from a given list. When the interviewee was introduced as an introvert, the subjects chose questions that presumed introversion, such as, "What do you find unpleasant about noisy parties?" When the interviewee was described as extroverted, almost all the questions presumed extroversion, such as, "What would you do to liven up a dull party?" These loaded questions gave the interviewees little or no opportunity to falsify the hypothesis about them. However, a later version of the experiment gave the subjects less presumptive questions to choose from, such as, "Do you shy away from social interactions?" Subjects preferred to ask these more diagnostic questions, showing only a weak bias towards positive tests. This pattern, of a main preference for diagnostic tests and a weaker preference for positive tests, has been replicated in other studies.

Another experiment gave subjects a particularly complex rule-discovery task involving moving objects simulated by a computer. Objects on the computer screen followed specific laws, which the subjects had to figure out. They could "fire" objects across the screen to test their hypotheses. Despite making many attempts over a ten-hour session, none of the subjects worked out the rules of the system. They typically sought to confirm rather than falsify their hypotheses, and were reluctant to consider alternatives. Even after seeing evidence that objectively refuted their working hypotheses, they frequently continued doing the same tests. Some of the subjects were instructed in proper hypothesis-testing, but these instructions had almost no effect.

Biased Interpretation

Confirmation biases are not limited to the collection of evidence. Even if two individuals have the same information, the way they interpret it can be biased.

A team at Stanford University ran an experiment with subjects who felt strongly about capital punishment, with half in favour and half against. Each of these subjects read descriptions of two studies; a comparison of U.S. states with and without the death penalty, and a comparison of murder rates in a state before and after the introduction of the death penalty. After reading a quick description of each study, the subjects were asked whether their opinions had changed. They then read a much more detailed account of each study's procedure and had to rate how well-conducted and convincing that research was. In fact, the studies were fictional. Half the subjects were told that one kind of study supported the deterrent effect and the other undermined it, while for other subjects the conclusions were swapped.

The subjects, whether proponents or opponents, reported shifting their attitudes slightly in the direction of the first study they read. Once they read the more detailed descriptions of the two studies, they almost all returned to their original belief regardless of the evidence provided, pointing to details that supported their viewpoint and disregarding anything contrary. Subjects described studies supporting their pre-existing view as superior to those that contradicted it, in detailed and specific ways. Writing about a study that seemed to undermine the deterrence effect, a death penalty proponent wrote, "The research didn't cover a long enough period of time", while an opponent's comment on the same study said, "No strong evidence to contradict the researchers has been presented". The results illustrated that people set higher standards of evidence for hypotheses that go against their current expectations. This effect, known as "disconfirmation bias", has been supported by other experiments.

A study of biased interpretation took place during the 2004 US presidential election and involved subjects who described themselves as having strong feelings about the candidates. They were shown apparently contradictory pairs of statements, either from Republican candidate George W. Bush, Democratic candidate John Kerry or a politically neutral public figure. They were also given further statements that made the apparent contradiction seem reasonable. From these three pieces of information, they had to decide whether or not each individual's statements were inconsistent. There were strong differences in these evaluations, with subjects much more likely to interpret statements by the candidate they opposed as contradictory.

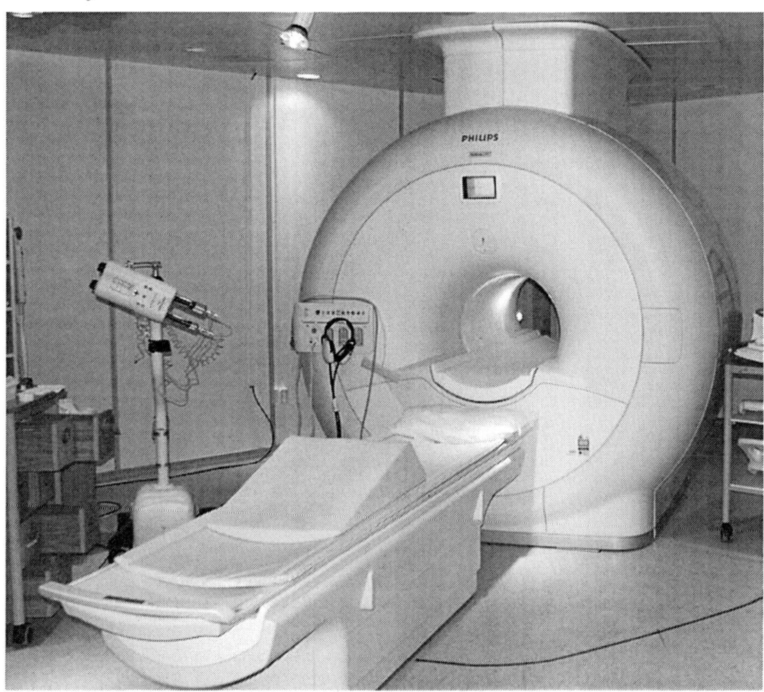

Figure: *An MRI scanner allowed researchers to examine how the human brain deals with unwelcome information.*

In this experiment, the subjects made their judgements while in a magnetic resonance imaging (MRI) scanner which monitored their brain activity. As subjects evaluated contradictory statements by their favoured candidate, emotional centres of their brains were aroused. This did not happen with the statements by the other figures. The experimenters inferred that the different responses to the statements were not due to passive reasoning errors. Instead, the subjects were actively reducing the cognitive dissonance induced by reading about their favoured candidate's irrational or hypocritical behaviour.

Biased interpretation is not restricted to emotionally significant topics. In another experiment, subjects were told a story about a theft. They had to rate the evidential importance of statements arguing either for or against a particular character being responsible. When they hypothesized that character's guilt, they rated statements supporting that hypothesis as more important than conflicting statements.

Biased Memory

Even if people have sought and interpreted evidence in a neutral manner, they may still remember it selectively to reinforce their expectations. This effect is called "selective recall", "confirmatory memory" or "access-biased memory". Psychological theories differ in their predictions about selective recall.

Schema theory predicts that information matching prior expectations will be more easily stored and recalled. Some alternative approaches say that surprising information stands out more and so is more memorable. Predictions from both these theories have been confirmed in different experimental contexts, with no theory winning outright.

In one study, subjects read a profile of a woman which described a mix of introverted and extroverted behaviours. They later had to recall examples of her introversion and extroversion. One group was told this was to assess the woman for a job as a librarian, while a second group were told it was for a job in real estate sales.

There was a significant difference between what these two groups recalled, with the "librarian" group recalling more examples of introversion and the "sales" groups recalling more extroverted behaviour. A selective memory effect has also been shown in experiments that manipulate the desirability of personality types. In one of these, a group of subjects were shown evidence that extroverted people are more successful than introverts. Another group were told the opposite.

In a subsequent, apparently unrelated, study, they were asked to recall events from their lives in which they had been either introverted or extroverted. Each group of subjects provided more memories connecting themselves with the more desirable personality type, and recalled those memories more quickly.

One study showed how selective memory can maintain belief in extrasensory perception (ESP). Believers and disbelievers were each shown descriptions of ESP experiments. Half of each group were told that the experimental results supported the existence of ESP, while the others were told they did not. In a subsequent test, subjects recalled the material accurately, apart from believers who had read the non-supportive evidence. This group remembered significantly less information and some of them incorrectly remembered the results as supporting ESP.

Related Effects

Backfire Effect: A similar cognitive bias found in individuals is the *backfire effect*, in which individuals challenged with evidence contradictory to their beliefs tend to reject the evidence and instead become an even firmer supporter of their initial belief. The phrase was first coined by Brendan Nyhan and Jason Reifler in a paper entitled "When Corrections Fail: The persistence of political misperceptions".

Polarization of Opinion

When people with opposing views interpret new information in a biased way, their views can move even further apart. This is called "attitude polarization". The effect was demonstrated by an experiment that involved drawing a series of red and black balls from one of two concealed "bingo baskets". Subjects knew that one basket contained 60% black and 40% red balls; the other, 40% black and 60% red. The experimenters looked at what happened when balls of alternating colour were drawn in turn, a sequence that does not favour either basket. After each ball was drawn, subjects in one group were asked to state out loud their judgements of the probability that the balls were being drawn from one or the other basket.

These subjects tended to grow more confident with each successive draw—whether they initially thought the basket with 60% black balls or the one with 60% red balls was the more likely source, their estimate of the probability increased. Another group of subjects were asked to state probability estimates only at the end of a sequence of drawn balls, rather than after each ball. They did not show the polarization effect, suggesting that it does not necessarily occur when people simply hold opposing positions, but rather when they openly commit to them.

A less abstract study was the Stanford biased interpretation experiment in which subjects with strong opinions about the death penalty read about mixed experimental evidence. Twenty-three percent of the subjects reported that their views had become more extreme, and this self-reported shift correlated strongly with their initial attitudes. In later experiments, subjects also reported their opinions becoming more extreme in response to ambiguous information. However, comparisons of their attitudes before and after the new evidence showed no significant change, suggesting that the self-reported changes might not be real. Based on these experiments, Deanna Kuhn and Joseph Lao concluded that polarization is a real phenomenon but far from inevitable, only happening in a small minority of cases. They found that it was prompted not only by considering mixed evidence, but by merely thinking about the topic.

Charles Taber and Milton Lodge argued that the Stanford team's result had been hard to replicate because the arguments used in later experiments were too abstract or confusing to evoke an emotional response. The Taber and Lodge study used the emotionally charged topics of gun control and affirmative action. They measured the attitudes of their subjects towards these issues before and after reading arguments on each side of the debate. Two groups of subjects showed attitude polarization; those with strong prior opinions and those who were politically knowledgeable. In part of this study, subjects chose which information sources to read, from a list prepared by the experimenters. For example they could read the National Rifle Association's and the Brady Anti-Handgun Coalition's arguments on gun control. Even when instructed to be even-handed, subjects were more likely to read arguments that supported their existing attitudes. This biased search for information correlated well with the polarization effect.

Persistence of Discredited Beliefs

Confirmation biases can be used to explain why some beliefs remain when the initial evidence for them is removed. This belief perseverance effect has been shown by a series of experiments using what is called the "debriefing paradigm": subjects read fake evidence for a hypothesis, their attitude change is measured, then the fakery is exposed in detail. Their attitudes are then measured once more to see if their belief returns to its previous level.

A typical finding is that at least some of the initial belief remains even after a full debrief. In one experiment, subjects had to distinguish between real and fake suicide notes. The feedback was random: some were told they had done well while others were told they had performed badly. Even after being fully debriefed, subjects were still influenced by the feedback. They still thought they were better or worse than average at that kind of task, depending on what they had initially been told.

In another study, subjects read job performance ratings of two firefighters, along with their responses to a risk aversion test. These fictional data were arranged to show either a negative or positive association: some subjects were told that a risk-taking firefighter did better, while others were told they did less well than a risk-averse colleague. Even if these two case studies had been true, they would have been scientifically poor evidence for a conclusion about firefighters in general. However, the subjects found them subjectively persuasive. When the case studies were shown to be fictional, subjects' belief in a link diminished, but around half of the original effect remained. Follow-up interviews established that the subjects had understood the debriefing and taken it seriously. Subjects seemed to trust the debriefing, but regarded the discredited information as irrelevant to their personal belief.

Preference for Early Information

Experiments have shown that information is weighted more strongly when it appears early in a series, even when the order is unimportant. For example, people form a more positive impression of someone described as "intelligent, industrious, impulsive, critical, stubborn, envious" than when they are given the same words in reverse order. This *irrational primacy effect* is independent of the primacy effect in memory in which the earlier items in a series leave a stronger memory trace. Biased interpretation offers an explanation for this effect: seeing the initial evidence, people form a working hypothesis that affects how they interpret the rest of the information.

One demonstration of irrational primacy involved coloured chips supposedly drawn from two urns. Subjects were told the colour distributions of the urns, and had to estimate the probability of a chip being drawn from one of them. In fact, the colours appeared in a pre-arranged order. The first thirty draws favoured one urn and the next thirty favoured the other. The series as a whole was neutral, so rationally, the two urns were equally likely. However, after sixty draws, subjects favoured the urn suggested by the initial thirty.

Another experiment involved a slide show of a single object, seen as just a blur at first and in slightly better focus with each succeeding slide. After each slide, subjects had to state their best guess of what the object was. Subjects whose early guesses were wrong persisted with those guesses, even when the picture was sufficiently in focus that other people could readily identify the object.

Illusory Association Between Events

Illusory correlation is the tendency to see non-existent correlations in a set of data. This tendency was first demonstrated in a series of experiments in the late 1960s. In one experiment, subjects read a set of psychiatric case studies, including responses to the Rorschach inkblot test. They reported that the homosexual men in the set were more likely to report seeing buttocks, anuses or sexually ambiguous figures in the inkblots. In fact the case studies were fictional and, in one version of the experiment, had been constructed so that the homosexual men were less likely to report this imagery. In a survey, a group of experienced psychoanalysts reported the same set of illusory associations with homosexuality.

Another study recorded the symptoms experienced by arthritic patients, along with weather conditions over a 15-month period. Nearly all the patients reported that their pains were correlated with weather conditions, although the real correlation was zero.

This effect is a kind of biased interpretation, in that objectively neutral or unfavourable evidence is interpreted to support existing beliefs. It is also related to biases in hypothesis-testing behaviour. In judging whether two events, such as illness and bad weather, are correlated, people rely heavily on the number of *positive-positive* cases: in this example, instances of both pain and bad weather. They pay relatively little attention to the other kinds of observation (of no pain and/or good weather). This parallels the reliance on positive tests in hypothesis testing. It may also reflect selective recall, in that people may have a sense that two events are correlated because it is easier to recall times when they happened together.

Example

Days	***Rain***	***No rain***
Arthritis	14	6
No arthritis	7	2

In the above fictional example, arthritic symptoms are more likely on days with no rain. However, people are likely to focus on the relatively large number of days which have both rain and symptoms. By concentrating on one cell of the table rather than all four, people can misperceive the relationship, in this case associating rain with arthritic symptoms.

History

Informal Observation: Before psychological research on confirmation bias, the phenomenon had been observed anecdotally by writers, including the Greek historian Thucydides (c. 460 BC – c.

395 BC), Italian poet Dante Alighieri (1265–1321), English philosopher and scientist Francis Bacon (1561–1626), and Russian author Leo Tolstoy (1828–1910). Thucydides, in *The Peloponnesian War* wrote: "...for it is a habit of mankind to entrust to careless hope what they long for, and to use sovereign reason to thrust aside what they do not fancy." In the *Divine Comedy*, St. Thomas Aquinas cautions Dante when they meet in Paradise, "opinion—hasty—often can incline to the wrong side, and then affection for one's own opinion binds, confines the mind." Bacon, in the *Novum Organum*, wrote,

The human understanding when it has once adopted an opinion ... draws all things else to support and agree with it. And though there be a greater number and weight of instances to be found on the other side, yet these it either neglects or despises, or else by some distinction sets aside or rejects[.]

Bacon said that biased assessment of evidence drove "all superstitions, whether in astrology, dreams, omens, divine judgements or the like". In his essay "What Is Art?", Tolstoy wrote,

I know that most men—not only those considered clever, but even those who are very clever, and capable of understanding most difficult scientific, mathematical, or philosophic problems—can very seldom discern even the simplest and most obvious truth if it be such as to oblige them to admit the falsity of conclusions they have formed, perhaps with much difficulty—conclusions of which they are proud, which they have taught to others, and on which they have built their lives.

Wason's Research on Hypothesis-testing

The term "confirmation bias" was coined by English psychologist Peter Wason. For an experiment published in 1960, he challenged subjects to identify a rule applying to triples of numbers. At the outset, they were told that (2,4,6) fits the rule. Subjects could generate their own triples and the experimenter told them whether or not each triple conformed to the rule.

While the actual rule was simply "any ascending sequence", the subjects had a great deal of difficulty in finding it, often announcing rules that were far more specific, such as "the middle number is the average of the first and last". The subjects seemed to test only positive examples—triples that obeyed their hypothesized rule. For example, if they thought the rule was, "Each number is two greater than its predecessor", they would offer a triple that fit this rule, such as (11,13,15) rather than a triple that violates it, such as (11,12,19).

Wason accepted falsificationism, according to which a scientific test of a hypothesis is a serious attempt to falsify it. He interpreted his results as showing a preference for confirmation over falsification, hence the term "confirmation bias". Wason also used confirmation bias to explain the results of his selection task experiment. In this task, subjects are given partial information about a set of objects, and have to specify what further information they would need to tell whether or not a conditional rule ("If A, then B") applies. It has been found repeatedly that people perform badly on various forms of this test, in most cases ignoring information that could potentially refute the rule.

Klayman and Ha's Critique

A 1987 paper by Joshua Klayman and Young-Won Ha argued that the Wason experiments had not actually demonstrated a bias towards confirmation. Instead, Klayman and Ha interpreted the results in terms of a tendency to make tests that are consistent with the working hypothesis. They called this the "positive test strategy". This strategy is an example of a heuristic: a reasoning shortcut that is imperfect but easy to compute. Klayman and Ha used Bayesian probability and information theory as their standard of hypothesis-testing, rather than the falsificationism used by Wason.

According to these ideas, each answer to a question yields a different amount of information, which depends on the person's prior beliefs. Thus a scientific test of a hypothesis is one that is expected to produce the most information. Since the information content depends on initial probabilities, a positive test can either be highly informative or uninformative. Klayman and Ha argued that when people think about realistic problems, they are looking for a specific answer with a small initial probability. In this case, positive tests are usually more informative than negative tests. However, in Wason's rule discovery task the answer—three numbers in ascending order—is very broad, so positive tests are unlikely to yield informative answers. Klayman and Ha supported their analysis by citing an experiment that used the labels "DAX" and "MED" in place of "fits the rule" and "doesn't fit the rule". This avoided implying that the aim was to find a low-probability rule. Subjects had much more success with this version of the experiment.

In light of this and other critiques, the focus of research moved away from confirmation versus falsification to examine whether people test hypotheses in an informative way, or an uninformative but positive way. The search for "true" confirmation bias led psychologists to look at a wider range of effects in how people process information.

Explanations

Confirmation bias is often described as a result of automatic, unintentional strategies rather than deliberate deception. According to Robert Maccoun, most biased evidence processing occurs through a combination of both "cold" (cognitive) and "hot" (motivated) mechanisms.

Cognitive explanations for confirmation bias are based on limitations in people's ability to handle complex tasks, and the shortcuts, called *heuristics*, that they use. For example, people may judge the reliability of evidence by using the *availability heuristic*, i.e. how readily a particular idea comes to mind. It is also possible that people can only focus on one thought at a time, so find it difficult to test alternative hypotheses in parallel. Another heuristic is the positive test strategy identified by Klayman and Ha, in which people test a hypothesis by examining cases where they expect a property or event to occur. This heuristic avoids the difficult or impossible task of working out how diagnostic each possible question will be. However, it is not universally reliable, so people can overlook challenges to their existing beliefs.

Motivational explanations involve an effect of desire on belief, sometimes called "wishful thinking". It is known that people prefer pleasant thoughts over unpleasant ones in a number of ways: this is called the "Pollyanna principle". Applied to arguments or sources of evidence, this could explain why desired conclusions are more likely to be believed true.

According to experiments that manipulate the desirability of the conclusion, people demand a high standard of evidence for unpalatable ideas and a low standard for preferred ideas. In other words, they ask, "Can I believe this?" for some suggestions and, "Must I believe this?" for others. Although consistency is a desirable feature of attitudes, an excessive drive for consistency is another potential source of bias because it may prevent people from neutrally evaluating new, surprising information. Social psychologist Ziva Kunda combines the cognitive and motivational theories, arguing that motivation creates the bias, but cognitive factors determine the size of the effect. Explanations in terms of cost-benefit analysis assume that people do not just test hypotheses in a disinterested way, but assess the costs of different errors. Using ideas from evolutionary psychology, James Friedrich suggests that people do not primarily aim at truth in testing hypotheses, but try to avoid the most costly errors. For example, employers might ask one-sided questions in job interviews because they are focused on weeding out unsuitable candidates. Yaacov Trope and Akiva Liberman's refinement of this theory assumes that people compare the two different kinds of error: accepting a false hypothesis or rejecting a true hypothesis. For instance, someone who underestimates a friend's honesty might treat him or her suspiciously and so undermine the friendship. Overestimating the friend's honesty may also be costly, but less so. In this case, it would be rational to seek, evaluate or remember evidence of their honesty in a biased way. When someone gives an initial impression of being introverted or extroverted, questions that match that impression come across as more empathic. This suggests that when talking to someone who seems to be an introvert, it is a sign of better social skills to ask, "Do you feel awkward in social situations?" rather than, "Do you like noisy parties?" The connection between confirmation bias and social skills was corroborated by a study of how college students get to know other people. Highly self-monitoring students, who are more sensitive to their environment and to social norms, asked more matching questions when interviewing a high-status staff member than when getting to know fellow students.

Psychologists Jennifer Lerner and Philip Tetlock distinguish two different kinds of thinking process. *Exploratory thought* neutrally considers multiple points of view and tries to anticipate all possible objections to a particular position, while *confirmatory thought* seeks to justify a specific point of view.

Lerner and Tetlock say that when people expect to need to justify their position to other people, whose views they already know, they will tend to adopt a similar position to those people, and then use confirmatory thought to bolster their own credibility. However, if the external parties are overly aggressive or critical, people will disengage from thought altogether, and simply assert their personal opinions without justification. Lerner and Tetlock say that people only push themselves to think critically and logically when they know in advance they will need to explain themselves to others who are well-informed, genuinely interested in the truth, and whose views they don't already know. Because those conditions rarely exist, they argue, most people are using confirmatory thought most of the time.

Consequences

In Finance: Confirmation bias can lead investors to be overconfident, ignoring evidence that their strategies will lose money. In studies of political stock markets, investors made more profit when they resisted bias. For example, participants who interpreted a candidate's debate performance in a neutral rather than partisan way were more likely to profit. To combat the effect of confirmation bias, investors can try to adopt a contrary viewpoint "for the sake of argument". In one technique, they imagine that their investments have collapsed and ask themselves why this might happen.

In Physical and Mental Health

Raymond Nickerson, a psychologist, blames confirmation bias for the ineffective medical procedures that were used for centuries before the arrival of scientific medicine. If a patient recovered, medical authorities counted the treatment as successful, rather than looking for alternative explanations such as that the disease had run its natural course. Biased assimilation is a factor in the modern appeal of alternative medicine, whose proponents are swayed by positive anecdotal evidence but treat scientific evidence hyper-critically.

Cognitive therapy was developed by Aaron T. Beck in the early 1960s and has become a popular approach. According to Beck, biased information processing is a factor in depression. His approach teaches people to treat evidence impartially, rather than selectively reinforcing negative outlooks. Phobias and hypochondria have also been shown to involve confirmation bias for threatening information.

In Politics and Law

Nickerson argues that reasoning in judicial and political contexts is sometimes subconsciously biased, favouring conclusions that judges, juries or governments have already committed to. Since the evidence in a jury trial can be complex, and jurors often reach decisions about the verdict early on, it is reasonable to expect an attitude polarization effect. The prediction that jurors will become more extreme in their views as they see more evidence has been borne out in experiments with mock trials. Both inquisitorial and adversarial criminal justice systems are affected by confirmation bias.

Confirmation bias can be a factor in creating or extending conflicts, from emotionally charged debates to wars: by interpreting the evidence in their favour, each opposing party can become overconfident that it is in the stronger position. On the other hand, confirmation bias can result in people ignoring or misinterpreting the signs of an imminent or incipient conflict. For example, psychologists Stuart Sutherland and Thomas Kida have each argued that US Admiral Husband E. Kimmel showed confirmation bias when playing down the first signs of the Japanese attack on Pearl Harbor.

A two-decade study of political pundits by Philip E. Tetlock found that, on the whole, their predictions were not much better than chance. Tetlock divided experts into "foxes" who maintained multiple hypotheses, and "hedgehogs" who were more dogmatic. In general, the hedgehogs were much less accurate. Tetlock blamed their failure on confirmation bias—specifically, their inability to make use of new information that contradicted their existing theories.

In the Paranormal

One factor in the appeal of psychic "readings" is that listeners apply a confirmation bias which fits the psychic's statements to their own lives. By making a large number of ambiguous statements in each sitting, the psychic gives the client more opportunities to find a match. This is one of the techniques of cold reading, with which a psychic can deliver a subjectively impressive reading without any prior information about the client. Investigator James Randi compared the transcript of a reading to the client's report of what the psychic had said, and found that the client showed a strong selective recall of the "hits".

As a striking illustration of confirmation bias in the real world, Nickerson mentions numerological pyramidology: the practice of finding meaning in the proportions of the Egyptian pyramids. There are many different length measurements that can be made of, for example, the Great Pyramid of Giza and many ways to combine or manipulate them. Hence it is almost inevitable that people who look at these numbers selectively will find superficially impressive correspondences, for example with the dimensions of the Earth.

In Science

A distinguishing feature of scientific thinking is the search for falsifying as well as confirming evidence. However, many times in the history of science, scientists have resisted new discoveries by selectively interpreting or ignoring unfavourable data. Previous research has shown that the assessment of the quality of scientific studies seems to be particularly vulnerable to confirmation bias. It has been found several times that scientists rate studies that report findings consistent with their prior beliefs more favourably than studies reporting findings inconsistent with their previous beliefs. However, assuming that the research question is relevant, the experimental design adequate and the data are clearly and comprehensively described, the found results should be of importance to the scientific community and should not be viewed prejudicially, regardless of whether they conform to current theoretical predictions. Confirmation bias may thus be especially harmful to objective evaluations regarding nonconforming results since biased individuals may regard opposing evidence to be weak in principle and give little serious thought to revising their beliefs. Scientific innovators often meet with resistance from the scientific community, and research presenting controversial results frequently receives harsh peer review.

In the context of scientific research, confirmation biases can sustain theories or research programmes in the face of inadequate or even contradictory evidence; the field of parapsychology has been particularly affected. An experimenter's confirmation bias can potentially affect which data are reported. Data that conflict with the experimenter's expectations may be more readily discarded as unreliable, producing the so-called file drawer effect. To combat this tendency, scientific training teaches ways to prevent bias. For example, experimental design of randomized controlled trials (coupled with their systematic review) aims to minimize sources of bias. The social process of peer review is thought to mitigate the effect of individual scientists' biases, even though the peer review process itself may be susceptible to such biases.

Role of Confirmation Bias in Self-Image

Self-verification theory predicts that people's self-views will cause them to see the world as more supportive of these self-views than it really is. That is, individuals process information in a biased manner. These biases may be conscious and deliberate, but are probably more commonly done effortlessly and non-consciously. Through the creative use of these processes, people may dramatically increase their chances of attaining self-verification. There are at least three relevant aspects of information processing in self-verification:

1. Attention: People will attend to evaluations that are self-confirming while ignoring non-confirming evaluations.
2. Memory retrieval: self-views bias memory recall to favour self-confirming material over non-confirming elements.

3. Interpretation of information: people tend to interpret information in ways that reinforce their self-views.

These distinct forms of self-verification may often be implemented sequentially. For example, in one scenario, people may first strive to locate partners who verify one or more self-views. If this fails, they may redouble their efforts to elicit verification for the self-view in question or strive to elicit verification for a different self-view. Failing this, they may strive to "see" more self-verification than actually exists. And, if this strategy is also ineffective, they may withdraw from the relationship, either psychologically or in actuality.

Related Processes

Preference for Novelty: People seem to prefer modest levels of novelty; they want to experience phenomena that are unfamiliar enough to be interesting, but not so unfamiliar as to be frightening or too familiar as to be boring.

The implications of people's preference for novelty for human relationships are not straightforward and obvious. Evidence that people desire novelty comes primarily from studies of people's reactions to art objects and the like. This is different when it concerns human beings and social relationships because people can shift attention away from already familiar novel objects, while doing so in human relationships is difficult or not possible. But novel art objects are very different from people. If a piece of art becomes overly stimulating, we can simply shift our attention elsewhere. This is not a viable option should our spouse suddenly begin treating us as if we were someone else, for such treatment would pose serious questions about the integrity of people's belief systems. Consequently, people probably balance competing desires for predictability and novelty by indulging the desire for novelty within contexts in which surprises are not threatening (e.g., leisure activities), while seeking coherence and predictability in contexts in which surprises could be costly—such as in the context of enduring relationships.

Tension with Self-enhancement

People's self-verification strivings are apt to be most influential when the relevant identities and behaviours matter to them. Thus, for example, the self-view should be firmly held, the relationship should be enduring, and the behaviour itself should be consequential. When these conditions are not met, people will be relatively unconcerned with preserving their self-views and they will instead indulge their desire for self-enhancement. In addition, self-reported emotional reactions favour self-enhancement while more thoughtful processes favour self-verification.

But if people with firmly held negative self-views seek self-verification, this does not mean that they are masochistic or have no desire to be loved. In fact, even people with very low self-esteem want to be loved. What sets people with negative self-views apart is their ambivalence about the evaluations they receive. Just as positive evaluations foster joy and warmth initially, these feelings are later chilled by incredulity. And although negative evaluations may foster sadness that the "truth" could not be kinder, it will at least reassure them that they know themselves. Happily, people with negative self-views are the exception rather than the rule. That is, on the balance, most people tend to view themselves positively. Although this imbalance is adaptive for society at large, it poses a challenge to researchers interested in studying self-verification. That is, for theorists interested in determining if behaviour is driven by self-verification or positivity strivings, participants with positive self-views will reveal nothing because both motives compel them to seek positive evaluations. If researchers want to learn if people prefer verification or positivity in a giving setting, they must study people with negative self-views.

Self-concept Change

Although self-verification strivings tend to stabilize people's self-views, changes in self-views may still occur. Probably the most common source of change is set in motion when the social environment recognizes a significant change in a person's age (e.g., when adolescents become adults), status (e.g., when students become teachers), or social role (e.g., when someone is convicted of a crime). Suddenly, the community may change the way that it treats the person. Eventually the target of such treatment will bring his or her self-view into accord with the new treatment.

Alternatively, people may themselves conclude that a given self-view is dysfunctional or obsolete and take steps to change it. Consider, for example, a woman who decides that her negative self-views have led her to tolerate abusive relationship partners. When she realizes that such partners are making her miserable, she may seek therapy. In the hands of a skilled therapist, she may develop more favourable self-views which, in turn, steer her toward more positive relationship partners with whom she may cultivate healthier relationships.

Alternatively, when a woman who is uncertain about her negative self-concept enters a relationship with a partner who is certain that she deserves to view herself more positively, that woman will tend to improve the self-concept.

Criticism

Critics have argued that self-verification processes are relatively rare, manifesting themselves only among people with terribly negative self views. In support of this viewpoint, critics cite hundreds of studies indicating that people prefer, seek and value positive evaluations more than negative ones. Such skeptical assessments overlook three important points. First, because most people have relatively positive self-views, evidence of a preference for positive evaluations in unselected samples may in reality reflect a preference for evaluations that are self-verifying, because for such individuals self-verification and positivity strivings are indistinguishable. No number of studies of participants with positive self-views can determine whether self-verification or self-enhancement strivings are more common. Second, self-verification strivings are not limited to people with globally negative self-views; even people with high self-esteem seek negative evaluations about their flaws. Finally, even people with positive self-views appear to be uncomfortable with overly positive evaluations. For example, people with moderately positive self-views withdraw from spouses who evaluate them in an exceptionally positive manner.

Other critics have suggested that when people with negative self-views seek unfavourable evaluations, they do so as a means of avoiding truly negative evaluations or for purposes of self-improvement, with the idea being that this will enable them to obtain positive evaluations down the road. Tests of this idea have failed to support it. For example, just as people with negative self-views choose self-verifying, negative evaluators even when the alternative is being in another experiment, they choose to be in another experiment rather than interact with someone who evaluates them positively. Also, people with negative self-views are most intimate with spouses who evaluate them negatively, despite the fact that these spouses are relatively unlikely to enable them to improve themselves. Finally, in a study of people's thought processes as they chose interaction partners, people with negative self-views indicated that they chose negative evaluators because such partners seemed likely to confirm their self-views (an epistemic consideration) and interact smoothly with them (a pragmatic consideration); self-improvement was rarely mentioned.

Recent criticism challenges the notion of a motive to self-verify. Raison Oblige Theory putatively accounts for all examples of self-verifying behaviour and offers an alternate explanation of why people appear to verify their self view.

The Years of Decline: Adjustment to a New Self.

Career Development is a "continuous lifelong process of developmental experiences that focuses on seeking, obtaining and processing information about self, occupational and educational alternatives, life styles and role options" (Hansen, 1976). Put another way, career development is the process through which people come to understand them as they relate to the world of work and their role in it. This career development process is where an individual fashions a work identity. In America, we are what we do, thus it becomes a person's identity. It is imperative when educating our young people that our school systems assist and consider the significance of this responsibility for our youth and their future. The influences on and outcomes of career development are one aspect of socialization as part of a broader process of human development.

Why Study Theory?

Theories and research describing career behaviour provide the "conceptual glue" for as well as describe where, when and for what purpose career counselling, career education, career guidance and other career interventions should be implemented.

The process of career development theory comes from four disciplines:

- Differential Psychology- interested in work and occupations
- Personality- view individuals as an organizer of their own experiences
- Sociology- focus on occupational mobility
- Developmental Psychology- concerned with the "life course"

"Theory is a picture, an image, a description, a representation of reality. It is not reality itself. It is a way we can think about some part of reality so that we can comprehend it"

(Krumboltz)

Career Development Theories for the past 75 years fall into four categories:

1. Trait Factor - Matching personal traits to occupations-Frank Parson's (1920's)
2. Psychological - Personality types matching work environment-Holland (1980's)
3. Decision - Situational or Sociological- Bandura (Self Efficacy-1970's)
4. Developmental - Self Concept over life span-Super (1950's)

Holland Codes

The Holland Codes or the Holland Occupational Themes (RIASEC), is a theory of careers and vocational choice based upon personality types. It was developed by the psychologist John L. Holland. Each letter or code stands for a particular "type": Realistic (Doers), Investigative (Thinkers), Artistic (Creators), Social (Helpers), Enterprising (Persuaders), and Conventional (Organizers)."

According to the *Committee on Scientific Awards,* Holland's "research shows that personalities seek out and ûourish in career environments they ût and that jobs and career environments are classiûable by the personalities that ûourish in them." Holland also wrote of his theory that "the choice of a vocation is an expression of personality." Furthermore, while Holland suggests that people can be "categorized as one of six types, " he also argues that "a six-category scheme built on the assumption that there are only six kinds of people in the world is unacceptable on the strength of common sense alone. But a six category scheme that allows a simple ordering of a person's resemblance to each of the six models provides the possibility of 720 different personality patterns."

Holland Theory of Vocational Types

This approach gives explicit attention to behavioural style or personality types as the major influence in career choice development. This is described as structurally interactive.

Common Themes:

- Occupation choice is an expression of personality and not random
- Members of an occupational group have similar personalities
- People in each group will respond to situations an problems similarly
- Occupational achievement, stability and satisfaction depends on congruence between one's personality and job environment

Holland Types

1. Realistic - work with hands, machines, tools, active, practical, adventurous

High traits - practical, masculine, stable

Low traits - sensitive, feminine, stable

Occupations - construction, farming, architecture, truck driving, mail carrier

2. Investigative – thought, analytical approaches, explore, knowledge, ideas, not social

High traits – scholarly, intellectual, critical

Low traits – powerful, ambitious, adventurous

Occupations – biologist, chemist, dentist, veterinarian, programmer

3. Artistic – literary, musical, artistic activities, emotional, creative, open

High traits – expressive, creative, spontaneous

Low traits – orderly, efficient, conventional, social, masculine

Occupations – artist, musician, poet, interior designer, writer

4. Social – train, inform, educate, help, supportive, avoid technical skills, empathy, relationships

High traits – cooperative, friendly, humanistic

Low traits – ambitious, creative, strong,

Occupations – social work, counselling, police officer, LPN

5. Enterprising – verbally skilled, persuasive, direct, leader, dominant

High traits – ambitious, adventurous, energetic

Low traits – intellectual, creative, feminine

Occupations – lawyer, business executive, politician, TV producer

6. Conventional – rules and routines, provide order or direct structure, great self control, respect power and status, punctual, orderly

High traits – stable, efficient, dependable, controlled

Low traits – intellectual, adventurous, creative

Occupations – bank teller, clerk typist, cashier, data entry

Advantages of Holland Types for Career Counselling

Types are intuitively appealing and easily shared with students. Helps students get oriented to the worlds of work that isn't overwhelming. Provides helpful way of understanding varied work environments.

Disadvantages of Holland Types for School Counselling

Theory doesn't provide insights into how one develops a type or guidance for working with student.

Bandura's Social Cognitive Theory

The concept of self efficacy is the focal point of Albert Bandura's social cognitive theory. By means of the self system, individuals exercise control over their thoughts, feelings, and actions. Among the beliefs with which an individual evaluates the control over his/her actions and environment, self-efficacy beliefs are the most influential predictor of human behaviour. The level and strength of self-efficacy will determine:

- whether coping behaviour will be initiated;
- how much effort will result;
- how long the effort will be sustained in the face of obstacles.

Self-Efficacy - the belief in one's capabilities to organize and execute the courses of action required to produce given attainments- is constructed on the basis of:

Four most influential sources where self-efficacy is derived:

- Personal Performance - Accomplishments-previous successes or failures (most influential)
- Vicarious Experience - Watching others, modelling, mentoring
- Verbal Persuasion - Verbal encouragement or discouragement
- Physiological and Emotional Factors - Perceptions of stress reactions in the body

Self-Efficacy plays the central role in the cognitive regulation of motivation, because people regulate the level and distribution of effort they will expend in accordance with the effects they are expecting from their actions.

It is Important to Understand the Distinction between Self Esteem and Self Efficacy.

- Self esteem relates to a person's sense of self worth.
- Self efficacy relates to a person's perception of their ability to reach a goal.

How Self Efficacy Affects Human Function

Choices regarding behaviour-People will be more inclined to take on a task if they believe they can succeed. People generally avoid tasks where their self efficacy is low, but engage when it is high. Self efficacy significantly higher than ability can lead to psychological damage. Significantly low self efficacy leads to an inability to grow and expand skills. Optimum levels of self efficacy are a little above ability, which encourages people to tackle challenging tasks and gain valuable experience.

Motivation- People with higher self efficacy in a task are likely to expend more effort and persist longer than with low efficacy. On the other hand, low self efficacy may provide an incentive to learn more and prepare better than a person with higher self efficacy.

Thought Patterns and Responses- Low self efficacy can lead people to believe tasks are harder than they actually are. This leads to poor planning and stress. A person with higher self efficacy will attribute a failure to external factors, whereas a person with lower self efficacy will attribute it to low ability. (Example: Math Test)

The Destiny Idea- Bandura successfully showed that people with differing self-efficacy perceive the world in fundamentally different ways. People with a high self efficacy are generally of the opinion that they are in control of their own lives: that their own actions and decisions shape their lives. On the other hand, people with low self-efficacy may see their lives as somewhat out of their hands and with fate.

Efficacy vs. Outcome Expectations

Bandura distinguishes between outcome expectancy and efficacy expectancy.

Outcome expectation refers to the person's estimate that a given behaviour will lead to particular outcomes.

Efficacy expectation is an estimate that one can successfully execute the behaviour required to produce the outcomes sought.

Self-beliefs about abilities play a central role in the career decision-making process. People move toward those occupations requiring capabilities they think they either have or can develop. People move away from those occupations requiring capabilities they think they do not possess or they cannot develop.

Personal goals also influence career behaviours in important ways. Personal goals relate to one's determination to engage in certain activities to produce a particular outcome. Goals help to organize and guide behaviour over long periods of time.

The relationship among goals, self-efficacy, and outcome expectations is complex and occurs within the framework of:

Bandura's Triadic Reciprocal Model of Causality – these factors are all affecting each other simultaneously

- personal attributes,
- external environmental factors
- overt behaviour

In essence, a person inputs (e.g. gender, race) interact with contextual factors (e.g. culture, family geography) and learning experiences to influence self-efficacy beliefs and outcome expectations.

Self-efficacy beliefs and outcome expectations in turn shape people's interests, goals, actions, and eventually their attainments.

However, these are also influenced by contextual factors (e.g. job opportunities, access to training opportunities, financial resources).

In this theory providing opportunities, experiences and significant adults to impact self-efficacy in all children becomes vital. Strategic career development interventions will positively impact young people in the context of this theory.

Super's Developmental Self-Concept Theory

Vocational development is the process of developing and implementing a self-concept. As the self-concept becomes more realistic and stable, so does vocational choice and behaviour. People choose occupations that permit them to express their self-concepts. Work satisfaction is related to the degree that they've been able to implement their self-concepts.

Career Maturity - Similarity between one's actual vocational behaviour and what is expected for that stage of development. Career maturity includes readiness to cope with developmental tasks at a given stage. It is both affective and cognitive.

Most career education programmes have been affected by Super's ideas. They provide gradual exposure to self-concepts and work concepts in curriculum that represents Super's ideas of career development/ vocational maturity.

Stages

Growth (Birth to mid teens) - Major developmental tasks are to develop a self-concept and to move from play to work orientation.

Sub stages

- Fantasy (4-10 years old) - needs dominate career fantasies and little reality orientation.
- Interest (11-12 years old) - identifies likes/dislikes as basis for career choices
- Capacity (13-14 years old) - more reality incorporated; can relate own skills to specific requirements of jobs.

Exploration (Mid teens through early 20's) - major tasks are to develop a realistic self-concept and implement a vocational preference though role tryouts and exploration; there is a gradual narrowing of choices leading to implementation of a preference. Preferences become CHOICES when acted upon.

Sub Stages

- Tentative (15-17 years old) - tentative choices incorporating needs, interests, abilities are tried out in fantasy, coursework, part time work, volunteer, shadowing.
  - o May identify field and level of work at this sub stage.
- Crystallization of Preference (18-21 years old) - General preference is converted into specific choice. Reality dominates as one enters the job market or training after high school. Choosing a college major or field of training.
- Specifying a Vocational Preference (early 20's) - trial/little commitment; first job is tried out as life's work but the implemented choice is provisional and person may cycle back through crystallizing and specifying if not appropriate.

Establishment (mid 20's through mid 40's) - major tasks are to find secure niche in one's field and advance within it.

Sub Stages

- Trial and Stabilization (25-30 years old) - process of settling down, if unsatisfactory may make 1-2 more changes before the right job is found.
- Advancement (30-40 years old) - efforts directed at securing one's position, acquiring seniority, developing skills, demonstrating superior performance, resume building actions.

Maintenance (40's through early 60's) - Major task is to preserve one's gains and develop non-occupational roles for things one always wanted to do; Little new ground is broken, one continues established work patterns. One faces competition from younger workers. Could be a plateau.

Disengagement or Decline (Late 60's through retirement) - Tasks are deceleration of the career, gradual disengagement from world of work and retirement. One is challenged to find other sources of satisfaction. May shift to part time to suit declining capacities.

Development Tasks

Crystallization	Forming a general vocational goal
Specification	Move from tentative to specific preference
Implementation	Complete training, enter employment
Stabilization	Confirm choice through work experience
Consolidation	Advance in career

Implications of Super's Theory for Career Counselling

- Identify the career development stage and set goals for mastery of the tasks unique to each stage.
- Help student clarify self-concept because any task that enhances self-knowledge will increase vocational maturity. Then help them relate their self-knowledge to occupational information.
- Expose students to a wider range of careers because occupational options narrow over time. Consider lifestyle implications and consider the vocational and avocational relevance of subjects studied in school.
- Direct work experiences are vital. Try on roles in real worlds of work.

Supers developmental view of career development in the context of the self allows for changes over time. This is very appropriate in the 21 Century workplace.

Career Development: Whose Responsibility is It ?

Many organizations are avoiding facing the growing challenges of career management by throwing the full responsibility on the shoulders of employees. Others still act like puppet masters and believe they can map everyone's career. And some are trying to strike the right balance that meets employers and employees aspirations. So really, whose responsibility is it?

Modern day career management seems to be reaching a paradox: employees want and feel more empowered as they can easily access external opportunities, but yet complain that their organizations don't help them enough in their quest; managers are becoming more accountable for talent development but often are not provided the support to do so, and HR is always stuck in the middle mediating rather than facilitating. These are the four critical forces for effective career management, and equilibrium is the key.

The Accountability "Matrix"

Career management must be a collaborative effort between Employees, Managers, HR and the Organization.

Employees must take individual responsibility for their careers by maintaining their individual talent profiles, focusing on personal development, demonstrating company values, and building their professional networks. Employees should understand their strengths and capabilities, outline career goals, identify development needs, create an individual development plan to close gaps, and be proactive in watching out for potential career opportunities.

The Organization provides an infrastructure in terms of the human and financial resources, business processes and technology that support career management. Sets and communicates strategy, values, goals and objectives, provides information about staffing needs, consistently supports and funds developmental programmes, and promotes an environment in which employees and managers are recognized for their efforts in talent development.

Managers are responsible for providing career coaching and candid performance feedback to employees, identifying opportunities for development and advising employees about potential job opportunities. Managers should actively support employees in setting clear goals and personal objectives, assessing potential, identifying career options, and providing growth opportunities through assignments, developmental programmes, exposure and visibility to other parts of the organization and leaders. HR's role is to provide the tools and resources for employees to manage their careers and for managers to help employees in going so, aligned with organizational and business needs. HR acts as a facilitator, providing clear information of what it takes to get to the next level, visibility to developmental initiatives and job opportunities, offer career counselling, and implement technologies that allow access to talent information.

Through the powerful collaboration of the different forces in career management, employees and employers can take benefits in the three strategic elements that must be considered when designing a career management solution:

- Transparency: for the employee, transparency means enabling employees to understand the career opportunities that may be open to them. For the employer, transparency means visibility into employee capabilities and career aspirations as well as understanding how these align with what the organization needs its workforce to look like.
- Control: for the employee, control means providing the tools that enable employees to fully participate in the decisions about the progression of their careers. For the employer, this means having the right career management processes in place to ensure that they fill their key roles with the right talent.
- Velocity: for the employee, velocity means being able to flex the speed of career advancement to meet his or her career aspirations. For the employer, it means having a ready talent pool that advances at the speed needed to fuel the talent pipelines.

Whatever your philosophy is, these are strategic elements that all organizations struggle with and often do not get them right. Balancing the accountabilities between the four key stakeholders in career management – Employees, Managers, HR and the Organization – will foster a collaborative environment that drives successful talent development, engagement and retention.

Taking Responsibility for Your own Career Development

During the recent economic crunch, many companies have placed Learning and Development on hiatus as a way of channeling available coffers into more short-term activities. Ironically, this temporary abandonment of training initiatives comes at a time when leadership development is most needed.

As millions of Baby Boomers prepare for retirement, organizations are scrambling to prepare for the giant vacuum of experience and wisdom about to envelop the corporate landscape. Succession planning and Individual Development Planning are returning to the forefront of business survival strategies. But whose responsibility is a career plan for development: the individual, the manager, or both?

Naturally, every person needs to actively engage in their own career planning. Who better knows the aspirations, inspirations, and values of individuals than themselves? A leader cannot read minds, nor force an unwanted career direction for very long. In order for individuals to have realistic chances at maximizing their potential and achieving their goals, they must first become clear about what their goals are, both short and long-term, and design a detailed map on how to reach their dreams.

No amount of direction, ambition, or planning by an individual can lead to success without the support and guidance from the manager. It is the responsibility of the manager to understand individuals' visions of their relationship with the organization, and positively influence effective career planning. While the individual must be clear about who they are and where they want to go, the manager must see the bigger picture, and find avenues that best capitalize on the individual's strengths and passions in the context of the organization's best interests. Managers play a critical (and sometimes delicate) role of channelling individuals' inherent talents into pragmatic applications. Managers cannot blaze the trail for the individual, but they can help illuminate the path.

There are myriad tools to assist managers and individuals with career planning, from self and 360-assessments to old-fashioned reflection and analysis. But the best place to start is always with a simple, honest conversation. Who is the individual? What matters to him or her? What is their vision of the ideal future? What about the manager, where does he or she see the greatest potential for development? Does the manager's vision align with both the individual's personal growth and the future success of the organization? These are important questions, and the result of the conversation should be the synergistic linking of goals to action plans. Once the vision is clear and the plan is set, the individual's development will foster greater engagement and loyalty. The individual understands that he or she is not stagnant or adrift, but highly focused and actively influencing the future. People may not stay with a company forever, but while they are there, the organization has their hearts and minds.

The Right Person for Every Job and the Right Job for Every Person

Selecting the right person for the job has never been more important than it is today. Organizations and businesses spend an enormous amount of time and money in a never ending effort to train, coach, motivate, or develop marginal employees to a level of performance that is merely adequate. In organizations and businesses throughout the world, there are people who are not performing at the levels expected. At some time or another, virtually every person has been in a job that was not right for him or her. All the same, organizations hired each of these people with careful thoughts and positive expectations. Most people took those same jobs with every intention of succeeding.

It is very difficult and expensive to train your way out of a bad hiring decision. The process by which individuals are selected is clearly the most critical and controllable variable in the development of a productive and successful work team. However, traditional selection methods have several limitations for the accurate understanding of people and their performance.

Traditionally, organizations have viewed people and their performance within the context of ability. Those with lots of ability can do almost anything well, and those with less are often assigned to jobs in which they won't cause significant damage. This type of thinking supports the belief that education, experience, training, and more training will enhance ability and, therefore, performance. If a person with perceived ability does not perform well after being trained, his or her problem is assumed to be motivational.

In reality, three factors may have impact on a person's ability potential: attitude (organizational match); technical competence (skills match); and cognitive ability, personality structure, and interests (job match).

Organizational Match

Organizational match is the degree to which the candidate's attitudes, values, ethics, and grooming fit those required by the job position. Face-to-face interviews are typically used to evaluate these things. Being honest, drug-free, and not prone to hostility are also important factors, and are usually determined by use of various paper-and-pencil, electronic, and chemical tests, as well as by background checks. The perception intuition, and experience-based observations of a well-trained interviewer are invaluable in assessing certain qualities of attitude and match with an organization's culture. There are problems, however, with relying wholly on the face-to-face interview process.

One such problem, the halo effect, occurs when the interviewer sees a part of himself or herself in a job candidate. The interviewer may focus on a common experience, part of growing up, school, or some other aspect of background that he and the applicant share.

A similar personality characteristic in the interviewee could generate a positive feeling of recognition within the interviewer. This self-recognition generates a "halo" that can cause a relatively mediocre candidate to glow with merit. On the other hand, another potential pitfall of the interview process is the unconscious bias, which is the opposite of the halo effect. The more a candidate is different from the interviewer, the more conscious effort is required on the interviewer's part to regard the candidate in a positive or neutral light.

This is a fundamental characteristic of being human: when a candidate appears to be different in some way, there is always some effect. This effect may be large or small, good or bad. The important thing is that interviewers recognize the subjective nature of face-to-face interviewing.

Unfortunately, outstanding verbal and communication skills during an interview Or their opposite, lackluster responses do not necessarily translate into job performance, just as the ability to talk knowledgeably about baseball and look good in a uniform would not necessarily translate into the ability to throw or hit a 95-mph fastball.

Skills Match

Skills match is the degree to which a candidate's educational background, technical skills, previous job experience, and particular expertise matches those required for the position. There are many job positions that demand specific sets of knowledge or technical skills. Research has shown that people charged with selecting for these positions are often tremendously biased toward thinking that expertise highly important. On a broader scale, one of the common hiring myths is that highly intelligent people can do anything. Job match research has proven that people actually perform best when they are fully engaged by the challenges of a job. Unless highly intelligent people are provided with a steady source of intellectual challenges, they may not only become poor performers, but may even become counterproductive.

If organizational match or skills match, or both, are unsatisfactory, improvement of an individual's long-term job performance with training or coaching is almost impossible.

Job Match

Job match is an integral part of a candidate's actual on-the-job success. Job match refers to how well an individual's cognitive abilities, interests, and personality traits match those required for success in a particular job.

Knowing an individual's strengths and weaknesses, a manager can amplify (on the job) that person's strong points while minimizing (or avoiding) weak areas, thereby helping build the employee's self-esteem and increasing his job performance. A manager who hires a person without a natural job match and thinks he can overcome the new hire's shortcomings with training might as well be trying to train a rabbit to swim instead of hiring a fish.

The degree to which a candidate's cognitive abilities, interests, and personality fit those required by a particular position determines the degree of job match. People fail in a job not because they can't do the job, but rather because they don't match the job.

Cognitive Abilities

Cognitive abilities are factors such as how quickly a person learns and what type of learning is most effective. In a business sense, this is a far more useful measurement than what is generally called intelligence. It is critical to match an employee's cognitive abilities with those required for the job. For example, exceptionally fast problem solvers thrive in a challenging environment. When placed in relatively routine situations, these same people quickly become bored, resulting in low performance or unexpected turnover.

In comparison, slow learners become frustrated in environments that do not allow sufficient time to assimilate key information about the job.

Interests

Whether a person has an interest in or preference for working with people, data, or things is important. An individual may be capable of performing certain tasks, but may not be interested in those tasks. If that is the case, the person will probably not perform the tasks well for very long.

Personality

Personality of the candidate consists of measurable characteristics of behaviour that determine how an employee will behave in particular situations. Core personality is made up of traits that have been conditioned over many years. Such traits are critical in assessing a candidate's ability to function as part of a team, ability to close, ability to make decisions, ability to handle customers, and ability to perform virtually any aspect of any job.

Understanding organizational match, skills match, and job match is integral to understanding job performance. Each is a necessary part of any hiring or performance-enhancement decision. The idea of predicting job performance through the use of assessment tools has long been a dream of the business world, and until recently, an elusive dream. With the advent of fifth-generation assessment tools, organizations and businesses now have an instrument that offers remarkable accuracy and reliability, enabling information to be used in a number of applications that were not possible with older technologies. If management can acquire better information on people, it will inevitably make better decisions.

Assessment Tools

First-generation assessment tools have two fundamental problems: they are easy to fake and they are ipsative (describing tendencies without using any point of reference).

Second-generation tools add some evaluation elements that are normative (using established units of measure), but most are still ipsative. Third-generation tools offer vast improvements; however, the normal manager cannot use them because they must be administered by licensed psychologists, and further, they contain questions that legally cannot be asked of employees, or on job applications. Fourth-generation tools do measure cognitive skills and personality characteristics; however, the fact that their validity base was developed in 1972 causes significant validation errors when current applicants and employees are measured for the twenty-first century. In addition, several scales in the mental abilities section measure crystallized knowledge (specific knowledge that is dependent on cultural environment and education) versus fluid knowledge (fundamental reasoning ability independent of specific content).

Fifth-generation assessment tools, which produce quantified scales (normative) and evaluate the total person, can be used accurately and effectively by non-experts to generate job patterns. Developed in compliance with legal requirements of the United States, Canada, and Great Britain, fifth-generation instruments can also serve to document nondiscriminatory hiring practices. Fifth-generation tools measure

- Mental abilities (cognitive ? can the person do the job?)
- Interests (conative?is the person interested in doing the job?), and
- Twenty-four personality factors. (Does the person have what it takes to do the job and does the person fit the organization's culture?)

Legalities of Using Testing and Assessments

The reality is that the proper and consistent use of effective testing and assessment systems can dramatically strengthen an organization's legal position. Job-related testing and assessments are essentially the only ways to document objective and nondiscriminatory hiring practices. In the three parts of the selection process, the area most susceptible to bias or discrimination is organizational match, which is largely determined by interviewing. Only the testing components are purely objective. Skills match may or may not be measurable, depending on the job.

In the selection process, the greatest advantage of assessments is the potential use of the information that results to predict the future performance of applicants. Testing may be used

1. To screen out those applicants who are not likely to be able to perform the job successfully,
2. To group applicants in accordance with the likelihood of their successful performance, and
3. To rank applicants, selecting those with the highest scores for employment.

It is important that the instrument used in the selection process meet certain standards:

1. The instrument should be copyrighted no earlier than 1991.
   - Two pieces of legislation that have directly impacted testing are the Civil Rights Act of 1991 and the Americans with Disabilities Act of 1990.
   - The provisions of both of these acts must have been considered in the construction of any psychometric instrument used in making business decisions involving people.
2. The instrument must have been designed for use in a selection process.

- Validation is a major element of compliance.
- That the instrument measures what it claims to measure must be demonstrable.
- The instrument can demonstrate its validity under the same circumstances in which it is being used.
- Many instruments that were originally validated for use in counselling and self-development cannot be validated as hiring tools.

3. The technical manual for the instrument must provide thorough documentation of

- The development of the scales used.
- The development of the norms.
- The diversity of the population used in the studies. (A robust sample would include several thousand people, representing a mixture of appropriate ages, sexes, cultures, and races.)
- The psychometric studies that generated the original norms should be revisited once every 3 years or so to allow the instrument to adjust to changes in demographics and social values and attitudes.

Using Job Match Assessments With Existing Employees

Have you ever worked with someone whose performance was not what you expected? Today, job match assessments can tell you why that happened and whether it can be changed. The accuracy of higher-generation assessment instruments has created extraordinary possibilities for analyzing and understanding the performance of existing employees.

Almost all managers or supervisors know who their best and worst employees are. What they generally do not know is why people hired by the same methods, doing the same job, and managed by the same person perform so differently. For centuries, businesses and organizations have relied on observation, opinion, and emotion to solve their people problems. At the same time, system solutions were based on objective data, quantified data, and common frame of reference. Modern assessment instruments can provide this same level of data about people.

The concept of the three cornerstones of job performance for selecting new employees is also essential to understanding the performance of existing employees. In the case of successful current employees, job attitude is a more precise terminology than organization match. Successful current employees typically have a can-do attitude and believe in the value of the contribution of each employee. They are positive and enthusiastic and are happy with their work place. Many factors affect this attitude, such as organizational leadership, work environment, and personal issues.

If job attitude is the only problem within an organization, motivational programmes can work well toward improving performance. If, however, there is a more fundamental cause reducing performance, motivational programmes can prove to be expensive and frustrating.

The second part of the puzzle of existing employees' performance is skills match.

Well-constructed training programmes may have a tremendously positive effect on skills match. The difficulty arises when training is viewed without consideration of job match.

Job match, as described earlier, is the degree to which the employee has the cognitive abilities, interests, and measurable personality traits that are necessary to perform the job successfully. When job match is determined prior to training, the most effective training programme is usually clear. The critical point is that unless job match is known, the best training is a hit-or-miss proposition: it can be frustrating for the employee and expensive for the organization.

Team Engineering Versus Team Building

Personality assessments have been used for team-building exercises since the first half of this century. Often four personality types are identified: dominant, influencing, stable, and compliant, or driver, expressive, amiable, and analytical. Other assessments may identify eight or nine types.

All of these typing methodologies are based on behaviourism, or behavioural style theory, a concept that is no longer supported in mainstream psychology. Team-building exercises based on these four quadrants, however, can be often very productive. The concepts are simple and easily understood. The construct is valid and accurate. The exercise normally does a superb job of describing each type and how each type relates or communicates with other types. The problem is that there is no accurate way for these instruments to sort people into types. It is unlikely that just four sizes fit all.

The most recent generations of assessment tools incorporate a total picture of cognitive abilities, interests, and personality. All of these factors play key roles in team interaction. More importantly, these newer instruments measure a range of discrete elements with considerable accuracy. This enables specific analysis of team fit. It also has the capability to deal with teams that are relatively homogenous or with work teams composed of specialized positions. The level of specificity possible is reflected in the designation of the process as team engineering.

Reorganization or Restructuring

The concept of job match is integral to any plan for reorganizing a work force. Without it, the outcome of the process becomes largely a matter of luck or hope. Job match assessments can be used to statistically analyze both the old system and the new configuration. The existing population of employees can then be compared to the new requirements of job match, and a strategic plan for transition can be developed. Some employees will fit easily into the new design, others will be phased in with training, and the ones that cannot make the change can be identified.

Succession Planning

Succession planning is basically a matter of an internal selection process. Job match assessments allow the analysis of an executive's career path relative to the various job matches that are available. Even when experience demands a period of time in a position of marginal benefit, that analysis enables a temporary adjustment of the expectations of performance during that period. This information can also be used to design individual training curriculum.

It is important to note that the numbers 1 through 10 make up the range of a scale. A person's holding any position(s) on the scale does not imply good or bad about that person. The numbers in the range are used to relate an individual's match to the requirements of a particular job. Everyone is a good match with some jobs and a bad match with others. In other words, accurate assessment tools do not judge a person good or bad; they only assess whether a person does or does not match the requirements of a particular job.

Mentors : The Key to a Career Development Culture

A mentor is an individual with expertise who can help develop the career of a mentee. A mentor often has two primary functions for the mentee. The career-related function establishes the mentor as a coach who provides advice to enhance the mentee's professional performance and development. The psychosocial function establishes the mentor as a role model and support system for the mentee. Both functions provide explicit and implicit lessons related to professional development as well as general work–life balance.

Stages of Mentoring

In the initiation stage, two individuals enter into a mentoring relationship. For informal mentoring, the matching process occurs through professional or social interactions between potential mentors and mentees. Potential mentees search for experienced, successful people whom they admire and perceive as good role models. Potential mentors search for talented people who are "coachable." Mentoring research describes this stage as a period when a potential mentee proves him- or herself worthy of a mentor's attention. Both parties seek a positive, enjoyable relationship that would justify the extra time and effort required in mentoring Formal mentoring programmes manage the matching process instead of letting these relationships emerge on their own. Good matching programmes are sensitive to demographic variables as well as common professional interests. The assignment of a mentee to a mentor varies greatly across formal mentoring programmes. Mentors may review mentee profiles and select their mentees or programme administrators may match mentors and mentees. Regardless of the method, a good formal mentoring programme would require both parties to explore the relationship and evaluate the appropriateness of the mentor–mentee match.

The Cultivation Stage is the Primary Stage of Learning and Development.

Assuming a successful initiation stage, during the cultivation stage, the mentee learns from the mentor. Two broad mentoring functions are at their peak during this stage. The career-related function often emerges first when the mentor coaches the mentee on how to work effectively and efficiently. Coaching may be active within the mentee's organization when a mentor assigns challenging assignments to the mentee, maximizes the mentee's exposure and visibility in the organization, and actively sponsors the mentee through promotions and recognition. Mentors outside of the mentee's organization can also provide valuable advice on how to thrive and survive; although they lack organizational power to directly intervene on behalf of the mentee. The psychosocial function emerges after the mentor and mentee have established an interpersonal bond. Within this function, the mentor accepts and confirms the mentee's professional identity and the relationship matures into a strong friendship.

The cultivation stage is generally a positive one for both mentor and mentee. The mentor teaches the mentee valuable lessons gained from the mentor's experience and expertise. The mentee may also teach the mentor valuable lessons related to new technologies, new methodologies, and emerging issues in the field.

The separation stage generally describes the end of a mentoring relationship.The relationship may end for a number of reasons. There may be nothing left to learn, the mentee may want to establish an independent identity, or the mentor may send the mentee off on his or her own the way a parent sends off an adult child. If the relationship's end is not accepted by both parties, this stage can be stressful with one party unwilling to accept the loss. Problems between the mentor and mentee arise when only one party wants to terminate the mentoring relationship. Mentees may feel abandoned, betrayed, or unprepared if they perceive the separation to be premature. Mentors may feel betrayed or used if the mentee no longer seeks their counsel or support.

During the redefinition stage, both mentor and mentee recognize that their relationship can continue but that it will not be the same as their mentoring relationship. If both parties successfully negotiate through the separation stage, the relationship can evolve into a collegial relationship or social friendship. Unlike the cultivation stage, the focus of the relationship is no longer centred on the mentee's career development. The former mentor may establish mentoring relationships with new mentees. Likewise, the former mentee may serve as a mentor to others.

Forms of Mentoring

The mentoring relationship is inherently flexible and can vary tremendously in its form and function. The mentoring relationship exists between one individual in need of developmental guidance and another individual who is both capable and willing to provide that guidance. Further, the mentoring relationship represents an important developmental relationship for the mentee as it supports and facilitates his or her professional development. Given the wide variety of mentoring relation-ships, they are broadly classified as formal or informal according to the manner in which the relationship formed.

Below are some of the possible needs of mentees, roles and characteristics of mentors, and settings for the relationship, which can be combined to create a wide variety of relationships.

Mentee Needs

- Guidance in a general or specific professional area
- Series of questions or issues
- Broad career development
- Early career development
- Ethical and moral guidance
- Assistance in navigating professional settings, institutions, structures, and politics
- Professional identity development guidance
- Roles and Characteristics of Mentors
- Acts as an experienced role model
- Provides acceptance, encouragement, and moral support
- Provides wisdom, advice, counsel, coaching
- Acts as a sponsor in professional organizations, supports networking efforts
- Assists with the navigation of professional settings, institutions, structures, and politics
- Facilitates professional development
- Challenges and encourages appropriately to facilitate growth
- Provides nourishment, caring, and protection
- Integrates professional support with other areas such as faith, family, and community
- Accepts assistance from mentee in mentor's professional responsibilities within appropriate limits
- Enjoys the opportunity to pass on their wisdom and knowledge and collaboration with early career professionals

Settings

- Professional settings
- Organizations (e.g., APA)
- Community
- Internet, e-mail, telephone
- Informal national and international networks within specialties

Relationship Types

- Established career and early career
- Professor to student
- Professional to professional
- Peer mentoring (same developmental level with specific experiential differences)
- Friendship
- Parent-like features can be present
- Task-focused versus relationship-based
- Daily contact versus less frequent contact
- Short- versus long-term mentorships
- Collegial collaborations

Informal Mentoring

Informal mentoring relationships develop spontaneously and are not managed or specifically recognized as a mentoring relationship within a larger organization. A mentor reaches out to a mentee (or vice versa) and a relationship develops which benefits the mentee's professional development. Due to the spontaneous development, these relationships depend somewhat more on the individuals having things in common and feeling comfortable with each other from the beginning. The relationship may develop out of a specific need by the mentee around a task or situation for guidance, support, or advice. The relationship is most likely to be initiated by the mentee as she or he seeks support around a specific task. This type of relationship might also develop when an established professional needs an early career professional to complete certain tasks within an office or project setting.

Formal Mentoring

Formal mentoring relationships develop within organizational structures that are specifically designed to facilitate the creation and maintenance of such relationships.

Six primary characteristics of formal mentoring programmes that can directly influence the programme's effectiveness: (a) programme objectives, (b) selection of participants, (c) matching of mentors and mentees, (d) training for mentors and mentees, (e) guidelines for frequency of meeting, and (f) a goal-setting process. Programme objectives may vary from socializing newcomers into an organization to intense career development of a target population (e.g., high potential people, women, ethnic minorities). These objectives affect the scope of the mentoring and will help drive goal-setting and training objectives. Formal mentoring programmes are generally more effective when mentors voluntarily participate (rather than being dragged or coerced) and are intrinsically motivated to help mentees.

Formal programmes vary widely in their methods to match mentors and mentees, and in their preparation of individuals to engage in mentoring. Programmes that solicit important matching criteria from both parties are more likely to initiate successful mentorships. Matching criteria may include professional interests, demographics, geographical location, human interest factors (e.g., hobbies, lifestyles), personality, values, and learning orientation.

Orientation or training programmes for mentors and mentees can help both parties establish a psychological contract for the relationship. Training objectives can include clear communications of expectations of the relationship, goal-setting procedures, conflict resolution skills, and general structure of the mentoring programme.

Furthermore, these programmes often suggest guidelines for frequency of meetings. Finally, a goal-setting process provides structure to the relationship. Good goals are specific, measurable, attainable, relevant, and time-bound.

4

Peer Mentoring

Peer mentoring is a form of mentorship that usually takes place between a person who has lived through a specific experience (peer mentor) and a person who is new to that experience (the peer mentee). An example would be an experienced student being a peer mentor to a new student, the peer mentee, in a particular subject, or in a new school. Peer mentors are also used for health and lifestyle changes. For example, clients, or patients, with support from peers, may have one-on-one sessions that meet regularly to help them recover or rehabilitate. Peer mentoring provides individuals who have suffered from a specific life experience the chance to learn from those who have recovered, or rehabilitated, following such an experience. Peer mentors provide education, recreation and support opportunities to individuals. The peer mentor may challenge the mentee with new ideas, and encourage the mentee to move beyond the things that are most comfortable. Most peer mentors are picked for their sensibility, confidence, social skills and reliability.

Critics of peer mentoring insist that little is known of the nature of peer mentoring relationships and that there are few consistent studies indicating the outcomes of peer mentoring beyond good feelings among peers and the development of friendships. Peer mentoring led by senior students may discourage diversity and prevent critical analysis of the higher education system.

Programme Design Characteristics

The frequency with which peer mentors and mentees meet varies according to the particular mentoring programme. Some pairs may make contact once a month, while others may meet 3-4 times per month or more. It is usually advised that mentors and mentees meet more often in the beginning of the relationship in order to establish a good foundation. Mentors and mentees may maintain contact through email, telephone or in-person meetings. Peer mentoring organizations may also set up social events for those participating in the programme. These events provide good opportunities for increased social interaction between mentors and mentees.

The compatibility of mentor and mentee is a factor that should be taken into consideration when choosing pairs. Mentors and mentees may benefit from having similar backgrounds, interests and life experiences. Age, gender, ethnicity, language preferences, and education may be taken into consideration when pairing mentors with mentees.

The quality of the peer mentoring relationship is important for mentees to experience positive results. A mentor relationship is more successful when the mentor cares for the whole person and not just the academic or career side of a person. Successful mentors tend to be available, knowledgeable, educated in diversity issues, empathic, personable, encouraging, supportive, and passionate. Although this is not an exhaustive list of qualities, they have been shown to be important for successful mentoring relationships. It is important to keep qualities like this in mind when recruiting and training mentors.

The objectives of a peer mentoring programme should be well-defined and measurable. The effectiveness of the programme should be monitored to ensure that the objectives are being met. One way to monitor the effectiveness of a programme is to administer evaluations to the mentors and mentees.

In Education

Peer Mentoring in Education was Promoted During the 1960s by Educator and Theorist Paulo Freire: "The fundamental task of the mentor is a liberatory task. It is not to encourage the mentor's goals and aspirations and dreams to be reproduced in the mentees, the students, but to give rise to the possibility that the students become the owners of their own history. This is how I understand the need that teachers have to transcend their merely instructive task and to assume the ethical posture of a mentor who truly believes in the total autonomy, freedom, and development of those he or she mentors."

Peer mentors appear mainly in secondary schools where students moving up from primary schools may need assistance in settling into the new schedule and lifestyle of secondary school life, however peer mentoring can occur at the grade school level, the undergraduate level, and the graduate school level. The goals of the programme may vary according to the level, the educational institution or the discipline.

Peer mentors in secondary schools aid in the transition of younger students from primary school to secondary school. They may assist mentees with their school work and study skills, peer pressure (such as pressure to use drugs or have sex), issues with attendance and behaviour, and typical family problems. Youth mentors are persons for children or adolescents to spend time with, often to compensate for absent family members or an inadequate home environment. Mentoring programmes for youth can be especially useful for students who are suffering from a lack of social support, and who therefore may be susceptible to delinquency.

Peer mentors for undergraduates may assist newly admitted students with time management, study skills, organizational skills, curriculum planning, administrative issues, test preparation, term paper preparation, goal setting, and grade monitoring. Additionally, such mentors may provide other forms of social support for the student, such as friendship, networking, and aiding the student's adjustment to college life.

A peer mentor at the graduate school level may assist new students in selecting an advisor, negotiating the advisor/advisee relationship, preparation for major examinations, publishing articles, searching for jobs, and adjusting to the rigors of graduate school life.

In Higher Education

Peer mentoring in higher education has enjoyed a good name and is seen favourably by both educational administrators and students. During the last decade, peer mentoring has expanded and is found in most colleges and universities, frequently as a means to outreach, retain, and recruit minority students. Peer mentoring is used extensively in higher education for several reasons:

- Benefits attributed to *classical mentoring* (when an older adult mentors a younger person) can translate to peer mentoring relationships, mainly when the peer mentor and the mentee have similar backgrounds;

- The lack of role models or volunteers forces administrators and student leaders to use students as peer mentors of other students—usually first year students, ethnic minorities, and women—in order to guide, support, and instruct junior students;
- Because peer mentoring programmes require a low budget for administration and/or development, they become a cheap alternative to support students perceived as likely to fail.

Advantages in Education

Peer mentoring may help new students adapt to a new academic environment faster. The relationship between the mentor and mentee gives the mentee a sense of being connected to the larger community where they may otherwise feel lost. Mentors are chosen because they are academically successful and because they possess good communication, social and leadership skills. As a consequence, mentors serve as positive role models for the students, guiding them towards academic and social success. Mentors provide support, advice, encouragement, and even friendship to students. Peer mentoring may improve student retention rates.

Mentors also stand to benefit from the mentor/mentee relationship. Mentors develop friendships through their participation in mentoring programmes and usually derive satisfaction from helping a younger student, and possibly shaping his or her life in a positive way. Mentors may also be paid, and they may receive other benefits such as prioritized registration, course credit, and references.

In higher education tutorial settings, the benefits of peer mentoring programmes also extend to class tutors. Using grounded theory techniques, Outhred and Chester found that five themes underlie their experiences: role exploration, sharing responsibility, regulation of the peer-tutored groups, harnessing the peer tutors' role, and community.

Criticisms

Peer mentoring programmes usually target ethnic minorities, people with disabilities and women. This approach tends to be conceived out of the "deficiency model" where multi-ethnic students, women and students with disabilities are perceived as being in need of help and unlikely to succeed unless senior students or successful adults help them. One of the main criticisms of peer mentoring is the lack of research to show how peer mentoring relationships work, how they develop, and what their outcomes are. Also, the nature of being either a mentor or mentee and at the same time a peer can make the relationship a dual one where other identities also converge. Some peer mentoring programmes promote assimilation among ethnic minority students because of the use of student role models who are perceived as successful in social and educational environments characterized by majority students. These role models then become the people that peer mentees strive to imitate or emulate. A more subtle criticism of peer mentoring refers to their lack of supervision and structure: most peer mentoring programmes led by undergraduate students rarely have direct supervision of full-time university staff.

Given the fact that students are led by other students who serve as peer mentors, critics say that university staff may free themselves from their responsibility to listen and help first year students classified as peer mentees, the group with the largest attrition rate in higher education. Without extensive training and supervision, senior students who serve as mentors may offer unreliable guidance to peer mentees. There is little research on what happens within peer mentoring relationships. Maryann Jacobi, in an extensive meta-analysis of mentoring research, concludes by asking, "Does mentoring help students succeed in college? If so, how? Both theoretical and empirical answers to these questions are lacking." Stephanie Budge states:

"The concept of mentoring has become increasingly popular over the past few decades. Mentoring has been advertised as necessary in order for students and employees to flourish in their environment. However, the lack of research concerning peer mentoring programmes in particular is surprising.

While there is an abundance of articles on the topic of mentoring in the educational setting, authors must be held to more stringent research standards and more definitional consistency. In addition to higher quality research, the fundamental flaws within peer mentoring programmes need to be corrected before these programmes can reach their full potential on college campuses."

Peer mentoring in higher education usually focuses on social, academic, and cultural skills that can help students graduate from colleges and universities, and how the educational system works (e.g. how to apply for financial aid, how to register for classes, how to write papers, how to choose a major, etc.). The knowledge students receive usually comes from senior students who serve as peer mentors.

Although peer mentoring programmes are appealing to most people and seem easy to implement and develop, there is little research to suggest that peer mentoring gives the same results as classical mentoring.

Vs. classical Mentoring

Morton-Cooper and Palmer distinguish between *classical mentoring* (also known as *primary mentoring*) and *contract or facilitated mentoring*. Classical mentoring is characterized as an informal, often spontaneous enabling relationship between an older mentor and a younger mentee, based on a shared wish to work together, usually for a long period, without financial compensation for the mentor.

Peer mentoring differs from classical mentoring in two aspects. First, in peer mentoring mentors and mentees are close in age, experience, educational level, and they may also overlap in their personal identities, which are usually the criteria for matching, but this may leave junior students vulnerable to peer pressure and unsupervised rivalry. Second, peer mentoring programmes are semi-structured planned programmes with specific guidelines and frequently with a set number of meetings and activities within a predetermined amount of time. Students who enroll in peer mentoring programmes tend to be matched mostly according to major, gender, language of preference, and ethnic background, and those students who share the largest number of similarities tend to become peers in the peer mentoring relationship. Little research is available to know what happens between peer mentors and peer mentees who have different characteristics.

Cross-age Peer Mentoring

The Handbook of Youth Mentoring provides the following definition of cross-age peer mentoring:

"Peer mentoring involves an interpersonal relationship between two youths of different ages that reflects a greater degree of hierarchical power imbalance than is typical of a friendship and in which the goal is for the older youth to promote one or more aspects of the younger youth's development. Peer mentoring refers to a sustained (long-term), usually formalized (i.e. programme-based), developmental relationship. The relationship is "developmental" in that the older peer's goal is to help guide the younger mentee's development in domains such as interpersonal skills, self-esteem and conventional connectedness and attitudes (e.g. future motivation, hopefulness)."

Cross-age mentoring can be distinguished from peer mentoring by the fact that the mentor is in a higher grade level and/or is older than the mentee, whereas in peer mentoring students of the same age are paired together based on varying levels of achievement. Karcher (2007) also notes:

"Cross-age peer mentoring programmes utilize structure, meet for more than ten meetings, do not focus primarily on deficit or problem reduction, and require an age span of at least two years."

Advantages

In general, cross-age mentoring programmes can involve a tutoring or teaching component, personal mentorship and guidance, or both, and they incorporate many of the advantages of other forms of peer mentorship. Because student mentors are closer in age, knowledge, authority and cognitive development than adult mentors, mentees often feel freer to express ideas, ask questions, and take risks. These similarities also make it easier for mentors to understand personal and academic problems that the mentee may be experiencing, and present solutions in a more understandable and relevant way. Furthermore, unlike same-age peer mentoring, cross-age programmes can prevent feelings of inferiority on the part of the mentee when they are mentored or tutored by a student of the same age or status. Thus, mentors who are slightly older than their mentees can take advantage of the higher status provided by their age difference while enjoying increased compatibility with their students. The specific benefits of cross-age mentoring/tutoring are numerous, and are briefly described here in three main categories: increased academic achievement, improved interpersonal skills, and personal development.

Cross-age mentorship, and tutoring programmes in particular, support the academic achievement and learning process of both the mentor and the mentee. Mentees benefit from increased personalized attention in a one-on-one setting and can work at their own pace. Sessions are customized for the mentee's individual questions, needs, and learning styles, and mentees gain a greater mastery of the material and concepts while developing creativity and critical thinking skills. The mentor may also gain a deeper understanding of the material or subject that they are teaching, as this relationship often encourages a deeper dedication to their own studies so that they may more effectively communicate what they've learned. The mentor gains a deeper sense of responsibility, dedication, and pride in being able to help a peer, while both students take pride in mutual accomplishments and successes. Ultimately, cross-age mentorship programmes may increase retention and graduation rates, especially among minority students.

In addition to improved learning and transmission of information, the mentorship process allows both students to develop more effective interpersonal communication skills. Mentees learn how to effectively form and pose questions, seek advice, and practice active listening and concentration. Similarly, the mentors gain valuable practice in effective teaching strategies. This format fosters increased self-esteem, empathy and patience in both participants, potentially creating new friendships and breaking down social barriers for students struggling to adjust to a new academic setting. Often the mentor will serve as an important role-model, and can model academic skills and work habits as well as personal values (e.g. dedication to service, empathy, and internal motivation). This relationship can be pivotal for the success of new or underserved students in academia by providing an opportunity for peers to discuss academic issues, career choices, research ideas, and personal matters.

Monitoring and Evaluation

Cross-age mentoring programmes require careful consideration of the goals, objectives and the available human, physical and financial resources in order to ultimately assess the progress made by the participants and the overall usefulness of the programme. Frequent assessment is important as it gives valuable insight into how well the cross-age mentoring curriculum is organized and implemented, and provides positive reinforcement for both the mentor and mentee. Mentors should be pre-screened according to their academic proficiency and attitudes to ensure that they will be able to meet the needs of a mentee. Moreover, mentors will also benefit from ongoing training, supervision and psychological support by teachers, administrators, parents and other members of the community.

An example: The Coca-Cola Valued Youth Programme

One established cross-age mentoring programme is the Coca-Cola Valued Youth Programme (VYP), which originated in San Antonio, Texas through the Intercultural Development Research Association (IDRA). In an effort to decrease truancy, the need for disciplinary actions and drop-out rates of students, this programme paired up "at-risk" middle school students to tutor "at-risk" elementary school students, both primarily of Hispanic origin with limited English proficiency. In this case, the tutors who participated were not only rewarded by getting paid and receiving course credit, but also by receiving recognition for their service and by improving their own academic and tutoring skills through special tutoring classes. These VYP programme benefits, in turn, resulted in a positive impact on school success and lowered the dropout rates of these tutors.

In the Workplace

Peer mentoring can offer employees a valuable source of support and information in the workplace. Peer mentoring offers a low cost way to train new employees or to upgrade the skills of less experienced workers.

Mentees may feel more comfortable learning from a peer than in a hierarchical setting. Mentors as well as mentees may also benefit from the bonds they form with colleagues. In 1978 Edgar Schein described multiple roles for successful mentors in the work setting. New employees who are paired with a mentor are twice as likely to remain in their job than those who do not receive mentorship.

In Health Care

Peer mentoring has been shown to increase resistance to stress-related anxiety and depression in patients, or clients, affected by chronic illness or mental health issues. Mental health peer mentors and peer support groups help clients change their lifestyle and adhere to a more productive healthy lifestyle by adjusting habits and helping them realize helpful ways of coping and taking on personal responsibility, for example, the Wildflowers' Movement.

Peer mentors can also help patients prepare for medical and surgical procedures and adhere to treatment regimes. Peer mentoring has been implemented in programmes to support survivors of traumatic brain injury, cancer patients, dialysis patients, diabetics persons with spinal cord injuries, and to reduce HIV transmission and increase adherence to treatment in HIV-positive IV drug users. Peer mentoring is also used in training health care workers.

Other Applications

Peer mentoring has also been used to prevent gang violence in schoolchildren and teens, to improve the quality of child care among economically disadvantaged first-time mothers, and to improve performance in military recruits.

Developmental Networks and Mentoring

Mentees often have more than one mentor throughout their careers. With multiple mentors, a mentee can benefit from different mentors who have a variety of experiences and skill strengths to share. A developmental network perspective is used to expand our understanding of mentoring. Different mentors may be able to address different developmental needs of mentees in order to facilitate career progress.

Filstad (2004) observed that most organizational newcomers had multiple role models that served different needs during the work adjustment process. Although most of the mentoring research has focused on only one mentor–mentee relationship, Kram (1985) recognized relationship constellations that provide multiple sources of developmental support for a mentee. More recently, Higgins, Chandler, and Kram (in press) provide a theoretical framework to reconceptualize mentoring. The typology of developmental networks is described by two dimensions: (a) the diversity of social systems from which mentees draw upon to form developmental relationships, and (b) the strength of these relationships.

Types of Mentors

A mentor's position, relative to the mentee, is typically superior in status and power, although some mentors may be peers and others may even be subordinate to the mentee. Mentors who have professional roles that are superior to the mentee often have power to affect the mentee's career development. They may be in positions of authority to evaluate the career progress of the mentee or to provide resources and experiences that enhance the mentee's development. These mentors also can use their power indirectly, by influencing people who are directly responsible for the mentee. In contrast, peer mentors typically do not exercise formal power over mentees, but they often provide support and both partners share lessons learned as their careers progress. Their similar positions and shared developmental needs provide a common ground for peer mentoring. Finally, subordinate mentors can be rich sources of information about people and procedures. Mentees who are new to an organization may be more comfortable asking a subordinate or staff person for help because making the request and receiving evaluations are generally less threatening.

In addition to superior, peer, and subordinate types of mentors, these relationships can be distinguished by the key criteria that match a mentor with a mentee.

Typically mentees are drawn to mentors who have key experiences in a particular professional speciality or interest area. The professional area is an obvious matching criterion, but it is not the only one. Mentees often seek mentors who share important demographic characteristics such as gender, race, religion, and sexual orientation.

Furthermore, mentees can identify with particular mentors who have values, attitudes, and experiences that the mentee holds or aspires to have.

The Etiquette of Mentoring

Many psychologists are familiar with the necessity of rapport development with clients for positive therapeutic outcomes. The therapeutic relationship plays a pivotal role in the experience for both client and practitioner. Successful mentoring also depends on the quality of the relationship between mentor and mentee.

Mentoring relationships may involve sharing more personal information related to professional growth whereas in therapeutic relationships, the therapist is likely to have stricter boundaries of self-disclosure. Training programmes for counselors do not assume that trainees come with the knowledge necessary to develop strong rapport with clients, however little guidance is offered to mentors or mentees about the dos and don'ts of establishing a healthy mentoring relationship. The mentoring relationship mirrors in many ways a relationship between a counsellor and a client, however it differs significantly in other ways. Areas in which the two overlap include positive regard, seeing boundaries, active listening, and ethical behaviour. However, one important area in which the mentoring relationship does not parallel a therapeutic relationship is that it is specifically not therapy.

In an effort to facilitate the development of functional and successful mentor relationships, articulating the rules of etiquette for these encounters may prove beneficial for both mentors and mentees. Although not intended to be comprehensive, this outlines key points that are essential to the development of rapport and the evolution of functional mentor relationships. Some points may be more appropriate for mentor relationships between two professionals and others more appropriate for mentor relationships between a student and a professional. These points are stated under the rubric of etiquette, along the lines of the conduct agreed upon by professionals to be observed in social and professional life.

Frequently both parties come to a mentor relationship with divergent expectations. Mentors may enter a mentor relationship to pass on wisdom received from their mentors. Mentees may solicit a mentor for counsel on career development.

Some mentors may conceptualize the relationship as a business arrangement in which both parties benefit and some mentees may feel entitled to the attention of the mentor. What mentor does not have a story about a mentee who turned into a nightmare and a drain on resources? What mentee has not had a less than stellar mentor with stories about the hardships suffered under a tyrannical mentor? With some forethought and empathy, the mentoring experience can prove not only beneficial for all involved, but also lay the groundwork for a lifelong professional relationship.

Carl Rogers argued that all that was necessary for a successful therapeutic encounter was unconditional positive regard. Although this may not be sufficient to guarantee a successful mentor relationship, any relationship without a shared sense of respect is likely to quickly become dysfunctional.

Respect is a cornerstone of the mentoring process. In a world where resources are in short supply and stress levels at all-time highs, respect can serve as a social lubricant for mentoring—respect for both mentor and mentee. Without shared positive regard, encounters become taxing and productivity levels fall. However, it is from a place of respect that a mentor understands the multiple forces involved in the struggle for professional identity development in the mentee and it is from a place of respect that the mentee understands the time limitations under which a mentor struggles. Although respect is earned and develops over time, it is a wise mentor and mentee who enter their relationship from a respectful stance.

A mentor who is clear and upfront about what the mentee can expect from a mentoring relationship, who guides the process, and who sets appropriate boundaries, creates an environment in which the relationship can thrive. A mentor who can provide perspective during critical incidents, and encourage the mentee to find balance, enables growth through the relationship. From the mentee's perspective, respectful behaviours such as punctuality, reliability, and the development of an independent work style, create an environment in which the mentor can best meet the needs of the mentee. This broad perspective may help a mentee to understand and value that the mentor relationship can be the start of a long-term, mutual, professional relationship that changes over time. The number of complex circumstances and interactions in a mentor relationship are limitless, but basic social etiquette can be applied successfully in most cases.

Mentoring and Ethics

Most professions have an established code of conduct, often called an ethics code. The general principles can be seen as an aspirational guide to appropriate interactions with others in many situations, including mentoring. They do not, however, dictate what is good and bad mentoring.

Potential Problems in Mentor Relationships

Although mentoring is generally defined as a relationship that helps the mentee and the mentor, problems in the relationship may hinder the career development of either individual. If the bounds of the relationship are not clearly understood, a mentee may be overly dependent on a mentor, asking for micromanagement instead of career advice and counsel. A mentee may also ask for personal favours or expect involvement and credit with the mentor's work. Such a relationship would not help the mentee establish his or her own independence and would intensify difficulties in the separation stage. Mentors should not use nor exploit their mentees, nor should they take credit for the mentee's work. They may resist the separation stage and insist on some voice in the mentee's career decisions. Severe interpersonal problems with the relationship may mitigate the value of many mentoring lessons.

Perhaps the most visible interpersonal problem in mentoring occurs when the relationship moves from a professional one to a personal one. Research on cross-gender mentoring has identified sexual relationships as a potential problem. Although sexual relationships are not confined to cross-gender mentoring, no research on sexual relationships in same-gender mentoring has been published to date.

If the personal relationships are substantiated within a single organization, the organization will generally terminate any formal relationship between the two individuals and may even terminate one or both participants employment.

In addition to problems within the relationship, mentors and mentees may experience problems with performance issues. Mentors may be jealous when their mentees outshine them. In addition, one partner may struggle as a result of errors made by the other. For example, a mentee's reputation may be tarnished if his or her mentor commits a serious breach of ethics. Likewise, a mentor may be viewed negatively if his or her mentee's performance is not meeting expectations. The mentor's judgement in selecting a good mentee may be questioned as well as the quality of the mentor's counsel and advice.

Problems with mentoring may be minimized when both parties have clear expectations of what the professional relationship can do and what it should not do.

Formal mentoring programmes often include a training component for both parties to understand the expectations. Specific content of these training programmes depends on the form of mentoring and purpose of the mentoring programme.

In general, personal reflection about the mentor relationship both before initiating it and throughout its course, by both the mentor and mentee, will contribute to a robust, growth-oriented relationship. Finally, although obvious but often forgotten, both the mentor and mentee are human beings who strive to meet personal needs and goals in a complex world. Everyone has bad days, and forgiveness and patience will aid in overcoming what may appear to be barriers to a successful mentor relationship.

Does Age Matter?

Today's multi-generational workforce has become a topic of interest at workplaces across the country. This is not the first time in history that people from different generations have worked "side-by-side." In agrarian societies, children, parents, and grandparents all contributed to productive work that was necessary for sustenance. Toward the end of the middle ages, guilds developed as a way to ensure the transfer of knowledge from one generation to the next. Many of the manufacturing sites established during the early years of industrialization structured their organizations to recruit from within extended families, assuming that the elders in the families would socialize and supervise the younger and less experienced workers.

How Age Matters

Age Can Have an Impact on Employees. For Example: Age can affect employees' decisions about labour force participation, as well as the employment opportunities and options which are offered to them. It has been widely recognized, for instance, that the labour force participation rates of women in the United States have historically declined during the traditional child bearing and children rearing years.

Employees' work experiences, attitudes and behaviours can be shaped by age and age-related factors. As a result, age can impact employee engagement, performance and productivity. For example, feeling valued at the workplace is a key driver of engagement. According to the Institute for Employment Studies, workers aged 50 and older tend to feel less valued and less involved in their organizations than those under 30.

In response to the changing age demographics of the workforce, some employers have started to assess how age might affect the effectiveness of their strategies for recruitment, on-boarding, training and development, and employee engagement.

Employers may adopt HR policies and programmes in an effort to be sure that employees (or potential employees) of different ages view the company as an employer of choice. A recent study completed by the American Business Collaborative found, for instance, that the top 3 factors contributing to job satisfaction among exempt men in their 30s were salary, flexible work options, and job security whereas salary, job security and advancement were reported as being the most important for exempt men in their 40s.

Managers who are interested in harnessing the creativity and business effectiveness of multi-generational work groups and minimizing possible conflict may want to gain a better understanding of the effects of age at the workplace.

Age-old Ways to Think about Age: Age, Generation, Life Course and Career Stage"Age" can mean more than just how old an employee is.In fact, there are at least four ways to think about age as it is relevant to the workplace: chronological age; generation; life course; and career stage. During the last century, there was more congruence between a person's age (and, therefore, the generation to which they belonged), key life course events (such as the average age when mothers gave birth to their first child), and career stages (such as entry into the workforce).

In the past, therefore, employers may have found that it was less important to make careful distinctions among these different perspectives of age. Today, however, the relationships among chronological age, generation, key life events, and career stage are less tightly coupled. For example, there is more variability in the age when people begin their careers – or beginning a second or third career – than was true in the past.

Employers can no longer assume that chronological age "predicts" employees' life stage or career stage. And, the differences between meanings of chronological age, generation, life stage, and career stage can matter. Each of these different perspectives of age can help employers to get deeper insights about how age diversity might affect their employees and work processes

There are many dimensions to human development, including: physical development, cognitive development, emotional development, and social development.

Although workplaces across the country provide resources, such as Employee Assistance Programmes, to their employees in an effort to support their emotional and social health, employers focus particular attention on employees' cognitive and physical abilities. Employers may implement training programmes and wellness initiatives in an effort to enhance their employees' intellectual and physical competencies.

Research confirms that there are some relationships between age and changes in both physical and mental abilities and skills, particularly among the very young and the very old. As noted by Hedge, Borman, and Lammlein (2006), "Overall, research on aging suggests that physical and cognitive abilities do decline in older age. However...these declines may not always generalize to deficits in on-the-job performance.....older workers generally seem to adapt well and to compensate for declining abilities by adjusting their approach to the job."

In part, many older workers are able to use their experience and accumulated knowledge as a strategy to successfully complete tasks. Indeed, many of these declines tend to occur after people withdraw from the labour force either because employees reach retirement age before there are noticeable declines in their abilities; or because the declines in employees' physical health precipitates withdrawal from the labour force. Some research has even found that certain types of cognitive abilities can improve with age.

It is important to underscore the observation that although some research confirms that age can be one factor that explains physical and cognitive changes over time, other factors are also important.

Several studies have explored possible differences in the productivity of employees of different ages. Recent investigations have demonstrated that variations in opportunities and barriers to career development that affect employee motivation explain performance outcomes as more than just age alone.

Employers might also want to consider how employees' functioning might reflect the fit between characteristics of the work assigned to employees and their interests/abilities. There are indications that the complexity of tasks completed by workers can affect intellectual functioning.

If the responsibilities of older workers are routine and no longer interesting or challenging, it is possible that any resultant decreased productivity might reflect both dis-engagement as well as some declines in ability that result from working on less challenging tasks.

Generation

There is, of course, a correspondence between chronological age and generation because generational labels designate population groups that were born within a specified time period.

Generational terms are often used as "easy-to-remember" labels for particular cohorts. There are some important differences, however, between the lens associated with chronological age and the generational perspective. Whereas the focus on chronological age makes it possible to ask the question, "How are individuals of a particular age alike?", the generational framework places the experiences of individuals and groups of individuals (that is, age cohorts) in the context of significant historical, social, or cultural events. Therefore, the compelling question for the generational framework is, "How are all individuals of a certain age during a certain historical period in a particular place alike?"

Historians and sociologists use the term "generation" to refer to groups of people who not only share their membership in a particular age cohort but who have also been exposed to significant events at a particular time, even though there is bound to be significant variation in the impact of these events on different individuals who belong to the same generation.

Although there is some controversy among demographers about how to establish the years which separate one generation from another, popular literature suggests that there are currently four generations in the labour force: Millennials/Gen Y, Gen X, Baby Boomers, and members of the Traditionalists/Silent Generation who have either not yet retired or have retired but have re-entered the labour force.

Looking at age from the perspective of generation can be a helpful, short-hand way to factor-in historical events or culture that may have a long-lasting impact on a specific age cohort. For example, observations about the technological competencies of many of the Millenials implicitly reflect the recognition that these young people were the first generation to grow up with computers and the internet as a natural part of their environments. The generational framework of age helps employers to consider questions such as, "How might the prevailing cultures or the historical experiences shared by many members of a particular generation affect how employees perceive their work experiences?"

The generational lens has been used for many workplace-based training sessions that explore age diversity.

It should be noted, however, that there are some limitations associated with the generational lens of age.

It is sometimes easy to gloss over how specific types of events might affect individuals in profoundly different ways. For example, the Baby Boomers "came of age" during the era of the Vietnam War. However, some of their lives were shaped by direct articipation in the war, others by the loss of loved ones killed during the war, and others by involvement in active protest against the war.

The key events shared by a generation tend to occur in a specific regional or national context. Therefore, the terms used to designate different generations may be meaningless in a global context. Because the term "Baby Boomer" designates the increased fertility experienced in the U.S. right after World War II, this generational label is not appropriate to adults in the same age cohort who live in other countries that were affected in different ways by the end of that war.

It can be difficult to separate out whether the characteristics of a particular generation at a specific "moment in time" reflect the fact that they are members of a generation or whether most of the members of that generation are sharing an important life stage experience. For example, it is often noted that the Millenials want jobs that are socially impactful.

But, isn't that an observation that was also made about the Baby Boomers in the 1960s and 1970s when they were in their 20s?

It is always tricky to accurately identify characteristics and values of younger generations because it is difficult to determine whether these characteristics will "stand the test of time." Perhaps the most difficult challenge associated with using the lens of generation when thinking about age is that it is very easy to begin to over-generalize the characteristics of different age cohorts, focusing primarily on the differences, whether these differences are small or large. For example, although some research suggests that the extent and level of intergenerational differences and conflict may not be widespread, there has been a lot of attention focused on "generation wars".

Life Course

The life course perspective focuses attention on individuals' "personal histories" in the context of the wider social-historical-cultural context. In addition, this perspective considers how resources, demands, and events in the individual's environment might affect the past, present and future course of personal histories. The life course perspective sharpens our focus on transitions, such as entrance into school (at different ages including during adulthood) or the formation and changes in family structures.

The life course perspective also explicitly acknowledges that not every individual will experience each life course event (such as marriage). Even though some life course events tend to happen in certain age ranges, the life course perspective does not specify the timing of life events. The life course perspective helps employers to address questions such as, "How might the life transitions experienced by employees and their families, such as the retirement of a spouse, affect our employees?"

Many workplaces have integrated a life course perspective for their work/life policies and programmes. For example, employers wanting to increase the retention rates among employees who are parents of young children have expanded dependent care resources and flexible work options.

Given today's context of an aging workforce, a life course perspective can help employers consider the challenges that their older employees face (e.g., demands for parent care, etc.).

Career Stage

The fourth way to think about employees' age-related experiences is to adopt a special type of developmental perspective which focuses on career stages. Although the term career is sometimes used as a referent only for professional occupations, for the purposes of this discussion, we consider the word to refer to a sustained "line of work," regardless of the occupational category.

Career trajectories reflect a combination of factors including education, experience, and opportunities as well as individual's personal characteristics.

Although some people assume that most employees experience careers as a steady upward progression, experts have observed that careers unfold in a variety of ways. In fact, the lock-step career has not been the norm for many people. For instance, the career patterns of most women and employees who have been more vulnerable to the vicissitudes of economic turbulence have never conformed to the "step climbing" metaphor.

The Bureau of Labour Statistics has reported that occupation mobility rates appear to have been relatively stable for the past 3 decades.

However, as many Baby Boomers get ready to extend their labour force participation, it is possible that some will want to change occupations or careers. In that case, it is entirely possible that an older worker who has recently changed careers (perhaps after taking a "retirement job") would be at an early career stage.

Therefore, the framework for career stages has moved from a linear notion to a cyclical construct. That is, employees may have the experience of being in "early career" several times over their life course and might skip some career stages entirely.

Today, employees in an early career stage might have a sense of exploration when they "try on" a specific career option. If they continue on that career trajectory, they might become established in that career where they develop and expand sets of career-related competencies. If the person continues in the same or a similar career, they might have "maintenance" experiences when they deepen their expertise. This is also a stage when some employees want to use their competencies in a generative fashion to benefit the next generation of employees as well as the organization. The stage of disengagement refers to the transitions during which individuals cut back or leave the job, the organization, the career, and/or the labour force. The career stage perspective helps employers to focus on questions such as, "What types of assignments are appropriate for specific employees, given the career-specific competencies they have? Which types of resources might enhance that employee's performance?" Employers use a career development perspective when they engage employees in conversations about the next opportunities appropriate for their careers – regardless of the employee's age.

The National Study of Business Strategy and Workforce

Development asked employers to describe employees in early career, mid career, and late career. Employers acknowledge that there is diversity within each career stage, as well as across career stages. However, the National Study of Business Strategy and Workforce Development found that employers feel that, in general, employees at different career stages may bring diverse sets of attributes to the work, recognizing of course that there can be significant diversity within the different groups.

For example, employers were more likely to report that late career employees had higher levels of skills than needed for their jobs and that they are more likely to want to lead or supervise others when compared to younger colleagues.

Employers are less likely to report that their younger adult/early career employees are productive (28.5% of the employers saying "very true") than their mid-life/mid career (42.1% of the employers saying "very true") or older adult/late career employees (38.5% of the employers saying "very true").

Implications for Employers

As noted in a report prepared by Ceridian, age can be related to "...differences in attitudes, values, workstyles and expectations can also cause miscommunication and misunderstandings, impact productivity and dampen the effect of teamwork and collaboration so critical to organizational effectiveness."

Savvy managers will consider how each of the four perspectives of age might lead to different strategies for motivation and engagement, different approaches to supervision and career development, as well as adjustments in benefits and supports.

Organizations interested in helping their supervisors strengthen their multi-generational competencies might find it useful to think about two different sets of competencies: supervising individual employees of different ages and supervising multi-generational work groups. The first set of competencies requires that supervisors can use the four perspectives of age to gain a better understanding of the experiences of individual employees. The second set of competencies demands that supervisors understand how age might affect the dynamics and interactions of group members, including the duration of the interactions, the status and power equality of employees engaged in the interaction, the closeness of the relationships within the groups, the complexity of the interactions, and the degree of cooperation/ conflict that characterizes the interactions.

Motivation

Motivation is a psychological feature that arouses an organism to act towards a desired goal and elicits, controls, and sustains certain goal-directed behaviours. It can be considered a driving force; a psychological one that compels or reinforces an action toward a desired goal. For example, hunger is a motivation that elicits a desire to eat. Motivation is the purpose or psychological cause of an action.

Motivation has been shown to have roots in physiological, behavioural, cognitive, and social areas. Motivation may be rooted in a basic impulse to optimize well-being, minimize physical pain and maximize pleasure. It can also originate from specific physical needs such as eating, sleeping or resting, and sex.

Motivation is an inner drive to behave or act in a certain manner. "It's the difference between waking up before dawn to pound the pavement and lazing around the house all day." These inner conditions such as wishes, desires, goals, activate to move in a particular direction in behaviour.

Types of Theories and Models

motivational theories A class of theories about why people do things seeks to reduce the number of factors down to one and explain all behaviour through that one factor. For example, economics has been criticized for using self-interest as a mono-motivational theory. Mono-motivational theories are often criticized for being too reductive or too abstract.

Conscious and Unconscious Motivations

A number of motivational theories emphasize the distinction between conscious and unconscious motivations. In evolutionary psychology, the "ultimate", unconscious motivation may be a cold evolutionary calculation, the conscious motivation could be more benign or even positive emotions. For example, while it may be in the best interest of a male's genes to have multiple partners and thus break up with or divorce one before moving onto the next, the conscious rationalization could be, "I loved her at the time".

Freud is associated with the idea that human beings have many unconscious motivations that cause them to make important decisions because of these unconscious forces, such as choosing a partner.

Non-psychological Theories

Platonic Theory of Motivation

In The Republic, Plato advances a tri-partite theory of the soul, which consists of three parts: reason, spirit and appetite. All parts of the soul have desires, however not all desires are the same. Desires take many different forms and have many different responses or results.

Machiavellianism

Machiavellism argues that human beings are motivated to seek power and status above all. Modern research argues that people who are high in this trait do indeed seek power and money, and are willing to use others as instruments towards that end.

5

Psychological Theories and Models

Rational Motivations

The idea that human beings are rational and human behaviour is guided by reason is an old one. However, recent research (on Satisficing for example) has significantly undermined the idea of homo economicus or of perfect rationality in favour of a more bounded rationality. The field of behavioural economics is particularly concerned with the limits of rationality in economic agents.

Intrinsic and Extrinsic Motivation

Motivation can be divided into two types: intrinsic (internal) motivation and extrinsic (external) motivation.

Intrinsic Motivation

Intrinsic motivation refers to motivation that is driven by an interest or enjoyment in the task itself, and exists within the individual rather than relying on external pressures or a desire for reward. Intrinsic motivation has been studied since the early 1970s. Students who are intrinsically motivated are more likely to engage in the task willingly as well as work to improve their skills, which will increase their capabilities. Students are likely to be intrinsically motivated if they:

- attribute their educational results to factors under their own control, also known as autonomy
- believe they have the skills to be effective agents in reaching their desired goals, also known as self-efficacy beliefs
- are interested in mastering a topic, not just in achieving good grades

Extrinsic Motivation

Extrinsic motivation refers to the performance of an activity in order to attain an outcome, whether or not that activity is also intrinsically motivated. Extrinsic motivation comes from outside of the individual. Common extrinsic motivations are rewards (for example money or grades) for showing the desired behaviour, and the threat of punishment following misbehaviour. Competition is in an extrinsic motivator because it encourages the performer to win and to beat others, not simply to enjoy the intrinsic rewards of the activity. A cheering crowd and the desire to win a trophy are also extrinsic incentives.

Comparison of intrinsic and extrinsic motivation

Social psychological research has indicated that extrinsic rewards can lead to overjustification and a subsequent reduction in intrinsic motivation. In one study demonstrating this effect, children who expected to be (and were) rewarded with a ribbon and a gold star for drawing pictures spent less time playing with the drawing materials in subsequent observations than children who were assigned to an unexpected reward condition.

While the provision of extrinsic rewards might reduce the desirability of an activity, the use of extrinsic constraints, such as the threat of punishment, against performing an activity has actually been found to increase one's intrinsic interest in that activity. In one study, when children were given mild threats against playing with an attractive toy, it was found that the threat actually served to increase the child's interest in the toy, which was previously undesirable to the child in the absence of threat.

For those children who received no extrinsic reward, self-determination theory proposes that extrinsic motivation can be internalized by the individual if the task fits with their values and beliefs and therefore helps to fulfill their basic psychological needs.

Operant Conditioning

Operant conditioning a term coined by B.F. Skinner, is a method of learning that occurs through rewards and punishments for behaviour. Skinner believed that internal thoughts and motivations could not be used to explain behaviour; instead to look at external, observable causes of human behaviour. His theory explained how we acquire the range of learned behaviours we exhibit each and every day.

Push and Pull

This model is usually used when discussing motivation within the context of tourism. Push factors determine the desire to go on holiday, whereas pull factors determine the choice of destination. Push motives are connected with internal forces, for example the need for relaxation or escapism, while pull factors are the external factors, such as landscape, cultural image or the climate of a destination, that induce a traveller to visit a certain location. Push factors can be stimulated by external and situational aspects of motivation in the shape of pull factors. Then again pull factors are issues that can arise from a location itself and therefore 'push' an individual to choose to experience it. Since then, a large number of theories have been developed over the years in many studies there is no single theory that illustrates all motivational aspects of travelling. Many researchers have highlighted that because several motives may occur at the same time it should not be assumed that only one motive drives an individual to perform an action, as was presumed in previous studies. On the other hand, since people are not able to satisfy all their needs at once, they usually seek to satisfy some or a few of them.

Self-control

The self-control aspect of motivation is increasingly considered to be a subset of emotional intelligence; it is suggested that although a person may be classed as highly intelligent (as measured by many traditional intelligence tests), they may remain unmotivated to pursue intellectual endeavours. Vroom's "expectancy theory" provides an account of when people may decide to exert self-control in pursuit of a particular goal.

Drives

A drive or desire can be described as *a deficiency or need that activates behaviour that is aimed at a goal or an incentive.* These drives are thought to originate within the individual and may not require external stimuli to encourage the behaviour. Basic drives could be sparked by deficiencies such as hunger, which motivates a person to seek food whereas more subtle drives might be the desire for praise and approval, which motivates a person to behave in a manner pleasing to others. Another basic drive is the sexual drive which like food motivates us because it is essential to our survival. The desire for sex is wired deep into the brain of all human beings as glands secrete hormones that travel through the blood to the brain and stimulates the onset of sexual desire. The hormone involved in the initial onset of sexual desire is called dihydroepiandosterone (DHEA). The hormonal basis of both men and women's sex drives is testosterone. Men naturally have more testosterone than women do and so are more likely than woman to think about sex, have sexual fantasies, seek sex and sexual variety (whether positions or partners), masturbate, want sex at an early point in a relationship, sacrifice other things for sex, have permissive attitudes for sex, and complain about low sex drive in their partners.

By contrast, the role of extrinsic rewards and stimuli can be seen in the example of training animals by giving them treats when they perform a trick correctly. The treat motivates the animals to perform the trick consistently, even later when the treat is removed from the process.

Drive Theory

In psychology, a drive theory or drive doctrine is a theory that attempt to define, analyze or classify the psychological drives. A drive is an "excitatory state produced by a homeostatic disturbance", an instinctual need that has the power of driving the behaviour of an individual.

Drive theory is based on the principle that organisms are born with certain psychological needs and that a negative state of tension is created when these needs are not satisfied. When a need is satisfied, drive is reduced and the organism returns to a state of homeostasis and relaxation. According to the theory, drive tends to increase over time and operates on a feedback control system, much like a thermostat.

Psychoanalysis

In Freudian psychoanalysis, drive theory (German: *Triebtheorie*, German: *Trieblehre*) refers to the theory of drives, motivations, or instincts, that have clear objects. In 1927 Freud said that a drive theory was what was lacking most in psychoanalysis. He was opposed to systematics in psychology, rejecting it as a form of paranoia, and instead classified drives with dichotomies like Eros/Thanatos drives, the drives toward Life and Death, respectively, and sexual/ego drives.

Freud's Civilization and Its Discontents was published in Germany in 1930 when the rise of fascism in that country was well under way, and the warnings of a second European war were leading to opposing calls for rearmament and pacifism. Against this background, Freud wrote "In face of the destructive forces unleashed, now it may be expected that the other of the two 'heavenly forces,' eternal Eros, will put forth his strength so as to maintain himself alongside of his equally immortal adversary.".

In 1947, Hungarian psychiatrist and psychologist Leopold Szondi, aimed instead to a systematic drive theory. Szondi Drive Diagram has been described as a revolutionary addition to psychology, and as paving the way for a theoretical psychiatry and a psychoanalytical anthropology.

Early Attachment Theory

In early attachment theory, behavioural drive reduction was proposed by Dollard and Miller (1950) as an explanation of the mechanisms behind early attachment in infants. Behavioural drive reduction theory suggests that infants are born with innate drives, such as hunger and thirst, which only the caregiver, usually the mother, can reduce. Through a process of classical conditioning, the infant learns to associate the mother with the satisfaction of reduced drive and is thus able to form a key attachment bond. However, this theory is challenged by the work done by Harlow, particularly the experiments involving the maternal separation of rhesus monkeys, which indicate that comfort possesses greater motivational value than hunger.

Social Psychology

In social psychology, drive theory was used by Robert Zajonc in 1965 as an explanation of the phenomenon of social facilitation. The audience effect notes that in some cases the presence of a passive audience will facilitate the better performance of a task, while in other cases the presence of an audience will inhibit the performance of a task. Zajonc's drive theory suggests that the variable determining direction of performance is whether the task is composed of a correct dominant response (that is, the task is perceived as being subjectively easy to the individual) or an incorrect dominant response (perceived as being subjectively difficult).

In the presence of a passive audience, an individual is in a heightened state of arousal. Increased arousal, or *stress*, causes the individual to enact behaviours that form dominant responses, since an individual's dominant response is the most likely response, given the skills which are available. If the dominant response is correct, then social presence enhances performance of the task. However, if the dominant response is incorrect, social presence produces an impaired performance.

Corroborative Evidence

Such behaviour was first noticed by Triplett (1898) while observing the cyclists who were racing together versus cyclists who were racing alone. It was found that the mere presence of other cyclists produced greater performance. A similar effect was observed by Chen (1937) in ants building colonies. However, it was not until Zajonc investigated this behaviour in the 1960s that any empirical explanation for the audience effect was pursued.

Zajonc's drive theory is based on an experiment involving the investigation of the effect of social facilitation in cockroaches. Zajonc devised a study in which individual cockroaches were released into a tube, at the end of which there was a light. In the presence of other cockroaches as spectators, cockroaches were observed to achieve a significantly faster time in reaching the light than those in the control, no-spectator group. However, when cockroaches in the same conditions were given a maze to negotiate, performance was impaired in the spectator condition, demonstrating that incorrect dominant responses in the presence of an audience impair performance.

Evaluation Apprehension

Cottrell's Evaluation Apprehension model later refined this theory to include yet another variable in the mechanisms of social facilitation. He suggested that the correctness of dominant responses only plays a role in social facilitation when there is an expectation of social reward or punishment based on performance. His study differs in design from Zajonc's as he introduced a separate condition in which participants were given tasks to perform in the presence of an audience that was blindfolded, and thus unable to evaluate the participant's performance. It was found that no social facilitation effect occurred, and hence the anticipation of performance evaluation must play a role in social facilitation Evaluation apprehension, however, is only key in human social facilitation and not observed in animals.

Incentive Theory

A reward, tangible or intangible, is presented after the occurrence of an action (i.e. behaviour) with the intention of causing the behaviour to occur again. This is done by associating positive meaning to the behaviour. Studies show that if the person receives the reward immediately, the effect is greater, and decreases as delay lengthens. Repetitive action-reward combination can cause the action to become habit. Motivation comes from two sources: oneself, and other people. These two sources are called intrinsic motivation and extrinsic motivation, respectively.

Reinforcers and reinforcement principles of behaviour differ from the hypothetical construct of reward. A reinforcer is any stimulus change following a response that increases the future frequency or magnitude of that response, therefore the cognitive approach is certainly the way forward as in 1973 Maslow described it as being the golden pineapple. Positive reinforcement is demonstrated by an increase in the future frequency or magnitude of a response due to in the past being followed contingently by a reinforcing stimulus. Negative reinforcement involves stimulus change consisting of the removal of an aversive stimulus following a response. Positive reinforcement involves a stimulus change consisting of the presentation or magnification of a positive stimulus following a response. From this perspective, motivation is mediated by environmental events, and the concept of distinguishing between intrinsic and extrinsic forces is irrelevant.

Applying proper motivational techniques can be much harder than it seems. Steven Kerr notes that when creating a reward system, it can be easy to reward A, while hoping for B, and in the process, reap harmful effects that can jeopardize your goals.

Incentive theory in psychology treats motivation and behaviour of the individual as they are influenced by beliefs, such as engaging in activities that are expected to be profitable. Incentive theory is promoted by behavioural psychologists, such as B.F. Skinner and literalized by behaviourists, especially by Skinner in his philosophy of Radical behaviourism, to mean that a person's actions always have social ramifications: and if actions are positively received people are more likely to act in this manner, or if negatively received people are less likely to act in this manner.

Incentive theory distinguishes itself from other motivation theories, such as drive theory, in the direction of the motivation. In incentive theory, stimuli "attract", to use the term above, a person towards them, as opposed to the body seeking to reestablish homeostasis and pushing towards the stimulus. In terms of behaviourism, *incentive theory* involves positive reinforcement: the reinforcing stimulus has been conditioned to make the person happier. For instance, a person knows that eating food, drinking water, or gaining social capital will make them happier. As opposed to in *drive theory*, which involves negative reinforcement: a stimulus has been associated with the removal of the punishment—the lack of homeostasis in the body. For example, a person has come to know that if they eat when hungry, it will eliminate that negative feeling of hunger, or if they drink when thirsty, it will eliminate that negative feeling of thirst.

Escape-seeking Dichotomy Model

Escapism and seeking are major factors influencing decision making. Escapism is a need to breakaway from a daily life routine, turning on the television and watching an adventure film, whereas seeking is described as the desire to learn, turning on the television to watch a documentary. Both motivations have some interpersonal and personal facets for example individuals would like to escape from family problems (personal) or from problems with work colleagues (interpersonal). This model can also be easily adapted with regard to different studies.

Drive-reduction Theory

There are a number of drive theories. The *Drive Reduction Theory* grows out of the concept that people have certain biological drives, such as hunger. As time passes the strength of the drive increases if it is not satisfied (in this case by eating). Upon satisfying a drive the drive's strength is reduced. The theory is based on diverse ideas from the theories of Freud to the ideas of feedback control systems, such as a thermostat.

Drive theory has some intuitive or folk validity. For instance when preparing food, the drive model appears to be compatible with sensations of rising hunger as the food is prepared, and, after the food has been consumed, a decrease in subjective hunger. There are several problems, however, that leave the validity of drive reduction open for debate. The first problem is that it does not explain how secondary reinforcers reduce drive. For example, money satisfies no biological or psychological needs, but a pay check appears to reduce drive through second-order conditioning. Secondly, a drive, such as hunger, is viewed as having a "desire" to eat, making the drive a homuncular being—a feature criticized as simply moving the fundamental problem behind this "small man" and his desires.

Drive reduction theory cannot be a complete theory of behaviour, or a hungry human could not prepare a meal without eating the food before he finished cooking it. The ability of drive theory to cope with all kinds of behaviour, from not satisfying a drive (by adding on other traits such as restraint), or adding additional drives for "tasty" food, which combine with drives for food in order to explain cooking render it hard to test.

Cognitive Dissonance Theory

Suggested by Leon Festinger, cognitive dissonance occurs when an individual experiences some degree of discomfort resulting from an inconsistency between two cognitions: their views on the world around them, and their own personal feelings and actions. For example, a consumer may seek to reassure themselves regarding a purchase, feeling in retrospect that another decision may have been preferable. Their feeling that another purchase would have been preferable is inconsistent with their action of purchasing the item. The difference between their feelings and beliefs causes dissonance, so they seek to reassure themselves. While not a theory of motivation, per se, the theory of cognitive dissonance proposes that people have a motivational drive to reduce dissonance. The cognitive miser perspective makes people want to justify things in a simple way in order to reduce the effort they put into cognition. They do this by changing their attitudes, beliefs, or actions, rather than facing the inconsistencies, because dissonance is a mental strain. Dissonance is also reduced by justifying, blaming, and denying. It is one of the most influential and extensively studied theories in social psychology.

Need Theories

Motivation, as defined by Pritchard and Ashwood, is the process used to allocate energy to maximize the satisfaction of needs.

Maslow's Hierarchy of Needs: Content theory of human motivation includes both Abraham Maslow's hierarchy of needs and Herzberg's two-factor theory. Maslow's theory is one of the most widely discussed theories of motivation.

The American motivation psychologist Abraham H. Maslow developed the hierarchy of needs consisting of five hierarchic classes. According to Maslow, people are motivated by unsatisfied needs. The needs, listed from basic (lowest-earliest) to most complex (highest-latest) are as follows:

- Physiology (hunger, thirst, sleep, etc.)
- Safety/Security/Shelter/Health
- Belongingness/Love/Friendship
- Self-esteem/Recognition/Achievement
- Self actualization

The basic requirements build upon the first step in the pyramid: physiology. If there are deficits on this level, all behaviour will be oriented to satisfy this deficit. Essentially, if you have not slept or eaten adequately, you won't be interested in your self-esteem desires. Subsequently we have the second level, which awakens a need for security. After securing those two levels, the motives shift to the social sphere, the third level. Psychological requirements comprise the fourth level, while the top of the hierarchy consists of self-realization and self-actualization.

Maslow's Hierarchy of Needs theory can be summarized as follows:

- Human beings have wants and desires which influence their behaviour. Only unsatisfied needs influence behaviour, satisfied needs do not.
- Needs are arranged in order of importance to human life, from the basic to the complex.
- The person advances to the next level of needs only after the lower level need is at least minimally satisfied.
- The further the progress up the hierarchy, the more individuality, humanness and psychological health a person will show.

Herzberg's Two-factor Theory

Frederick Herzberg's two-factor theory, a.k.a. intrinsic/extrinsic motivation, concludes that certain factors in the workplace result in job satisfaction, but if absent, they don't lead to dissatisfaction but no satisfaction. The factors that motivate people can change over their lifetime, but "respect for me as a person" is one of the top motivating factors at any stage of life.

He distinguished between:

- *Motivators*; (e.g. challenging work, recognition, responsibility) which give positive satisfaction, and
- *Hygiene factors*; (e.g. status, job security, salary and fringe benefits) that do not motivate if present, but, if absent, result in demotivation.

The name hygiene factors is used because, like hygiene, the presence will not improve health, but absence can cause health deterioration.

Herzberg's theory has found application in such occupational fields as information systems and in studies of user satisfaction such as computer user satisfaction.

Alderfer's ERG Theory

Alderfer, expanding on Maslow's hierarchy of needs, created the *ERG theory*. This theory posits that there are three groups of core needs — existence, relatedness, and growth, hence the label: ERG theory. The existence group is concerned with providing our basic material existence requirements. They include the items that Maslow considered to be physiological and safety needs. The second group of needs are those of relatedness- the desire we have for maintaining important personal relationships. These social and status desires require interaction with others if they are to be satisfied, and they align with Maslow's social need and the external component of Maslow's esteem classification. Finally, Alderfer isolates growth needs as an intrinsic desire for personal development. These include the intrinsic component from Maslow's esteem category and the characteristics included under self-actualization.

Self-determination Theory

Edward L. Deci and Richard M. Ryan, during the early nineties, proposed the theory of self-determination; focusing on the degree to which an individual's behaviour is self-motivated and self-determined. According to Deci and Ryan, the three psychological needs motivate the self to initiate specific behaviour and mental nutriments that are essential for psychological health and well-being for an individual. These needs are said to be universal, innate and psychological and include the need for competence, autonomy, and psychological relatedness.

When these needs are satisfied, there are positive consequence (e.g. well being and growth), we're motivated, productive and happy. When they're thwarted, our motivation, productivity and happiness plummet. Deci and Vansteenkiste claim that there are three essential elements to the theory: 1. Humans are inherently proactive with their potential and mastering their inner forces (such as drive and emotions). 2. Humans have an inherent tendency towards growth, development and integrated functioning. 3. Optimal development and actions are inherent in humans but they don't happen automatically. Whether this aspect of our humanity emerges in our lives depends on whether the conditions around us support it. The main mechanisms of Motivation 2.0 are more stifling than supportive. Of course these are necessary, as stated earlier, but the less salient they are made, the better. Instead, we should focus our efforts on creating environments (at our workplace, schools, home) for our innate psychological needs to flourish. Other researchers also reach the same conclusion, i.e. human beings have an innate drive to be autonomous, self-determined yet connected to one another. When these conditions are met, internet drive is liberated and people achieve more and live richer lives.

Temporal Motivation Theory

The latest approach in developing a broad, integrative theory of motivation is Temporal Motivation Theory. Introduced in a 2006 *Academy of Management Review* article, it synthesizes into a single formulation the primary aspects of several other major motivational theories, including Incentive Theory, Drive Theory, Need Theory, Self-Efficacy and Goal Setting. It simplifies the field of motivation and allows findings from one theory to be translated into terms of another. Another journal article that helped to develop the Temporal Motivation Theory, "The Nature of Procrastination, " received American Psychological Association's George A. Miller award for outstanding contribution to general science.

Achievement Motivation

Achievement motivation is an integrative perspective based on the premise that performance motivation results from the way broad components of personality are directed towards performance. As a result, it includes a range of dimensions that are relevant to success at work but which are not conventionally regarded as being part of performance motivation. The emphasis on performance seeks to integrate formerly separate approaches as Need for Achievement with, for example, social motives like dominance. Personality is intimately tied to performance and achievement motivation, including such characteristics as tolerance for risk, fear of failure, and others. The Achievement Motivation Inventory is based on this theory and assesses three factors (in 17 separated scales) relevant to vocational and professional success. This motivation has repeatedly been linked with adaptive motivational patterns, including working hard, a willingness to pick learning tasks with much difficulty, and contributing success to effort. Achievement motivation was studied intensively by David C. McClelland, John W. Atkinson and their colleagues since the early 1950s. Their research showed that business managers who were successful demonstrated a high need to achieve no matter the culture. There are three major characteristics of people who have a great need to achieve according to McClelland's research.

1. They would prefer a work environment in which they are able to assume responsibility for solving problems.
2. They would take calculated risk and establish moderate, attainable goals.
3. They want to hear continuous recognition, as well as feedback, in order for them to know how well they are doing.

Cognitive theories

Goal-setting Theory: Goal-setting theory is based on the notion that individuals sometimes have a drive to reach a clearly defined end state. Often, this end state is a reward in itself. A goal's efficiency is affected by three features: proximity, difficulty and specificity. Good goal setting incorporates the SMART criteria, in which goals are: specific, measurable, accurate, realistic, and timely. An ideal goal should present a situation where the time between the initiation of behaviour and the end state is close.

This explains why some children are more motivated to learn how to ride a bike than to master algebra. A goal should be moderate, not too hard or too easy to complete. In both cases, most people are not optimally motivated, as many want a challenge (which assumes some kind of insecurity of success). At the same time people want to feel that there is a substantial probability that they will succeed. Specificity concerns the description of the goal in their class. The goal should be objectively defined and intelligible for the individual. A classic example of a poorly specified goal is to get the highest possible grade. Most children have no idea how much effort they need to reach that goal.

Models of Behaviour Change

Social-cognitive models of behaviour change include the constructs of motivation and volition. Motivation is seen as a process that leads to the forming of behavioural intentions. Volition is seen as a process that leads from intention to actual behaviour. In other words, motivation and volition refer to goal setting and goal pursuit, respectively. Both processes require self-regulatory efforts. Several self-regulatory constructs are needed to operate in orchestration to attain goals. An example of such a motivational and volitional construct is perceived self-efficacy. Self-efficacy is supposed to facilitate the forming of behavioural intentions, the development of action plans, and the initiation of action. It can support the translation of intentions into action. John W. Atkinson, David Birch and their colleagues developed the theory of "Dynamics of Action" to mathematically model change in behaviour as a consequence of the interaction of motivation and associated tendencies toward specific actions. The theory posits that change in behaviour occurs when the tendency for a new, unexpressed behaviour becomes dominant over the tendency currently motivating action. In the theory, the strength of tendencies rises and falls as a consequence of internal and external stimuli (sources of instigation), inhibitory factors, and consummatory in factors such as performing an action. In this theory, there are three causes responsible for behaviour and change in behaviour:

1. Instigation (Ts) - increases tendency when an activity has intrinsic ability to satisfy;
2. Inhibition (Taf) - decreases tendency when there are obstacles to performing an activity; and
3. Consummation - decreases a tendency as it is performed.

Conscious Motivation

This is a kind of motivation that people are aware of.

Unconscious Motivation

Some psychologists believe that a significant portion of human behaviour is energized and directed by unconscious motives. According to Maslow, "Psychoanalysis has often demonstrated that the relationship between a conscious desire and the ultimate unconscious aim that underlies it need not be at all direct."

Thematic Appreception Test

Psychologists David C. McClelland and John W. Atkinson argued that motivation should be unconscious. They refined measures of motivation by means of content analysis of imaginative thought using, for example, the Thematic Apperception Test.'

Intrinsic Motivation and the 16 Basic Desires Theory

Starting from studies involving more than 6,000 people, Professor Steven Reiss has proposed a theory that found 16 basic desires that guide nearly all human behaviour. The 16 basic desires that motivate our actions and define our personalities are:

- Acceptance, the need for approval
- Curiosity, the need to learn
- Eating, the need for food
- Family, the need to raise children
- Honour, the need to be loyal to the traditional values of one's clan/ethnic group
- Idealism, the need for social justice
- Independence, the need for individuality
- Order, the need for organized, stable, predictable environments
- Physical activity, the need for exercise
- Power, the need for influence of will
- Romance, the need for sex and for beauty
- Saving, the need to collect
- Social contact, the need for friends (peer relationships)
- Social status, the need for social standing/importance
- Tranquility, the need to be safe
- Vengeance, the need to strike back and to compete

Attribution Theory

The attribution theory is a theory developed by psychologist, Fritz Heider that describes the processes by which individuals explain the causes of their behaviour and events. A form of attribution theory developed by psychologist, Bernard Weiner describes an individual's beliefs about how the causes of success or failure affect their emotions and motivations. Bernard Weiner's theory can be defined into two perspectives: intrapersonal or interpersonal. The intrapersonal perspective includes self-directed thoughts and emotions that are attributed to the self. The interpersonal perspective includes beliefs about the responsibility of others and other directed affects of emotions; the individual would place the blame on another individual.

Individuals formulate explanatory attributions to understand the events they experience and to seek reasons for their failures. When individuals seek positive feedback from their failures, they use the feedback as motivation to show improved performances. For example, using the intrapersonal perspective, a student who failed a test may attribute their failure for not studying enough and would use their emotion of shame or embarrassment as motivation to study harder for the next test. A student who blames their test failure on the teacher would be using the interpersonal perspective, and would use their feeling of disappointment as motivation to rely on a different study source other than the teacher for the next test.

Approach Versus Avoidance

Approach motivation is a motivation to experience a positive outcome. In contrast, avoidance motivation is a motivation *not* to experience a negative outcome. Research suggests that, all else being equal, avoidance motivations tend to be more powerful than approach motivations. Because people expect losses to have more powerful emotional consequences than equal-size gains, they will take more risks to avoid a loss than to achieve a gain.

Practical Applications

The control of motivation is only understood to a limited extent. There are many different approaches of *motivation training*, but many of these are considered pseudoscientific by critics. To understand how to control motivation it is first necessary to understand why many people lack motivation.

Employee Motivation

Workers in any organization need something to keep them working. Most of the time, the salary of the employee is enough to keep him or her working for an organization. An employee must be motivated to work for a company or organization. If no motivation is present in an employee, then that employee's quality of work or all work in general will deteriorate. People differ on a personality dimension called locus of control.

This variable refers to individual's beliefs about the location of the factors that control their behaviour. At one end of the continuum are high internals who believe that opportunity to control their own behaviour rests within themselves. At the other end of the continuum there are high externals who believe that external forces determine their behaviour. Not surprisingly, compared with internals, externals see the world as an unpredictable, chancy place in which luck, fate, or powerful people control their destinies. When motivating an audience, you can use general motivational strategies or specific motivational appeals. General motivational strategies include soft sell versus hard sell and personality type. Soft sell strategies have logical appeals, emotional appeals, advice and praise. Hard sell strategies have barter, outnumbering, pressure and rank. Also, you can consider basing your strategy on your audience personality. Specific motivational appeals focus on provable facts, feelings, right and wrong, audience rewards and audience threats.

Job Characteristics Model

The Job Characteristics Model (JCM), as designed by Hackman and Oldham attempts to use job design to improve employee motivation. They show that any job can be described in terms of five key job characteristics:

1. *Skill Variety* - the degree to which the job requires the use of different skills and talents
2. *Task Identity* - the degree to which the job has contributed to a clearly identifiable larger project
3. *Task Significance* - the degree to which the job has an impact on the lives or work of other people
4. *Autonomy* - the degree to which the employee has independence, freedom and discretion in carrying out the job
5. *Task Feedback* - the degree to which the employee is provided with clear, specific, detailed, *actionable* information about the effectiveness of his or her job performance

The JCM links the core job dimensions listed above to critical psychological states which results in desired personal and work outcomes. This forms the basis of this 'employee growth-need strength." The core dimensions listed above can be combined into a single predictive index, called the *Motivating Potential Score.*

Work Motivation

Work motivation "is a set of energetic forces that originate both within as well as beyond an individual's being, to initiate work-related behaviour, and to determine its form, direction, intensity, and duration" Understanding what motivates an organization's employees is central to the study of I–O psychology. Motivation is a person's internal disposition to be concerned with and approach positive incentives and avoid negative incentives. To further this, an *incentive* is the anticipated reward or aversive event available in the environment. While motivation can often be used as a tool to help predict behaviour, it varies greatly among individuals and must often be combined with ability and environmental factors to actually influence behaviour and performance. Because of motivation's role in influencing workplace behaviour and performance, it is key for organizations to understand and to structure the work environment to encourage productive behaviours and discourage those that are unproductive.

There is general consensus that motivation involves three psychological processes: arousal, direction, and intensity. Arousal is what initiates action. It is fueled by a person's need or desire for something that is missing from their lives at a given moment, either totally or partially. Direction refers to the path employees take in accomplishing the goals they set for themselves. Finally, intensity is the vigor and amount of energy employees put into this goal-directed work performance. The level of intensity is based on the importance and difficulty of the goal. These psychological processes result in four outcomes. First, motivation serves to direct attention, focusing on particular issues, people, tasks, etc. It also serves to stimulate an employee to put forth effort. Next, motivation results in persistence, preventing one from deviating from the goal-seeking behaviour. Finally, motivation results in task strategies, which as defined by Mitchell & Daniels, are "patterns of behaviour produced to reach a particular goal.

Theories

A number of various theories attempt to describe employee motivation within the discipline of I–O psychology. Most of these theories can be divided into the four broad categories of need-based, cognitive process, behavioural, and job-based.

Need-based Theories

Need-based theories of motivation focus on an employee's drive to satisfy a variety of needs through their work. These needs range from basic physiological needs for survival to higher psychoemotional needs like belonging and self-actualization.

Maslow's Hierarchy of Needs

Abraham Maslow's Hierarchy of Needs (1943) was applied to offer an explanation of how the work environment motivates employees. In accordance with Maslow's theory, which was not specifically developed to explain behaviour in the workplace, employees strive to satisfy their needs in a hierarchical order.

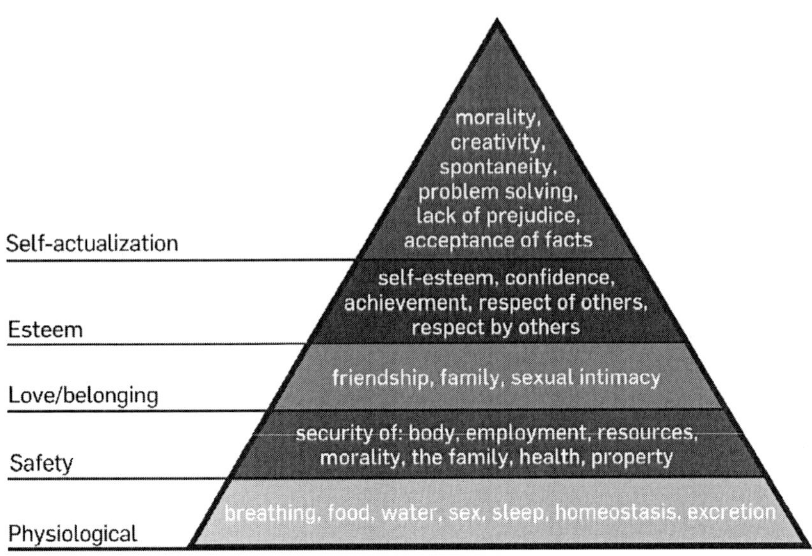

Figure: *An interpretation of Maslow's hierarchy of needs, represented as a pyramid with the more basic needs at the bottom.*

At the most basic level, an employee is motivated to work in order to satisfy basic physiological needs for survival, such as having enough money to purchase food.

The next level of need in the hierarchy is safety, which could be interpreted to mean adequate housing or living in a safe neighbourhood. The next three levels in Maslow's theory relate to intellectual and psycho-emotional needs: love and belonging, esteem (which refers to competence and mastery), and finally the highest order need, self-actualization.

Although Maslow's theory is widely known, in the workplace it has proven to be a poor predictor of employee behaviour. Maslow theorized that people will not seek to satisfy a higher level need until their lower level needs are met. There has been little empirical support for the idea that employees in the workplace strive to meet their needs only in the hierarchical order prescribed by Maslow.

Building on Maslow's theory, Clayton Alderfer (1959) collapsed the levels in Maslow's theory from five to three: existence, relatedness and growth. This theory, called the ERG theory, does not propose that employees attempt to satisfy these needs in a strictly hierarchical manner. Empirical support for this theory has been mixed.

Need for Achievement

Atkinson & McClelland's Need for Achievement Theory is the most relevant and applicable need-based theory in the I–O psychologist's arsenal. Unlike other need-based theories, which try to interpret every need, Need for Achievement allows the I–O psychologist to concentrate research into a tighter focus. Studies show those who have a high need for achievement prefer moderate levels of risk, seek feedback, and are likely to immerse themselves in their work. Achievement motivation can be broken down into three types:

- Achievement – seeks position advancement, feedback, and sense of accomplishment
- Authority – need to lead, make an impact and be heard by others
- Affiliation – need for friendly social interactions and to be liked.

Because most individuals have a combination of these three types (in various proportions), an understanding of these achievement motivation characteristics can be a useful assistance to management in job placement, recruitment, etc.

The theory is referred to as Need for Achievement because these individuals are theorized to be the most effective employees and leaders in the workplace. These individuals strive to achieve their goals and advance in the organization. They tend to be dedicated to their work and strive hard to succeed. Such individuals also demonstrate a strong desire for increasing their knowledge and for feedback on their performance, often in the form of performance appraisal .

The Need for Achievement is in many ways similar to the need for mastery and self-actualization in Maslow's hierarchy of needs and growth in the ERG theory. The achievement orientation has garnered more research interest as compared to the need for affiliation or power.

Cognitive Process Theories

Equity Theory: Equity Theory is derived from social exchange theory. It explains motivation in the workplace as a cognitive process of evaluation, whereby the employee seeks to achieve a balance between inputs or efforts in the workplace and the outcomes or rewards received or anticipated.

In particular, Equity Theory research has tested employee sentiments regarding equitable compensation. Employee inputs take the form of work volume and quality, performance, knowledge, skills, attributes and behaviours. The company-generated outcomes include rewards such as compensation, praise and advancement opportunities. The employee compares his inputs relative to outcomes; and, then, extrapolating to the social context, the employee compares his input/ outcome ratio with the perceived ratios of others. If the employee perceives an inequity, the theory posits that the employee will adjust his behaviour to bring things into balance. Equity Theory has proven relevance in situations where an employee is under-compensated. If an employee perceives that he is undercompensated, he can adjust his behaviour to achieve equilibrium in several different ways:

- reduce input to a level he believes better matches his level of compensation
- change or adjust the comparative standard to which he is comparing his situation
- cognitively adjust his perception of his inputs or the outcomes received
- withdraw
- address the situation with his employer by asking for a raise

If the employee is able to achieve a ratio of inputs to outputs that he perceives to be equitable, then the employee will be satisfied. The employee's evaluation of input-to-output ratios and subsequent striving to achieve equilibrium is an ongoing process. While it has been established that Equity Theory provides insight into scenarios of under-compensation, the theory has generally failed to demonstrate its usefulness in understanding scenarios of overcompensation. In this way, it could be said Equity Theory is more useful in describing factors that contribute to a lack of motivation rather than increasing motivation in the workplace. Concepts of organizational justice later expanded upon the fundamentals of Equity Theory and pointed to the importance of fairness perceptions in the workplace.

There are three fairness perceptions applied to organizational settings:

1. Distributive justice, or the perception of equality of an individual's outcomes
2. Procedural justice, or the fairness of the procedures used to determine one's outcomes

3. Interactional justice, or the perception that one has been treated fairly with dignity and respect
4. Informational Justice, or the perception that one has been given all the information he/she needs in order to best perform their jobs.

When workplace processes are perceived as fair, the benefits to an organization can be high. In such environments, employees are more likely to comply with policies even if their personal outcome is less than optimal. When workplace policies are perceived as unfair, risks for retaliation and related behaviours such as sabotage and workplace violence can increase.

Leventhal (1980) described six criteria for creating fair procedures in an organization. He proposed that procedures and policies should be:

1. consistently applied to everyone in the organization
2. free from bias
3. accurate
4. correctable
5. representative of all concerns
6. based on prevailing ethics

Expectancy Theory

According to Vroom's Expectancy Theory, an employee will work smarter and/or harder if he believes his additional efforts will lead to valued rewards. Expectancy theory explains this increased output of effort by means of the equation

$$F = E\ (\Sigma\ I \times V)$$

whereas: F (Effort or Motivational Force) = Effort the employee will expend to achieve the desired performance;

E (Expectancy) = Belief that effort will result in desired level of performance;

I (Instrumentality) = Belief that desired level of performance will result in desired outcome;

V (Valence) = Value of the outcome to the employee

Expectancy theory has been shown to have useful applications in designing a reward system. If policies are consistently, clearly and fairly implemented, then the instrumentality would be high. If the rewards are substantial enough to be meaningful to an employee, then the valence would be also considered high. A precursor to motivation is that the employee finds the reward(s) attractive. In some instances, the reward or outcome might inadvertently be unattractive, such as increased workload or demanding travel that may come with a promotion. In such an instance, the valence might be lower for individuals who feel work–life balance is important, for example.

Expectancy theory posits employee satisfaction to be an outcome of performance rather than the cause of performance. However, if a pattern is established whereas an employee understands his performance will lead to certain desired rewards, an employee's motivation can be strengthened based on anticipation. If the employees foresee a high probability that they can successfully carry out a desired behaviour, and that their behaviour will lead to a valued outcome, then they will direct their efforts toward that end. Expectancy theory has been shown to have greater validity in research in within-subject designs rather than between-subjects designs. That is, it is more useful in predicting how an employee might choose among competing choices for their time and energy, rather than predicting the choices two different employees might make.

Goal-setting Theory

An I–O psychologist can assist an employer in designing task-related goals for their employees that are

- attainable
- specific
- appropriately difficult,
- feedback providing

in hopes of rousing tunnel vision focus in the employees. Following S.M.A.R.T criteria is also suggested.

Letter	*Major Term*	*Minor Terms*
S	Specific	Significant, Stretching, Simple
M	Measurable	Meaningful, Motivational, Manageable
A	Attainable	Appropriate, Achievable, Agreed, Assignable, Actionable, Ambitious, Aligned, Aspirational, Acceptable, Action-focused
R	Relevant	Results-oriented, Realistic, Resourced, Resonant
T	Timely	Time-oriented, Time framed, Timed, Time-based, Timeboxed, Time-bound, Time-Specific, Timetabled, Time limited, Trackable, Tangible

Studies have shown both feedback from the employer and self-efficacy (belief in one's capabilities to achieve a goal) within the employee must be present for goal-setting to be effective. However, because of the tunnel vision focus created by goal-setting theory, several studies have shown this motivational theory may not be applicable in all situations. In fact, in tasks that require creative on-the-spot improvising, goal-setting can even be counterproductive. Furthermore, because clear goal specificity is essential to a properly designed goal-setting task, multiple goals can create confusion for the employee and the end result is a muted overall drive. Despite its flaws, Goal-setting Theory is arguably the most dominant theory in the field of I–O psychology; over one thousand articles and reviews published in just over thirty years.

Locke suggested several reasons why goals are motivating: they direct attention, lead to task persistence and the development of task strategies for accomplishing the goal. In order for a goal to be motivating, the employee or work group must first accept the goal. While difficult goals can be more motivating, a goal still needs to appear achievable, which in turn will lead to greater goal acceptance. The person or group should have the necessary skills and resources to achieve the goal, or goal acceptance could be negatively impacted. Specific goals that set a performance expectation are more motivating than those that are vague. Similarly, more proximal goals have greater motivation impact than those that are very long range or distal goals.

There are three types of factors that influence goal commitment:

- External- The external factors that affect it are authority, peer influence and external rewards. Complying with the dictates of an authority figure such as boss has been shown to be an inducement to high goal commitment. Goal commitment increases when the authority figure is physically present, supportive, pay increases, peer pressure and external rewards.
- Interactive- The factors that influence commitment here are competition and the opportunity to participate in setting goals. It has been shown to be an inducement to setting higher goals and working harder to reach them.
- Internal- these come from self-administered rewards and the expectation of success. The commitment decreases when the expectation to achieve is decreased.

From: Psychology and Work Today by Schultz and Schultz.

Feedback while the employee or group is striving for the goal is seen as crucial. Feedback keeps employees on track and reinforces the importance of the goal as well as supporting the employees in adjusting their task strategies.

Goal-setting Theory has strong empirical support dating back thirty years. However, there are some boundary conditions that indicate in some situations, goal-setting can be detrimental to performance on certain types of tasks. Goals require a narrowing of one's focus, so for more complex or creative tasks, goals can actually inhibit performance because they demand cognitive resources. Similarly, when someone is learning a new task, performance-related goals can distract from the learning process. During the learning process, it may be better to focus on mastering the task than achieving a particular result. Finally, too many goals can become distracting and counterproductive, especially if they conflict with one another.

Social Cognitive Theory

Bandura's Social Cognitive Theory is another cognitive process theory that offers the important concept of self-efficacy for explaining employee's level of motivation relative to workplace tasks or goals. Self-efficacy is an individual's belief in his or her ability to achieve results in a given scenario. Empirically, studies have shown a strong correlation between self-efficacy and performance. The concept has been extended to group efficacy, which is a group's belief that it can achieve success with a given task or project.

Self-efficacy is seen to mediate important aspects of how an employee undertakes a given task, such as the level of effort and persistence. An employee with high self-efficacy is confident that effort he or she puts forth has a high likelihood of resulting in success. In anticipation of success, an employee is willing to put forth more effort, persist longer, remain focused on the task, seek feedback and choose more effective task strategies.

The antecedents of self-efficacy may be influenced by expectations, training or past experience and requires further research. It has been shown that setting high expectations can lead to improved performance, known as the Pygmalian effect. Low expectations can lower self-efficacy and is referred to as the golem effect.

Relative to training, a mastery-oriented approach has been shown to be an effective way to bolster self-efficacy. In such an approach, the goal of training is to focus on mastering skills or tasks rather than focusing on an immediate performance-related outcome. Individuals who believe that mastery can be achieved through training and practice are more likely to develop greater self-efficacy than those who see mastery as a product of inherent talent than is largely immutable.

Behavioural Approach to Motivation

The behavioural approach to workplace motivation is known as Organizational Behavioural Modification. This approach applies the tenets of behaviourism developed by B.F. Skinner to promote employee behaviours that an employer deems beneficial and discourage those that are not. Any stimulus that increases the likelihood of a behaviour increasing is a reinforcer.

An effective use of positive reinforcement would be frequent praise while an employee is learning a new task. An employee's behaviour can also be shaped during the learning process if approximations of the ideal behaviour are praised or rewarded. The frequency of reinforcement is an important consideration. While frequent praise during the learning process can be beneficial, it can be hard to sustain indefinitely. A variable-ratio schedule of reinforcement, where the frequency of reinforcement varies unpredictably, can be also be highly effective if used in instances where it is ethical to do so. Providing praise on a variable-ratio schedule would be appropriate, whereas paying an employee on an unpredictable variable-ratio schedule would not be.

Compensation and other reward programmes provide behavioural reinforcement, and if carefully crafted, can provide powerful incentives to employees. Behavioural principles can also be used to address undesirable behaviours in the workplace, but punishment should be used judiciously. If overused, punishment can negatively impact employee's perception of fairness in the workplace.

In general, the less time that elapses between a behaviour and its consequence, the more impactful a consequence is likely to be.

Job-based Theories

The job-based theories hold that the key to motivation is within an employee's job itself. Generally, these theories say that jobs can be motivating by their very design. This is a particularly useful view for organizations, because the practices set out in the theories can be implemented more practically in an organization. Ultimately, according to the job-based theories, the key to finding motivation through one's job is being able to derive satisfaction from the job content.

Motivation–Hygiene Theory

It is impossible to discuss motivation and job attributes in I–O psychology without crediting Frederick Herzberg's Motivator–Hygiene Theory (also referred to as Herzberg's Two-factor theory). Published in 1968, Herzberg's Motivator–Hygiene Theory holds that the content of a person's job is the primary source of motivation. In other words, he argued against the commonly held belief that money and other compensation is the most effective form of motivation to an employee. Instead, Herzberg posed that high levels of what he dubbed hygiene factors (pay, job security, status, working conditions, fringe benefits, job policies, and relations with co-workers) could only reduce employee dissatisfaction (not create satisfaction). Motivation factors (level of challenge, the work itself, responsibility, recognition, advancement, intrinsic interest, autonomy, and opportunities for creativity) however, could stimulate satisfaction within the employee, provided that minimum levels of the hygiene factors were reached. For an organization to take full advantage of Herzberg's theory, they must design jobs in such a way that motivators are built in, and thus are intrinsically rewarding. While the Motivation–Hygiene Theory was the first to focus on job content, it has not been strongly supported through empirical studies. Frederick Herzberg also came up with the concept of job enrichment, which expands jobs to give employees a greater role in planning, performing, and evaluating their work, thus providing the chance to satisfy their motivators needs. some suggested ways would be to remove some management control, provide regular and continuously feedback. Proper job enrichment, therefore, involves more than simply giving the workers extra tasks to perform. It means expanding the level of knowledge and skills needed to perform the job.

Job Characteristics Theory

Shortly after Herzberg's Two-factor theory, Hackman and Oldham contributed their own, more refined, job-based theory; Job Characteristics Theory (JCT). JCT attempts to define the association between core job dimensions, the critical psychological states that occur as a result of these dimensions, the personal and work outcomes, and growth-need strength. Core job dimensions are the characteristics of a person's job. The core job dimensions are linked directly to the critical psychological states. According to JCT, an organization that provides sufficient levels of skill variety, task identity, and task significance to its employees will, in turn, provide experienced meaningfulness. That is, employees will feel that the work they do has meaning and value. Sufficient levels of autonomy will inspire felt responsibility for the employee, and proper feedback will provide the employee with knowledge of results. The combined effect of these psychological states results in desired personal and work outcomes: internal motivation, job satisfaction, performance quality, low absenteeism, and low turnover rate. Lastly, the glue of this theory is the "growth-need strength" factor which ultimately determines the effectiveness of the core job dimensions on the psychological states, and likewise the effectiveness of the critical psychological states on the affective outcomes.

Hackman and Oldman created the Job Diagnostic Survey (JDS) which measures three parts of their theory.

1. Employees views of the job characteristics
2. The level of growth needed by each employee
3. Employees overall job satisfaction

JDS is the most frequently and commonly used tool to measure job and work design. JDS is a self- report which has small detailed phrases for the different job characteristics. An employee will be asked to fill out the JDS and rate how precise each statement describes their job.

Self-Regulation Theory

A theory based in self-efficacy, Self Regulation is "A theory of motivation based on the setting of goals and the receipt of accurate feedback that is monitored to enhance the likelihood of goal attainment" It is presumed that people consciously set goals for themselves that guide and direct their behaviour toward the attainment of these goals. These people also engage in self-monitoring or self-evaluation. Self-evaluation can be helped along if feedback is given when a person is working on their goals because it can align how a person feels about how they are doing to achieve a goal and what they are actually doing to achieve their goals. In short, feedback provides an "error" message that a person who is off-track can reevaluate their goal.

This theory has been linked to Goal setting and Goal Setting Theory, which has been mentioned above.

Work Engagement

A new approach to work motivation is the idea of Work Engagement or "A conception of motivation whereby individuals are physically immersed in emotionally and intellectually fulfilling work." This theory draws on many aspects of I/O Psychology. This theory proposes that motivation taps into energy where it allows a person to focus on a task. According to Schaufeli and Bakker there are three dimensions to work engagement.

- Vigor- a sense of personal energy for work
- Dedication- experiencing a sense of pride in one's work and challenge from it
- Absorption- The Capacity to be engrossed in work and experiencing a sense of flow.

Work Engagement forwards the notion that individuals have the ability to contribute more to their own productivity than organizations typically allow. An example would be to allow workers to take some risks and not punish them if the risks leads to unsuccessful outcomes. "In short, work engagement can be thought of as an interaction of individuals and work. Engagement can occur when both facilitate each other, and engagement will not occur when either (or both) thwarts each other." Some critics of work engagement say that this is nothing new, just "old wine in a new bottle."

Applications of motivation

Organizational Reward Systems: Organizational reward systems have a significant impact on employees' level of motivation. Rewards can be either tangible or intangible. Various forms of pay, such as salary, commissions, bonuses, employee ownership programmes and various types of profit or gain sharing programmes, are all important tangible rewards. While fringe benefits have a positive impact on attraction and retention, their direct impact on motivation and performance is not well-defined.

Salaries play a crucial role in the tangible reward system. They are an important factor in attracting new talent to an organization as well as retaining talent. Compensating employees well is one way for an organization to reinforce an employee's value to the organization. If an organization is known for paying their employees top dollar, then they may develop a positive reputation in the job market as a result.

Through incentive compensation structures, employees can be guided to focus their attention and efforts on certain organizational goals. The goals that are reinforced through incentive pay should be carefully considered to make sure they are in alignment with the organizational objectives. If there are multiple rewards programmes, it is important to consider if there might be any conflicting goals. For example, individual and team-based rewards can sometime work at cross-purposes.

Important forms of intangible rewards include praise, recognition and rewards. Intangible rewards are ones from which an employee does not derive any material gain. Such rewards have the greatest impact when they soon follow the desired behaviour and are closely tied to the performance. If an organization wants to use praise or other intangible rewards effectively, praise should be offered for a high level of performance and for things that they employee has control over. Some studies have shown that praise can be as effective as tangible rewards.

Other forms of intangible performance include status symbols, such as a corner office, and increased autonomy and freedom. Increased autonomy demonstrates trust in an employee, may decrease stress and improve job satisfaction. Since it may be hard for an employee to achieve a similar level of trust in a new organization, increased autonomy may also help improve retention.

Motivation Through Design of Work

Reward-based systems are certainly the more common practice for attempting to influence motivation within an organization, but some employers strive to design the work itself to be more conducive. There are multiple ways an organization can leverage job design principles to increase motivation. Three of the predominant approaches will be discussed here: the Humanistic Approach, the Job Characteristics Approach, and the Interdisciplinary Approach.

Humanistic Approach

The Humanistic Approach to job design was a reaction to "worker dissatisfaction over Scientific Management" and focused on providing employees with more input and an opportunity to maximize their personal achievement as referenced by Jex and Britt. Jobs should also provide intellectual stimulation, opportunities for creativity, and greater discretion over work-related activities. Two approaches used in the Humanistic Approach to job design are job rotation and job enrichment. Job rotation allows employees to switch to different jobs which allows them to learn new skills and provides them with greater variety. According to Jex and Britt, this would be most effective for simple jobs that can become mundane and boring over time. Job enrichment is focused on leveraging those aspects of jobs that are labelled motivators, such as control, intellectual challenge, and creativity.

The most common form of job enrichment is vertical loading where additional tasks or discretion enhances the initial job design. While there is some evidence to support that job enrichment improves motivation, it is important to note that it is not effective for all people. Some employees are not more motivated by enriched jobs.

Job Characteristics Approach

The Job Characteristics Approach to job design is based on how core dimensions affect motivation. These dimensions include autonomy, variety, significance, feedback, and identity. The goal of JCT job design is to utilize specific interventions in an effort to enhance these core dimensions.

1. Vertical Loading – Like the tactic used in the Humanistic Job Enrichment approach, this intervention is designed to enhance autonomy, task identity, task significance, and skill variety by increasing the number of tasks and providing greater levels of control over how those tasks are completed.
2. Task Combination – By combining tasks into larger units of work and responsibility, task identity may be improved.
3. Natural Work Units – A form of task combination that represents a logical body of work and responsibility that may enhance both task significance and task identity.
4. Establishing Client Relationships – Designs interactions between employees and customers, both internal and external, to enhance task identity, feedback, and task significance. This is accomplished by improving the visibility of beneficial effects on customers.
5. Feedback – By designing open feedback channels, this intervention attempts to increase the amount and value of feedback received.

The process of designing work so as to enhance individual motivation to perform the work is called Job enrichment

While the JCT approach to job design has a significant impact on job satisfaction, the effects on performance are more mixed. Much of the success of implementation of JCT practices is dependent on the organization carefully planning interventions and changes to ensure impact throughout the organization is anticipated. Many companies may have difficulty implementing JCT changes throughout the organization due to its high cost and complexity.

Interdisciplinary Approach

One of the most recent approaches to work design, the Interdisciplinary Approach is based on the use of careful assessment of current job design, followed by a cost/benefit analysis, and finally changes based on the area in which a job is lacking. The assessment is conducted using the Multi-method Job Design Questionnaire, which is used to determine if the job is deficient in the areas of motivational, mechanistic, biological, or perceptual motor support. Motivational improvements are aligned with the Job Characteristics theory dimensions. Mechanistic improvements are focused on improving the efficiency of the job design.

Biological improvements focus on improvements to ergonomics, health conditions, and employee comfort. Finally, perceptual motor improvements focus on the nature and presentation of the information an employee must work with. If improvements are identified using the questionnaire, the company then evaluates the cost of making the improvements and determines if the potential gains in motivation and performance justify those costs. Because of the analysis and cost/benefit components of the Interdisciplinary Approach, it is often less costly for organizations and implementations can be more effective. Only changes deemed to be appropriate investments are made, thus improving motivation, productivity, and job satisfaction while controlling costs.

Other Factors Affecting Motivation

Creativity: On the cutting edge of research pertaining to motivation in the workplace is the integration of motivation and creativity. Essentially, according to Ambrose and Kulik, the same variables that predict intrinsic motivation are associated with creativity. This is a helpful conclusion in that organizations can measure and influence both creativity and motivation simultaneously. Further, allowing employees to choose creative and challenging jobs/tasks has been shown to improve motivation. In order to increase creativity, setting "creativity goals" can positively influence the process, along with allowing more autonomy (i.e., giving employees freedom to feel/be creative). Other studies have found that team support may enable more creativity in a group setting, also increasing motivation.

Groups and Teams

As the workplace is changing to include more group-based systems, researching motivation within these groups is of growing importance. To date, a great amount of research has focused on the Job Characteristics Theory and the Goal-setting Theory. While more research is needed that draws on a broader range of motivation theories, research thus far has concluded several things: (a) semi-autonomous groups report higher levels of job scope (related to intrinsic job satisfaction), extrinsic satisfaction, and organizational commitment; and (b) developmentally mature teams have higher job motivation and innovation. Further, voluntarily formed work teams report high work motivation. Though research shows that appropriate goal-setting influences group motivation and performance, more research is needed in this area (group goals, individual goals, cohesiveness, etc.). There are inseparable mediating variables consisting of group cohesiveness, commitment, and performance. As the workplace environment calls for more and more teams to be formed, research into motivation of teams is ever-pressing. Thus far, overarching research merely suggests that individual-level and team-level sources of motivation are congruent with each other. Consequently, research should be expanded to apply more theories of motivation; look at group dynamics; and essentially conclude how groups can be most impacted to increase motivation and, consequently, performance.

Culture

Organizational cultures can be broken down into three groups: Strong, Strategically Appropriate, and Adaptive. Each has been identified with high performing organizations and has particular implications on motivation in the workplace.

Strength

The most widely reported effect of culture on performance is that strong cultures result in high performance. The three reasons for this are goal alignment, motivation, and the resulting structure provided. Goal alignment is driven by the proposed unified voice that drives employees in the same direction. Motivation comes from the strength of values and principles in such a culture. And structure is provided by these same attributes which obviate the need for formal controls that could stifle employees. There are questions that concern researchers about causality and the veracity of the driving voice of a strong culture.

Strategic Appropriateness

A strategically appropriate culture motivates due to the direct support for performance in the market and industry: "The better the fit, the better the performance; the poorer the fit, the poorer the performance," state Kotter & Heskett. There is an appeal to the idea that cultures are designed around the operations conditions a firm encounters although an outstanding issue is the question of adapting culture to changes in the environment.

Adaptability

Another perspective in culture literature asserts that in order for an organization to perform at a high level over a long period of time, it must be able to adapt to changes in the environment. According to Ralph Kilmann, in such a culture "there is a shared feeling of confidence: the members believe, without a doubt, that they can effectively manage whatever new problems and opportunities will come their way." In effect, the culture is infused with a high degree of self-efficacy and confidence. As with the strong culture, critics point to the fact that the theory provides nothing in the way of appropriate direction of adaptation that leads to high performance.

Competing Values Framework

Another perspective on culture and motivation comes from the work of Cameron & Quinn and the Competing Values Framework. They divide cultures into four quadrants: Clan, Adhocracy, Market, Hierarchy, with particular characteristics that directly affect employee motivation.

- *Clan* cultures are collaborative and driven by values such as commitment, communication, and individual development. Motivation results from human development, employee engagement, and a high degree of open communication.
- *Adhocracy* cultures are creative and innovative. Motivation in such cultures arises from finding creative solutions to problems, continually improving, and empowering agility.
- *Market* cultures focus on value to the customer and are typically competitive and aggressive. Motivation in the market culture results from winning in the marketplace and creating external partnerships.
- And finally, *Hierarchy* cultures value control, efficiency, and predictability. Motivation in such a culture relies on

effectiveness, capability, and consistency. Effective hierarchy cultures have developed mature and capable processes which support smooth operations.

Culture has been shown to directly affect organizational performance. When viewed through the lens of accepted behaviours and ingrained values, culture also profoundly affects motivation. Whether one looks at the type of culture—strong, strategically appropriate, or adaptive—as Kotter & Heskett do, or at the style of culture—Clan, Adhocracy, Market, or Hierarchy—as Cameron & Quinn do, the connection between culture and motivation becomes clear and provides insights into how to hire, task, and motivate employees.

Motivating Potential Score

The motivating potential score (MPS) can be calculated, using the core dimensions discussed above, as follows:

$$\text{MPS} = \frac{\text{Skill Variety} + \text{Task Identity} + \text{Task Significance}}{3} \times \text{Autonomy} \times \text{Feedback}$$

Jobs that are high in motivating potential must be high on at least one of the three factors that lead to experienced meaningfulness, and also must be high on both Autonomy and Feedback. If a job has a high MPS, the job characteristics model predicts that motivation, performance and job satisfaction will be positively affected and the likelihood of negative outcomes, such as absenteeism and turnover, will be reduced.

Employee Recognition Programmes

Employee recognition is not only about gifts and points. It's about changing the corporate culture in order to meet goals and initiatives and most importantly to connect employees to the company's core values and beliefs. Strategic employee recognition is seen as the most important programme not only to improve employee retention and motivation but also to positively influence the financial situation. The difference between the traditional approach (gifts and points) and strategic recognition is the ability to serve as a serious business influencer that can advance a company's strategic objectives in a measurable way. "The vast majority of companies want to be innovative, coming up with new products, business models and better ways of doing things. However, innovation is not so easy to achieve. A CEO cannot just order it, and so it will be. You have to carefully manage an organization so that, over time, innovations will emerge."

Drugs

Some authors, especially in the transhumanist movement, have suggested the use of "smart drugs", also known as nootropics, as "motivation-enhancers". These drugs work in various ways to affect neurotransmitters in the brain. It is generally widely accepted that these drugs enhance cognitive functions, but not without potential side effects. The effects of many of these drugs on the brain are emphatically not well understood, and their legal status often makes open experimentation difficult.

Education

Motivation is of particular interest to educational psychologists because of the crucial role it plays in student learning. However, the specific kind of motivation that is studied in the specialized setting of education differs qualitatively from the more general forms of motivation studied by psychologists in other fields.

Motivation in education can have several effects on how students learn and how they behave towards subject matter. It can:

1. Direct behaviour toward particular goals
2. Lead to increased effort and energy
3. Increase initiation of, and persistence in, activities
4. Enhance cognitive processing
5. Determine what consequences are reinforcing
6. Lead to improved performance.

Because students are not always internally motivated, they sometimes need *situated motivation*, which is found in environmental conditions that the teacher creates.

If teachers decided to extrinsically reward productive student behaviours, they may find it difficult to extricate themselves from that path. Consequently student dependency on extrinsic rewards represents one of the greatest detractors from their use in the classroom.

The majority of new student orientation leaders at colleges and universities recognize that distinctive needs of students should be considered in regard to orientation information provided at the beginning of the higher education experience. Research done by Whyte in 1986 raised the awareness of counselors and educators in this regard. In 2007, the National Orientation Directors Association reprinted Cassandra B. Whyte's research report allowing readers to ascertain improvements made in addressing specific needs of students over a quarter of a century later to help with academic success. Generally, motivation is conceptualized as either *intrinsic* or *extrinsic*. Classically, these categories are regarded as distinct. Today, these concepts are less likely to be used as distinct categories, but instead as two ideal types that define a continuum:

- Intrinsic motivation occurs when people are internally motivated to do something because it either brings them pleasure, they think it is important, or they feel that what they are learning is significant. It has been shown that intrinsic motivation for education drops from grades 3-9 though the exact cause cannot be ascertained. Also, in younger students it has been shown that contextualizing material that would otherwise be presented in an abstract manner increases the intrinsic motivation of these students.
- Extrinsic motivation comes into play when a student is compelled to do something or act a certain way because of factors external to him or her (like money or good grades).

Cassandra B. Whyte researched and reported about the importance of locus of control and academic achievement. Students tending toward a more internal locus of control are more academically successful, thus encouraging curriculum and activity development with consideration of motivation theories.

Academic motivation orientation may also be tied with one's ability to detect and process errors. Fisher, Nanayakkara, and Marshall conducted neuroscience research on children's motivation orientation, neurological indicators of error monitoring (the process of detecting an error), and academic achievement. Their research suggests that students with high intrinsic motivation attribute performance to personal control and that their error-monitoring system is more strongly engaged by performance errors. They also found that motivation orientation and academic achievement were related to the strength in which their error-monitoring system was engaged.

Motivation has been found to be an important element in the concept of Andragogy (what motivates the adult learner), and in treating Autism Spectrum Disorders, as in Pivotal Response Therapy.

Doyle and Moeyn have noted that traditional methods tended to use anxiety as negative motivation (e.g. use of bad grades by teachers) as a method of getting students to work. However, they have found that progressive approaches with focus on positive motivation over punishment has produced greater effectiveness with learning, since anxiety interferes with performance of complex tasks.

Indigenous Education, Learning, and Motivation

For many indigenous students (such as Native American children), motivation may be derived from social organization; an important factor educators should account for in addition to variations in Sociolinguistics and Cognition. While poor academic performance among Native American students is often attributed to low levels of motivation, Top-down classroom organization is often found to be ineffective for children of many cultures, who depend on a sense of community purpose and competence to effectively engage in material. Horizontally-structured, community-based learning strategies often provide a more structurally supportive environment for motivating indigenous children, who tend to be driven by "social/affective emphasis, harmony, holistic perspectives, expressive creativity, and nonverbal communication." This drive is also traceable to a cultural tradition of community-wide expectations of participation in the activities and goals of the greater group, rather than individualized aspirations of success or triumph.

Structure for social learning in indigenous communities also often allows siblings to co-parent younger children in their acquisition of behaviours and traditions, which fosters the dynamic of community-motivated engagement from a young age. Furthermore, it is commonplace for children to assist and demonstrate for their younger counterparts without being prompted by authority figures. Observation techniques are demonstrated in such examples as weaving in Chiapas, Mexico, where it is commonplace for children to learn by "a more skilled other" within the community.

The assumption of responsibility amongst children is also apparent within Mayan weaving apprenticeships; often, when the "more skilled other" is tasked with multiple obligations, an older child will step in and guide the learner. Sibling guidance is supported from early youth, where learning through play encourages horizontally-structured environments through alternative educational models such as "Intent Community Participation." Research also suggests that that formal Westernized schooling can actually reshape the traditionally collaborative nature of social life in indigenous communities This research is supported cross-culturally, with variations in motivation and learning often reported higher between indigenous groups and their national Westernized counterparts than between indigenous groups across international continental divides.

Self-Determination in Education

Self-determination is the ability to make choices and exercise a high degree of control, such as what the student does and how they do it (Deci et al., 1991; Reeve, Hamm, & Nix, 2003; Ryan & Deci, 2002). Self-determination can be supported by providing opportunities for students to be challenged, such as leadership opportunities, providing appropriate feedback and fostering, establishing and maintaining good relationships between teachers and students. These strategies can increase students' interest, competence, creativity and desire to be challenged and ensure that students are intrinsically motivated to study. On the other hand, students who lack of self-determination are more likely to feel their success is out of their control. Such students lose motivation to study, which causes a state of "helpless learning". Students who feel helpless readily believe they will fail and therefore cease to try. Over time, a vicious circle of low achievement develops.

Physical Activity in Education

Physical activity is body movement that works your muscles and requires more energy than resting. According to the American Intercontinental University, college students should make time for exercise to maintain and increase motivation. AIU states that regular exercise has impeccable effects on the brain. With consistent running routines, there are more complex connections between neurons, meaning the brain is able to access its brain cells more flexibly. By performing well physically, motivation will be present in education because of how well the brain is performing. After exercising, the brain can have more desire to obtain knowledge and better retain the information. In addition, exercise can relieve stress. Exercising can ease anxiety and relieve negative effects of stress on the body. Without stress factors, individuals can perform better and more efficiently, since their minds will have a more positive outlook. This positive mood will help keep students motivated and more open and willing to succeed academically. Lastly, exercise increases focus and concentration that could also help students maintain their motivation and focus on their studies. AIU claims that exercise may have improved the students' ability to participate and retain information during the class after they had exercised. By being able to retain information and be more willing to participate will keep the students motivated and perform academically well.

Healthy Sleeping Habits in Education

Sleep is a natural periodic state of rest for the mind and body. According to the American Academy of Sleep Medicine, it is important and essential for students to obtain the right amount of sleep in order to succeed in academics. AASM states that getting good nights of sleep is one of the best ways to maximize performance on finals. It is possible that the more chaotic and sporadic one's sleeping schedule is, the harder it will be for that individual to get an A or B on an exam. Dr. Kushida from AASM proclaims that sleep loss may lead to learning and memory impairment.

In addition, she also comments that lack of sleep can lead to decreased attention and vigilance. So, with small amounts of sleep, individuals cannot maintain all their memory or focus needed to score well in their classes. Therefore, sleep is a requirement in education if the individual wants to succeed academically.

The right amount of sleep will enable individuals to keep their motivation and good grades in education. Without sleep, students and individual's memory capacity can become so minimal that it is possible for them not to even remember what they are supposed to do in a day's time. In addition, with a lack of sleep, students cannot physically withhold and function for a long time, since their bodies will not have the energy. So, with enough sleep, students' minds will be clearer and have more potential to contain information. At the same time, students would be granted with more motivation and energy since their minds and bodies will be more willing to obtain information.

Business

At lower levels of Maslow's hierarchy of needs, such as physiological needs, money is a motivator, however it tends to have a motivating effect on staff that lasts only for a short period (in accordance with Herzberg's two-factor model of motivation). At higher levels of the hierarchy, praise, respect, recognition, empowerment and a sense of belonging are far more powerful motivators than money, as both Abraham Maslow's theory of motivation and Douglas McGregor's theory X and theory Y (pertaining to the theory of leadership) demonstrate.

According to Maslow, people are motivated by unsatisfied needs. The lower level needs such as Physiological and Safety needs will have to be satisfied before higher level needs are to be addressed.

We can relate Maslow's Hierarchy of Needs theory with employee motivation. For example, if a manager is trying to motivate his employees by satisfying their needs; according to Maslow, he should try to satisfy the lower level needs before he tries to satisfy the upper level needs or the employees will not be motivated. Also he has to remember that not everyone will be satisfied by the same needs. A good manager will try to figure out which levels of needs are active for a certain individual or employee.

Maslow has money at the lowest level of the hierarchy and shows other needs are better motivators to staff. McGregor places money in his Theory X category and feels it is a poor motivator. Praise and recognition are placed in the Theory Y category and are considered stronger motivators than money.

- Motivated employees always look for better ways to do a job.
- Motivated employees are more quality oriented.
- Motivated workers are more productive.

The average workplace is about midway between the extremes of high threat and high opportunity. Motivation by threat is a dead-end strategy, and naturally staff are more attracted to the opportunity side of the motivation curve than the threat side. Motivation is a powerful tool in the work environment that can lead to employees working at their most efficient levels of production.

Nonetheless, Steinmetz also discusses three common character types of subordinates: ascendant, indifferent, and ambivalent who all react and interact uniquely, and must be treated, managed, and motivated accordingly. An effective leader must understand how to manage all characters, and more importantly the manager must utilize avenues that allow room for employees to work, grow, and find answers independently.

The assumptions of Maslow and Herzberg were challenged by a classic study at Vauxhall Motors' UK manufacturing plant. This introduced the concept of orientation to work and distinguished three main orientations: instrumental (where work is a means to an end), bureaucratic (where work is a source of status, security and immediate reward) and solidaristic (which prioritizes group loyalty).

Other theories which expanded and extended those of Maslow and Herzberg included Kurt Lewin's Force Field Theory, Edwin Locke's Goal Theory and Victor Vroom's Expectancy theory. These tend to stress cultural differences and the fact that individuals tend to be motivated by different factors at different times.

According to the system of scientific management developed by Frederick Winslow Taylor, a worker's motivation is solely determined by pay, and therefore management need not consider psychological or social aspects of work. In essence, scientific management bases human motivation wholly on extrinsic rewards and discards the idea of intrinsic rewards.

In contrast, David McClelland believed that workers could not be motivated by the mere need for money—in fact, extrinsic motivation (e.g., money) could extinguish intrinsic motivation such as achievement motivation, though money could be used as an indicator of success for various motives, e.g., keeping score. In keeping with this view, his consulting firm, McBer & Company, had as its first motto "To make everyone productive, happy, and free." For McClelland, satisfaction lay in aligning a person's life with their fundamental motivations.

Elton Mayo found that the social contacts a worker has at the workplace are very important and that boredom and repetitiveness of tasks lead to reduced motivation. Mayo believed that workers could be motivated by acknowledging their social needs and making them feel important. As a result, employees were given freedom to make decisions on the job and greater attention was paid to informal work groups. Mayo named the model the Hawthorne effect. His model has been judged as placing undue reliance on social contacts within work situations for motivating employees.

William Ouchi introduced Theory Z, a hybrid management approach consisting of both Japanese and American philosophies and cultures. Its Japanese segment is much like the clan culture where organizations focus on a standardized structure with heavy emphasis on socialization of its members. All underlying goals are consistent across the organization. Its American segment retains formality and authority amongst members and the organization. Ultimately, Theory Z promotes common structure and commitment to the organization, as well as constant improvement of work efficacy. In *Essentials of Organizational Behaviour*, Robbins and Judge examine recognition programmes as motivators, and identify five principles that contribute to the success of an employee incentive programme:

- Recognition of employees' individual differences, and clear identification of behaviour deemed worthy of recognition
- Allowing employees to participate
- Linking rewards to performance
- Rewarding of nominators
- Visibility of the recognition process

The Importance of Employee Motivation

The company believes in creating a highly committed and motivated workforce made up of people who achieve personal fulfilment through the freedom to act given to them in their daily work. The company sees its workforce as a prime organisational asset that is motivated through a positive organisational culture, pay and benefits, as well as training and development.

J D Wetherspoon recognises that many of its employees will not stay with it for all their working lives, but it wants its employees to develop a sense of loyalty. It pays a rate above that of its competitors, in the belief that employees are more likely to be motivated when they know they are being paid more than the minimum required. The company also bases its pay on reviews of performance, so that the higher pay reflects its positive view of the worth of its employees.

Employee Retention

The company does well at keeping its employees. It feels that its good rates of pay and proper treatment of its workforce are major contributors to this success, which reduces ongoing training costs and also creates a body of committed people. The company has a bonus scheme. All staff receive a bonus, dependant on the performance of the pub where they work. The company also runs a number of incentive schemes eg a monthly draw for examples of excellent customer care, with a paid holiday for two in New York for the winner.

The company also operates a share option scheme enabling employees to buy shares at a guaranteed price. By holding shares in the company, employees are likely to feel a greater sense of belonging and will want to see the company do well. Wetherspoon's training and development programme is a combination of 'on the job' and 'off the job' training courses. Wetherspoon's training focuses on career progression and links training to national qualifications. The company is justifiably proud of its record, in that:

- 54% of pub management began as hourly paid Associates
- 40% of area managers were once pub managers
- 50% of Wetherspoon's board were area managers.

The company encourages all employees to feel that if they show the right qualities then they will receive the support they need to advance their careers within the organisation.

Wetherspoon understands the importance of enabling employees to gain relevant qualifications recognised at a national level. In particular, training is closely linked to qualifications offered by the British Institute of Innkeeping, including areas such as licensing law, food hygiene and health and safety.

National Vocational Qualifications also feature heavily in training. Employees are encouraged to identify their own development needs and the company seeks to provide appropriate development opportunities. The company also supports professionally recognised training eg in the fields of accountancy, law and personnel management.

The Factorial Approach to Vocational Development

Parents are major partners in helping adolescents prepare for a career choice. Although several studies have examined links between general aspects of the parent-adolescent relationship and adolescents' career development, little research has addressed the mechanisms involved.

While parental support associated positively with career exploration, interference and lack of engagement associated with decision-making difficulties. Furthermore, interference and lack of engagement moderated the relationship between support and exploration. Support moderated the association between interference and decision-making difficulties.

6

Career Assessment

Career assessments are tools that are designed to help individuals understand how a variety of personal attributes (i.e., interests, values, preferences, motivations, aptitudes and skills), impact their potential success and satisfaction with different career options and work environments. Career assessments have played a critical role in career development and the economy in the last century. Assessments of some or all of these attributes are often used by individuals or organizations, such as university career service centres, career counselors, outplacement companies, corporate human resources staff, executive coaches, vocational rehabilitation counsellors, and guidance counsellors to help individuals make more informed career decisions.

In part, the popularity for this tool is due to the National Defence Education Act of 1958, which funded career guidance in schools. Focus was put onto tools that would help high school students determine which subjects they may want to focus on to reach a chosen career path. Since 1958, career assessment tool options have exploded.

Career Assessments

Career assessments come in many forms and vary along several dimensions. The assessments selected by individuals or administrators vary depending on their personal beliefs regarding the most important criteria when considering career choices, as well as the unique needs of the individual considering a career decision. Some common points of variance are:

- Methodology - Some assessments are quantitative in nature and precisely measure key attributes believed to influence an individuals potential success and satisfaction with a career. Others are qualitative exercises designed to help individuals clarify their goals and preferences, which can then be used to make more informed career decisions.

- Measured attributes - Assessments vary with regard to the specific personality attributes measured. Some assessments focus on an individual's interests, and perhaps aptitude, while others focus on skills or values.
- Validity - Many assessments, particularly those offered on the internet, lack evidence for "validity," which is the degree to which interpretation of the results of the assessment or decisions made from the results are useful. Typical evidence of validity is verified empirically. Users should evaluate any tests psychometric properties when assessing whether to use it for a particular purpose, and how much weight to give to the results. When the validity of the assessment for its intended purpose cannot be evaluated, results should be interpreted with appropriate caution.
- Target customer profile - Some assessments, such as the Strong Interest Inventory, the Myers Briggs Type Indicator, and Careerscope are designed to serve broad markets (i.e., virtually any individual choosing a vocational programme or Career Clusters, starting their career or considering a career change.

Benefits

Career assessments are designed to discover the skills, aptitude and talents of candidates. A self-assessment can be helpful in assessing the areas in which a candidate has strengths and where they are weak. The results can be useful in helping candidates to choose a career that is in tune with their goals and talents. While the validation of each instrument may vary from test to test, overall these types of assessments have been proven to introduce more career options, increase satisfaction in one's career plan and increase the understanding of oneself (Prince et al., 2003).

Data as to how often people change careers are unavailable while there's a considerable mythology about it, though no systematic studies have been undertaken. However, many people change careers more than once. Some make changes because the career path they chose is no longer viable (to wit, buggy whip makers are no longer in high demand). Or because as they mature throughout the lifespan their interests evolve. The biggest benefit of career assessment, therefore, is that it enables candidates to make the best career decision to grow both personally and professionally.

To make an assessment of their skills, candidates can pursue many avenues, the can take career interest tests such as the Strong Vocational Aptitude test, they can conduct a self-assessment, they can use the plethora of career books designed to help with this task. In fact, there are a myriad of helpful books, the most famous of which is, Richard Bolles, What Colour is Your Parachute.

In addition, they can seek expert help from career counsellors, or when warranted, psychologists or other mental health professionals. These professionals use a variety of techniques to determine the talents of candidates. Also, career counsellors can guide candidates on how to go about planning their career to achieve professional success.

Many people who are unhappy in their work find themselves uncertain as to where to turn for help. They may have seen career counsellors or career coaches or read self-help books or even obtained psychotherapy to address their career concerns—and, still found that their difficulties did not yield to these interventions. In response to this uncertainty in 2000, Dr. Lynn Friedman, a clinical psychologist, psychoanalyst who has devoted her career to work-life concerns pioneered an exciting new approach to career assessment; psychoanalytically-informed, career assessment. As a clinical psychologist, psychoanalyst working with people around work-life concerns, Friedman, a Washington DC Psychologist found that many people devoted considerable time, energy and money to unhelpful services because their difficulties were not properly assessed at the outset.

Friedman found that a careful psychological assessment aimed at asking the question, "what prompts these career difficulties" allowed the underlying nature of the difficulties to be clarified and understood. With this understanding a helpful intervention could be planned. For example, Friedman found that many people who sought psychotherapy when career coaching might have been the optimal intervention and conversely, many sought career coaching or career counselling when psychotherapy or even psychoanalysis would be more effective at resolving their difficulties. Unfortunately, most career coaches and counsellors are not trained to assess whether psychotherapy or psychoanalysis would be the appropriate intervention.

Drawbacks

Career assessment, in the form of tests and other structured and unstructured tools, can be very useful for those who are uncertain about the array of career possibilities. However, there are some drawbacks to each. At best, the results of individual career assessments provide targeted information that may not address a particular individual's needs. In addition, some of the best individual assessment tools require the help of a qualified professional to ensure the results are interpreted correctly and usefully.

Also, many of the tests are based on the person's view of himself or herself. If someone is not self-aware, the results may not be accurate. Many times they do not take into account that people have natural blind spots. The test is only as good as its user and individuals are often not clearly aware of their own strengths and weaknesses.

Myers-Briggs Type Indicator

The Myers-Briggs Type Indicator (MBTI) assessment is a psychometric questionnaire designed to measure psychological preferences in how people perceive the world and make decisions. These preferences were extrapolated from the typological theories proposed by Carl Gustav Jung and first published in his 1921 book *Psychological Types* (English edition, 1923). Jung theorized that there are four principal psychological functions by which we experience the world: sensation, intuition, feeling, and thinking. One of these four functions is dominant most of the time.

The original developers of the personality inventory were Katharine Cook Briggs and her daughter, Isabel Briggs Myers; these two, having studied extensively the work of Jung, turned their interest of human behaviour into a devotion of turning the theory of psychological types to practical use. They began creating the indicator during World War II, believing that a knowledge of personality preferences would help women who were entering the industrial workforce for the first time to identify the sort of war-time jobs that would be "most comfortable and effective". The initial questionnaire grew into the Myers-Briggs Type Indicator, which was first published in 1962. The MBTI focuses on normal populations and emphasizes the value of naturally occurring differences. Robert Kaplan and Dennis Saccuzzo believe "the underlying assumption of the MBTI is that we all have specific preferences in the way we construe our experiences, and these preferences underlie our interests, needs, values, and motivation".

Concepts

As the MBTI *Manual* states, the indicator "is designed to implement a theory; therefore the theory must be understood to understand the MBTI".

Fundamental to the Myers-Briggs Type Indicator is the theory of psychological type as originally developed by Carl Jung. Jung proposed the existence of two dichotomous pairs of cognitive functions:

- The "rational" (judging) functions: *thinking* and *feeling*
- The "irrational" (perceiving) functions: *sensation* and *intuition*

Jung believed that for every person each of the functions are expressed primarily in either an introverted or extraverted form. From Jung's original concepts, Briggs and Myers developed their own theory of psychological type, described below, on which the MBTI is based.

Type

Jung's typological model regards psychological type as similar to left or right handedness: individuals are either born with, or develop, certain preferred ways of perceiving and deciding. The MBTI sorts some of these psychological differences into four opposite pairs, or *dichotomies*, with a resulting 16 possible psychological types. None of these types are *better* or *worse*; however, Briggs and Myers theorized that individuals naturally *prefer* one overall combination of type differences. In the same way that writing with the left hand is hard work for a right-hander, so people tend to find using their opposite psychological preferences more difficult, even if they can become more proficient (and therefore behaviourally flexible) with practice and development.

The 16 types are typically referred to by an abbreviation of four letters—the initial letters of each of their four type preferences (except in the case of *intuition*, which uses the abbreviation *N* to distinguish it from Introversion). For instance:

- ESTJ: extraversion (E), sensing (S), thinking (T), judgement (J)
- INFP: introversion (I), intuition (N), feeling (F), perception (P)

This Method of Abbreviation is Applied to All 16 Types.

A related personality type model is the Personality Assessment System developed by John Gittinger. Like the MBTI, PAS identifies people's inherited tendencies, and it goes on to describe how people either accept and foster them, or compensate and modify them as functioning adults. With compensation and modification, Gittinger's PAS gives 512 types.

Four Dichotomies

	Dichotomies	
Extraversion (E)	–	(I) Introversion
Sensing (S)	–	(N) Intuition
Thinking (T)	–	(F) Feeling
Judging (J)	–	(P) Perception

The four pairs of preferences or *dichotomies* are shown in the table to the right.

Note that the terms used for each dichotomy have specific technical meanings relating to the MBTI which differ from their everyday usage. For example, people who prefer judgement over perception are not necessarily more *judgemental* or less *perceptive*. Nor does the MBTI instrument measure aptitude; it simply indicates for one preference over another. Someone reporting a high score for extraversion over introversion cannot be correctly described as *more* extraverted: they simply have a clear *preference*.

Point scores on each of the dichotomies can vary considerably from person to person, even among those with the same type. However, Isabel Myers considered the *direction* of the preference (for example, E vs. I) to be more important than the *degree* of the preference (for example, very clear vs. slight). The expression of a person's psychological type is more than the sum of the four individual preferences. The preferences interact through *type dynamics* and *type development*.

Attitudes: Extraversion/introversion (E/I)

Myers-Briggs literature uses the terms *extraversion* and *introversion* as Jung first used them. Extraversion means "outward-turning" and introversion means "inward-turning". These specific definitions vary somewhat from the popular usage of the words. Note that *extraversion* is the spelling used in MBTI publications.

The preferences for extraversion and introversion are often called "attitudes". Briggs and Myers recognized that each of the cognitive functions can operate in the external world of behaviour, action, people, and things ("extraverted attitude") or the internal world of ideas and reflection ("introverted attitude"). The MBTI assessment sorts for an overall preference for one or the other. People who prefer extraversion draw energy from action: they tend to act, then reflect, then act further. If they are inactive, their motivation tends to decline. To rebuild their energy, extraverts need breaks from time spent in reflection. Conversely, those who prefer introversion "expend" energy through action: they prefer to reflect, then act, then reflect again. To rebuild their energy, introverts need quiet time alone, away from activity.

The extravert's flow is directed outward toward people and objects, and the introvert's is directed inward toward concepts and ideas. Contrasting characteristics between extraverts and introverts include the following:

- Extraverts are "action" oriented, while introverts are "thought" oriented.
- Extraverts seek "breadth" of knowledge and influence, while introverts seek "depth" of knowledge and influence.
- Extraverts often prefer more "frequent" interaction, while introverts prefer more "substantial" interaction.
- Extraverts recharge and get their energy from spending time with people, while introverts recharge and get their energy from spending time alone.

Functions: Sensing/intuition (S/N) and Thinking/feeling (T/F)

Jung identified two pairs of psychological functions:

- The two *perceiving* functions, sensing and intuition
- The two *judging* functions, thinking and feeling

According to Jung's typology model, each person uses one of these four functions more dominantly and proficiently than the other three; however, all four functions are used at different times depending on the circumstances.

Sensing and *intuition* are the information-gathering (perceiving) functions. They describe how new information is understood and interpreted. Individuals who prefer *sensing* are more likely to trust information that is in the present, tangible, and concrete: that is, information that can be understood by the five senses. They tend to distrust hunches, which seem to come "out of nowhere". They prefer to look for details and facts. For them, the meaning is in the data. On the other hand, those who prefer *intuition* tend to trust information that is more abstract or theoretical, that can be associated with other information (either remembered or discovered by seeking a wider context or pattern). They may be more interested in future possibilities. For them, the meaning is in the underlying theory and principles which are manifested in the data.

Thinking and *feeling* are the decision-making (judging) functions. The thinking and feeling functions are both used to make rational decisions, based on the data received from their information-gathering functions (sensing or intuition). Those who prefer *thinking* tend to decide things from a more detached standpoint, measuring the decision by what seems reasonable, logical, causal, consistent, and matching a given set of rules.

Those who prefer *feeling* tend to come to decisions by associating or empathizing with the situation, looking at it 'from the inside' and weighing the situation to achieve, on balance, the greatest harmony, consensus and fit, considering the needs of the people involved. Thinkers usually have trouble interacting with people who are inconsistent or illogical, and tend to give very direct feedback to others. They are concerned with the truth and view it as more important than being tactful.

As noted already, people who prefer thinking do not necessarily, in the everyday sense, "think better" than their feeling counterparts; the opposite preference is considered an equally rational way of coming to decisions (and, in any case, the MBTI assessment is a measure of preference, not ability). Similarly, those who prefer feeling do not necessarily have "better" emotional reactions than their thinking counterparts.

Dominant Function

According to Jung, people use all four cognitive functions. However, one function is generally used in a more conscious and confident way. This dominant function is supported by the secondary (auxiliary) function, and to a lesser degree the tertiary function. The fourth and least conscious function is always the opposite of the dominant function. Myers called this inferior function the *shadow*.

The four functions operate in conjunction with the attitudes (extraversion and introversion). Each function is used in either an extraverted or introverted way. A person whose dominant function is extraverted intuition, for example, uses intuition very differently from someone whose dominant function is introverted intuition.

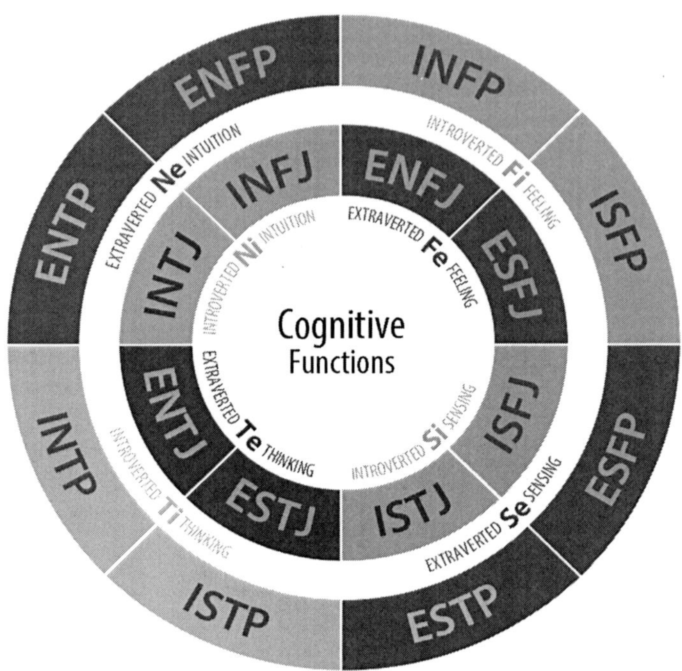

Figure: *A diagram depicting the cognitive functions of each type. A type's background colour represents its Dominant function, and its text colour represents its Auxiliary function.*

Lifestyle: Judging/perception (J/P)

Myers and Briggs added another dimension to Jung's typological model by identifying that people also have a preference for using either the *judging* function (thinking or feeling) or their *perceiving* function (sensing or intuition) when relating to the outside world (extraversion).

Myers and Briggs held that types with a preference for *judging* show the world their preferred judging function (thinking or feeling). So TJ types tend to appear to the world as logical, and FJ types as empathetic. According to Myers, judging types like to "have matters settled". Those types who prefer *perception* show the world their preferred perceiving function (sensing or intuition). So SP types tend to appear to the world as concrete and NP types as abstract. According to Myers, perceptive types prefer to "keep decisions open".

For extraverts, the J or P indicates their *dominant* function; for introverts, the J or P indicates their *auxiliary* function. Introverts tend to show their dominant function outwardly only in matters "important to their inner worlds". For example: Because the ENTJ type is extraverted, the J indicates that the *dominant* function is the preferred judging function (extraverted thinking). The ENTJ type introverts the auxiliary perceiving function (introverted intuition). The tertiary function is sensing and the inferior function is introverted feeling.

Because the INTJ type is introverted, however, the J instead indicates that the *auxiliary* function is the preferred judging function (extraverted thinking). The INTJ type introverts the dominant perceiving function (introverted intuition). The tertiary function is feeling and the inferior function is extraverted sensing.

Historical Development

Katharine Cook Briggs began her research into personality in 1917. Upon meeting her future son-in-law, she observed marked differences between his personality and that of other family members. Briggs embarked on a project of reading biographies, and she developed a typology based on patterns she found. She proposed four temperaments: Meditative (or Thoughtful), Spontaneous, Executive, and Social. Then, after the English translation of *Psychological Types* was published in 1923 (having first been published in German in 1921), she recognized that Jung's theory was similar to, yet went far beyond, her own. Briggs's four types were later identified as corresponding to the Is, EPs, ETJs and EFJs. Her first publications were two articles describing Jung's theory, in the journal *New Republic* in 1926 (*Meet Yourself Using the Personality Paint Box*) and 1928 (*Up From Barbarism*).

Briggs's daughter, Isabel Briggs Myers, added to her mother's typological research, which she would progressively take over entirely. Myers graduated first in her class from Swarthmore College in 1919 and wrote the prize-winning mystery novel *Murder Yet to Come* in 1929 using typological ideas. However, neither Myers nor Briggs were formally educated in psychology, and thus they lacked scientific credentials in the field of psychometric testing. So Myers apprenticed herself to Edward N. Hay, who was then personnel manager for a large Philadelphia bank and went on to start one of the first successful personnel consulting firms in the U.S. From Hay, Myers learned test construction, scoring, validation, and statistics. In 1942, the "Briggs-Myers Type Indicator" was created, and the *Briggs Myers Type Indicator Handbook* was published in 1944. The indicator changed its name to the modern form (*Myers-Briggs Type Indicator*) in 1956.

Myers' work attracted the attention of Henry Chauncey, head of the Educational Testing Service, and under these auspices, the first MBTI *Manual* was published in 1962. The MBTI received further support from Donald T. McKinnon, head of the Institute of Personality Research at the University of California; Harold Grant, professor at Michigan State and Auburn Universities; and Mary H. McCaulley of the University of Florida. The publication of the MBTI was transferred to Consulting Psychologists Press in 1975, and the Centre for Applications of Psychological Type (CAPT) was founded as a research laboratory. After Myers' death in May 1980, Mary McCaulley updated the MBTI *Manual*, and the second edition was published in 1985. The third edition appeared in 1998.

Differences from Jung

Judging vs. Perception: The most notable addition of Myers and Briggs to Jung's original thought is their concept that a given type's fourth letter (J or P) indicates a person's preferred extraverted function, which is the dominant function for extraverted types and the auxiliary function for the introverted types.

Orientation of the Tertiary Function: Jung theorized that the dominant function acts alone in its preferred world: exterior for the extraverts, and interior for the introverts. The remaining three functions, he suggested, operate together in the opposite world. If the dominant cognitive function is introverted, the other functions are extraverted, and vice versa. The MBTI *Manual* summarizes references in Jung's work to the balance in psychological type as follows:

> There are several references in Jung's writing to the three remaining functions having an opposite attitudinal character. For example, in writing about introverts with thinking dominant...Jung commented that the counterbalancing functions have an extraverted character.

However, many MBTI practitioners hold that the tertiary function is oriented in the same direction same as the dominant function. Using the INTP type as an example, the orientation would be as follows:

- Dominant introverted thinking
- Auxiliary extraverted intuition
- Tertiary introverted sensing
- Inferior extraverted feeling

From a theoretical perspective, psychologist Hans Eysenck called the MBTI a moderately successful quantification of Jung's original principles as outlined in *Psychological Types*.

Eysenck, However, Also Said: "This (the MBTI) creates 16 personality types which are said to be similar to Jung's theoretical concepts. I have always found difficulties with this identification, which omits one half of Jung's theory (he had 32 types, by asserting that for every conscious combination of traits there was an opposite unconscious one). Obviously the latter half of his theory does not admit of questionnaire measurement, but to leave it out and pretend that the scales measure Jungian concepts is hardly fair to Jung."

Both models remain theory, with no controlled scientific studies supporting either Jung's original concept of type or the Myers-Briggs variation.

Applications

The indicator is frequently used in the areas of pedagogy, career counselling, team building, group dynamics, professional development, marketing, family business, leadership training, executive coaching, life coaching, personal development and marriage counselling. .

Format and Administration

The current North American English version of the MBTI Step I includes 93 forced-choice questions (there are 88 in the European English version). *Forced-choice* means that the individual has to choose only one of two possible answers to each question. The choices are a mixture of word pairs and short statements. Choices are not literal opposites but chosen to reflect opposite preferences on the same dichotomy. Participants may skip questions if they feel they are unable to choose.

Using psychometric techniques, such as item response theory, the MBTI will then be scored and will attempt to identify the preference, and clarity of preference, in each dichotomy. After taking the MBTI, participants are usually asked to complete a *Best Fit* exercise and then given a readout of their Reported Type, which will usually include a bar graph and number to show how clear they were about each preference when they completed the questionnaire.

During the early development of the MBTI thousands of items were used. Most were eventually discarded because they did not have high *midpoint discrimination*, meaning the results of that one item did not, on average, move an individual score *away* from the midpoint. Using only items with high midpoint discrimination allows the MBTI to have fewer items on it but still provide as much statistical information as other instruments with many more items with lower midpoint discrimination. The MBTI requires five points one way or another to indicate a clear preference.

Additional Formats

Isabel Myers had noted that people of any given type shared differences as well as similarities. At the time of her death, she was developing a more in-depth method of measuring how people express and experience their individual type pattern.

In 1987, an advanced scoring system was developed for the MBTI. From this was developed the Type Differentiation Indicator (TDI) (Saunders, 1989) which is a scoring system for the longer MBTI, *Form J*, which includes the 290 items written by Myers that had survived her previous item analyses. It yields 20 subscales (five under each of the four dichotomous preference scales), plus seven additional subscales for a new Comfort-Discomfort factor (which purportedly corresponds to the missing factor of Neuroticism).

This factor's scales indicate a sense of overall comfort and confidence versus discomfort and anxiety. They also load onto one of the four type dimensions: guarded-optimistic (also T/F), defiant-compliant (also T/F), carefree-worried (also T/F), decisive-ambivalent (also J/P), intrepid-inhibited (Also E/I), leader-follower (Also E/I), and proactive-distractible (also J/P)

Also included is a composite of these called "strain." There are also scales for type-scale consistency and comfort-scale consistency. Reliability of 23 of the 27 TDI subscales is greater than 0.50, "an acceptable result given the brevity of the subscales" (Saunders, 1989).

In 1989, a scoring system was developed for only the 20 subscales for the original four dichotomies. This was initially known as Form K, or the Expanded Analysis Report (EAR).This tool is now called the MBTI Step II.

Form J or the TDI included the items (derived from Myers' and McCaulley's earlier work) necessary to score what became known as Step III. (The 1998 *MBTI Manual* reported that the two instruments were one and the same) It was developed in a joint project involving the following organizations: CPP, the publisher of the whole family of MBTI works; CAPT (Centre for Applications of Psychological Type), which holds all of Myers' and McCaulley's original work; and the MBTI Trust, headed by Katharine and Peter Myers. Step III was advertised as addressing type development and the use of perception and judgement by respondents.

Translations Into Other Languages

The MBTI has been successfully translated into over 20 languages, covering many countries across the world. However, it is more true to say that the creation of a new questionnaire language is adaptation, which includes translation; the other stages include reviews by subject matter experts fluent in the native language, and statistical analysis to check that the questions still measure the same psychological concepts as the original US English questionnaire.

Precepts and Ethics

The following precepts are generally used in the ethical administration of the Myers-Briggs Type Indicator:

Type Not Trait

The MBTI sorts for type; it does not indicate the strength of ability. The questionnaire allows the clarity of a preference to be ascertained (Bill *clearly* prefers introversion), but not the strength of preference (Jane *strongly* prefers extraversion) or degree of aptitude (Harry is *good* at thinking). In this sense, it differs from trait-based tools such as 16PF. Type preferences are polar opposites: a precept of MBTI is that people fundamentally prefer one thing over the other, not a bit of both.

Own Best Judge

Individuals are considered the best judge of their own type. While the MBTI questionnaire provides a *Reported Type*, this is considered only an indication of their probable overall Type. A *Best Fit Process* is usually used to allow respondents to develop their understanding of the four dichotomies, to form their own hypothesis as to their overall Type, and to compare this against the Reported Type. In more than 20% of cases, the hypothesis and the Reported Type differ in one or more dichotomies. Using the clarity of each preference, any potential for bias in the report, and often, a comparison of two or more whole Types may then help respondents determine their own Best Fit.

No Right or Wrong: No preference or total type is considered better or worse than another. They are all *Gifts Differing*, as emphasized by the title of Isabel Briggs Myers' book on this subject.

Voluntary: It is considered unethical to compel anyone to take the Myers-Briggs Type Indicator. It should always be taken voluntarily.

Confidentiality: The result of the MBTI Reported and Best Fit type are confidential between the individual and administrator and, ethically, not for disclosure without permission.

Not for selection: The results of the assessment should not be used to "label, evaluate, or limit the respondent in any way" (emphasis original). Since all types are valuable, and the MBTI measures *preferences* rather than *aptitude*, the MBTI is not considered a proper instrument for purposes of employment selection. Many professions contain highly competent individuals of different types with complementary preferences.

Importance of Proper Feedback: Individuals should always be given detailed feedback from a trained administrator and an opportunity to undertake a Best Fit exercise to check against their Reported Type. This feedback can be given in person or, where this is not practical, by telephone or electronically.

Type Dynamics and Development

The interaction of two, three, or four preferences is known as *type dynamics*. Although type dynamics has received little or no empirical support to substantiate its viability as a scientific theory, Myers and Briggs asserted that for each of the 16 four-preference types, one function is the most *dominant* and is likely to be evident earliest in life. A secondary or *auxiliary* function typically becomes more evident (*differentiated*) during teenage years and provides balance to the dominant. In normal development, individuals tend to become more fluent with a third, *tertiary* function during mid life, while the fourth, *inferior* function remains least consciously developed. The inferior function is often considered to be more associated with the unconscious, being most evident in situations such as high stress (sometimes referred to as being *in the grip* of the inferior function).

However the use of type dynamics is disputed: in the conclusion of various studies on the subject of type dynamics, James H. Reynierse writes that "Type dynamics has persistent logical problems and is fundamentally based on a series of category mistakes; it provides, at best, a limited and incomplete account of type related phenomena"; and that "type dynamics relies on anecdotal evidence, fails most efficacy tests, and does not fit the empirical facts". His studies gave the clear result that the descriptions and workings of type dynamics do not fit the real behaviour of people. He suggests getting completely rid of type dynamics, because it does not help but hinders understanding of personality. The presumed order of functions 1 to 4 did only occur in one out of 540 test results.

The sequence of differentiation of dominant, auxiliary, and tertiary functions through life is termed *type development*. Note that this is an idealized sequence that may be disrupted by major life events.

The dynamic sequence of functions and their attitudes can be determined in the following way:

- The overall *lifestyle preference* (J-P) determines whether the judging (T-F) or perceiving (S-N) preference is most evident in the outside world; i.e., which function has an extraverted attitude
- The *attitude* preference (E-I) determines whether the extraverted function is dominant or auxiliary
- For those with an overall preference for extraversion, the function with the *extraverted attitude* will be the dominant function. For example, for an ESTJ type the dominant function is the judging function, thinking, and this is experienced with an extraverted attitude. This is notated as a dominant Te. For an ESTP, the dominant function is the perceiving function, sensing, notated as a dominant Se.
- The *Auxiliary* function for extraverts is the secondary preference of the judging or perceiving functions, and it is experienced with an introverted attitude: for example, the auxiliary function for ESTJ is introverted sensing (Si) and the auxiliary for ESTP is introverted thinking (Ti).
- For those with an overall preference for introversion, the function with the extraverted attitude is the *auxiliary*; the dominant is the other function in the main four letter preference. So the dominant function for ISTJ is introverted sensing (Si) with the auxiliary (supporting) function being extraverted thinking (Te).
- The *Tertiary* function is the opposite preference from the Auxiliary. For example, if the Auxiliary is thinking then the Tertiary would be feeling. The attitude of the Tertiary is the subject of some debate and therefore is not normally indicated; i.e. if the Auxiliary was Te then the Tertiary would be F (not Fe or Fi)

- The *Inferior* function is the opposite preference and attitude from the Dominant, so for an ESTJ with dominant Te the Inferior would be Fi.

Note that for extraverts, the *dominant* function is the one most evident in the external world. For introverts, however, it is the *auxiliary* function that is most evident externally, as their dominant function relates to the interior world.

Some examples of whole types may clarify this further. Taking the *ESTJ* example above:

- Extraverted function is a judging function (T-F) because of the overall J preference
- Extraverted function is dominant because of overall E preference
- Dominant function is therefore extraverted thinking (Te)
- Auxiliary function is the preferred perceiving function: introverted sensing (Si)
- Tertiary function is the opposite of the Auxiliary: intuition (N)
- Inferior function is the opposite of the Dominant: introverted feeling (Fi)

The dynamics of the ESTJ are found in the primary combination of extraverted thinking as their dominant function and introverted sensing as their auxiliary function: the dominant tendency of ESTJs to order their environment, to set clear boundaries, to clarify roles and timetables, and to direct the activities around them is supported by their facility for using past experience in an ordered and systematic way to help organize themselves and others.

For instance, ESTJs may enjoy planning trips for groups of people to achieve some goal or to perform some culturally uplifting function. Because of their ease in directing others and their facility in managing their own time, they engage all the resources at their disposal to achieve their goals.

However, under prolonged stress or sudden trauma, ESTJs may overuse their extraverted thinking function and fall into the grip of their inferior function, introverted feeling.

Although the ESTJ can seem insensitive to the feelings of others in their normal activities, under tremendous stress, they can suddenly express feelings of being unappreciated or wounded by insensitivity.

Looking at the diametrically opposite four-letter type, *INFP*:

- Extraverted function is a perceiving function (S-N) because of the P preference
- Introverted function is dominant because of the I preference
- Dominant function is therefore introverted feeling (Fi)
- Auxiliary function is extraverted intuition (Ne)
- Tertiary function is the opposite of the Auxiliary: sensing (S)
- Inferior function is the opposite of the Dominant: extraverted thinking (Te)

The dynamics of the INFP rest on the fundamental correspondence of introverted feeling and extraverted intuition. The dominant tendency of the INFP is toward building a rich internal framework of values and toward championing human rights. They often devote themselves behind the scenes to causes such as civil rights or saving the environment. Since they tend to avoid the limelight, postpone decisions, and maintain a reserved posture, they are rarely found in executive-director type positions of the organizations that serve those causes. Normally, the INFP dislikes being "in charge" of things. When not under stress, the INFP radiates a pleasant and sympathetic demeanor; but under extreme stress, they can suddenly become rigid and directive, exerting their extraverted thinking erratically.

Every type, and its opposite, is the expression of these interactions, which give each type its unique, recognizable *signature*.

Cognitive Learning Styles

The test is scored by evaluating each answer in terms of what it reveals about the taker. Each question is relevant to one of the following cognitive learning styles. Each is not a polar opposite, but a gradual continuum.

E/I: The first continuum reflects what generically energizes a person. Extraverted types learn best by talking and interacting with others. By interacting with the physical world, extraverts can process and make sense of new information. Introverted types prefer quiet reflection and privacy. Information processing occurs for introverts as they explore ideas and concepts internally.

S/N: The second continuum reflects what a person focuses their attentions on. Sensing types enjoy a learning environment in which the material is presented in a detailed and sequential manner. Sensing types often attend to what is occurring in the present, and can move to the abstract after they have established a concrete experience. Intuitive types prefer a learning atmosphere in which an emphasis is placed on meaning and associations. Insight is valued higher than careful observation, and pattern recognition occurs naturally for Intuitive types.

T/F: The third continuum reflects the person's decision preferences. Thinking types desire objective truth and logical principles and are natural at deductive reasoning. Feeling types place an emphasis on issues and causes that can be personalized while they consider other people's motives.

J/P: The fourth continuum reflects how the person regards complexity. Judging types will thrive when information is organized and structured, and they will be motivated to complete assignments to gain closure. Perceiving types will flourish in a flexible learning environment in which they are stimulated by new and exciting ideas.

Correlations to Other Instruments

Keirsey Temperaments

David W. Keirsey mapped four "temperaments" to the existing Myers-Briggs system groupings: SP, SJ, NF and NT; this often results in confusion of the two theories. However, the Keirsey Temperament Sorter is not directly associated with the official Myers-Briggs Type Indicator.

IS_IT_EJ	IS_IF_EJ	IN_IF_EJ	IN_IT_EJ
Inspector	Protector	Counsellor	Mastermind
IS_ET_IP	IS_EF_IP	IN_EF_IP	IN_ET_IP
Crafter	Composer	Healer	Architect
ES_ET_IP	ES_EF_IP	EN_EF_IP	EN_ET_IP
Promoter	Performer	Champion	Inventor
ES_IT_EJ	ES_IF_EJ	EN_IF_EJ	EN_IT_EJ
Supervisor	Provider	Teacher	Fieldmarshal

Big Five

McCrae and Costa present correlations between the MBTI scales and the Big Five personality construct, which aims to organize the complete set of basic personality domains. The five personality characteristics are extraversion, openness, agreeableness, conscientiousness, and emotional stability (or neuroticism). The following study is based on the results from 267 men followed as part of a longitudinal study of aging. (Similar results were obtained with 201 women.)

	Extraversion	*Openness*	*Agreeableness*	*Conscientiousness*	*Neuroticism*
E-I	–0.74	0.03	–0.03	0.08	0.16
S-N	0.10	0.72	0.04	–0.15	–0.06
T-F	0.19	0.02	0.44	–0.15	0.06
J-P	0.15	0.30	–0.06	–0.49	0.11

The closer the number is to 1.0 or "1.0, the higher the degree of correlation. These data suggest that the four MBTI scales are subsumed within the Big Five personality traits, but that the MBTI lacks a measure for emotional stability dimension of the Big Five (though the TDI, discussed above, has addressed that dimension). Emotional stability (or neuroticism) is a core domain predictive of depression and anxiety disorders. These correlations refer to the second letter shown, i.e. the table shows that I and P have negative correlation to extraversion and conscientiousness respectively, while F and N have positive correlation to agreeableness and openness respectively.

These findings led McCrae and Costa, the formulators of the Five Factor Model (a Big Five theory), to conclude, "correlational analyses showed that the four MBTI indices did measure aspects of four of the five major dimensions of normal personality. The five-factor model provides an alternative basis for interpreting MBTI findings within a broader, more commonly shared conceptual framework." However, "there was no support for the view that the MBTI measures truly dichotomous preferences or qualitatively distinct types, instead, the instrument measures four relatively independent dimensions."

Personality Disorders

One study found personality disorders as described by the DSM overall to correlate modestly with I, N, T, and P, though the associations varied significantly by disorder. The only two disorders with significant correlations of all four MBTI dimensions were schizotypal (INTP) and obsessive-compulsive personality disorder (ISTJ).

Origins of the Theory

Jung's theory of psychological type, as published in his 1921 book, was not tested through controlled scientific studies. Jung's methods primarily included clinical observation, introspection and anecdote—

methods that are largely regarded as inconclusive by the modern field of psychology. Jung's type theory introduced a sequence of four cognitive functions (thinking, feeling, sensation, and intuition), each having one of two orientations (extraversion or introversion), for a total of eight dominant functions. The Myers-Briggs theory is based on these eight functions, although with some differences in expression. However, neither the Myers-Briggs nor the Jungian models offer any scientific, experimental proof to support the *existence*, the *sequence*, the *orientation*, or the *manifestation* of these functions.

Criticism

The statistical validity of the MBTI as a psychometric instrument has been the subject of criticism. It has been estimated that between a third and a half of the published material on the MBTI has been produced for conferences of the Centre for the Application of Psychological Type (which provides training in the MBTI) or as papers in the *Journal of Psychological Type* (which is edited by Myers-Briggs advocates). It has been argued that this reflects a lack of critical scrutiny. Many of the studies that endorse MBTI are methodologically weak. A 1996 review by Gardner and Martinko concluded "It is clear that efforts to detect simplistic linkages between type preferences and managerial effectiveness have been disappointing. Indeed, given the mixed quality of research and the inconsistent findings, no definitive conclusion regarding these relationships can be drawn."

For example, some researchers expected that scores would show a bimodal distribution with peaks near the ends of the scales, but found that scores on the individual subscales were actually distributed in a centrally peaked manner similar to a normal distribution. A cut-off exists at the centre of the subscale such that a score on one side is classified as one type, and a score on the other side as the opposite type. This fails to support the concept of *type*: the norm is for people to lie near the middle of the subscale. "*Although we do not conclude that the absence of bimodality necessarily proves that the MBTI developers' theory-based assumption of categorical "types" of personality is invalid, the absence of empirical bimodality in IRT-based MBTI scores does indeed remove a potentially powerful line of evidence that was previously available to "type" advocates to cite in defence of their position.*"

In 1991, the National Academy of Sciences committee reviewed data from MBTI research studies and concluded that only the I-E scale has high correlations with comparable scales of other instruments and low correlations with instruments designed to assess different concepts, showing strong validity. In contrast, the S-N and T-F scales show relatively weak validity. The 1991 review committee concluded at the time there was "not sufficient, well-designed research to justify the use of the MBTI in career counselling programmes". This study based its measurement of validity on "criterion-related validity (i.e., does the MBTI predict specific outcomes related to interpersonal relations or career success/job performance?)." Studies have found that there is insufficient evidence to make claims about utility, particularly of the four letter type given after the test.

The accuracy of the MBTI depends on honest self-reporting by the person tested. Unlike some personality measures, such as the Minnesota Multiphasic Personality Inventory or the Personality Assessment Inventory, the MBTI does not use validity scales to assess exaggerated or socially desirable responses. As a result, individuals motivated to do so can fake their responses, and one study found that the MBTI judgement/perception dimension correlates with the Eysenck Personality Questionnaire lie scale.

If respondents "fear they have something to lose, they may answer as they assume they *should*." However, the MBTI ethical guidelines state, "It is unethical and in many cases illegal to require job applicants to take the Indicator if the results will be used to screen out applicants." The intent of the MBTI is to provide "a framework for understanding individual differences, and ... a dynamic model of individual development".

Terminology

The terminology of the MBTI has been criticized as being very "vague and general", so as to allow any kind of behaviour to fit any personality type, which may result in the Forer effect, where individuals give a high rating to a positive description that supposedly applies specifically to them. Others argue that while the MBTI type descriptions are brief, they are also distinctive and precise. Some theorists, such as David Keirsey, have expanded on the MBTI descriptions, providing even greater detail. For instance, Keirsey's descriptions of his four temperaments, which he correlated with the sixteen MBTI personality types, show how the temperaments differ in terms of language use, intellectual orientation, educational and vocational interests, social orientation, self-image, personal values, social roles, and characteristic hand gestures.

Factor Analysis

With regard to factor analysis, one study of 1291 college-aged students found *six* different factors instead of the *four* used in the MBTI. In other studies, researchers found that the JP and the SN scales correlate with one another.

Correlates

According to Hans Eysenck: "The main dimension in the MBTI is called E-I, or extraversion-introversion; this is mostly a sociability scale, corelating quite well with the MMPI social introversion scale (negatively) and the Eysenck Extraversion scale (positively). Unfortunately, the scale also has a loading on neuroticism, which correlates with the introverted end. Thus introversion correlates roughly (i.e. averaging values for males and females) -.44 with dominance, -.24 with aggression, +.37 with abasement, +.46 with counselling readiness, -.52 with self-confidence, -.36 with personal adjustment, and -.45 with empathy. The failure of the scale to disentangle Introversion and Neuroticism (in fact there is no scale for neurotic and other psychopathological attributes in the MBTI) is its worst feature, only equalled by the failure to use factor analysis in order to test the arrangement of items in the scale."

Test-retest

There is a lack of test-retest reliability, with large numbers of individuals having different classifications after five weeks. There is also strong evidence that the different scales are correlated, and not independent as claimed. In *Fortune Magazine* on May 15, 2013, an article on the test, entitled "Have we all been duped by the Myers-Briggs Test", said that:

"The interesting — and somewhat alarming — fact about the MBTI is that, despite its popularity, it has been subject to sustained criticism by professional psychologists for over three decades. One problem is that it displays what statisticians call low "test-retest reliability." So if you retake the test after only a five-week gap, there's around a 50% chance that you will fall into a different personality category compared to the first time you took the test."

The consequence is that the scores of two people labelled "introvert" and "extravert" may be almost exactly the same, but they could be placed into different categories since they fall on either side of an imaginary dividing line.

Reliability

The MBTI is "one of the most popular personality questionnaires". Some researchers have interpreted the reliability of the test as being low. Studies have found that between 39% and 76% of those tested fall into different types upon retesting some weeks or years later.

One study reports that the MBTI dichotomies exhibit good split-half reliability; however, the dichotomy scores are distributed in a bell curve, and the overall *type* allocations are less reliable. Also, test-retest reliability is sensitive to the time between tests. Within each *dichotomy* scale, as measured on Form G, about 83% of categorizations remain the same when individuals are retested within nine months, and around 75% when individuals are retested after nine months. About 50% of people tested within nine months remain the same overall *type*, and 36% remain the same type after more than nine months. For Form M (the most current form of the MBTI instrument), the MBTI *Manual* reports that these scores are higher.

In one study, when people were asked to compare their preferred type to that assigned by the MBTI assessment, only half of people picked the same profile. Critics also argue that the MBTI lacks falsifiability, which can cause confirmation bias in the interpretation of results.

A number of scholars argue that criticisms regarding the MBTI mostly come down to questions regarding the validity of its origins, not questions regarding the validity of the MBTI's usefulness. Others argue that the MBTI can be a reliable measurement of personality; it just so happens that "like all measures, the MBTI yields scores that are dependent on sample characteristics and testing conditions".

Utility

In her research, Isabel Myers found that the proportion of different personality types varied by choice of career or course of study. However, some researchers examining the proportions of each type within varying professions report that the proportion of MBTI types within each occupation is close to that within a random sample of the population. Some researchers have expressed reservations about the relevance of type to job satisfaction, as well as concerns about the potential misuse of the instrument in labelling individuals.

CPP became the exclusive publisher of the Myers-Briggs instrument in 1975. They call it "the world's most widely used personality assessment", with as many as two million assessments administered annually. CPP and other proponents state that the indicator meets or exceeds the reliability of other psychological instruments and cite reports of individual behaviour.

Some studies have found strong support for construct validity, internal consistency, and test-retest reliability, although variation was observed. However, some academic psychologists have criticized the MBTI instrument, claiming that it "lacks convincing validity data", while some studies have shown the statistical validity and reliability to be low.

Studies suggest that the MBTI is not a useful predictor of job performance. As noted above under Precepts and ethics, the MBTI measures preference, not ability. The use of the MBTI as a predictor of job success is expressly discouraged in the *Manual*. However, the MBTI continues to be popular because many people are qualified to administer it, it is not difficult to understand, and there are many supporting books, websites and other useful sources which are readily available to the general public.

Interests and Vocational Development.

Interest is a feeling or emotion that causes attention to focus on an object, event, or process. In contemporary psychology of interest, the term is used as a general concept that may encompass other more specific psychological terms, such as curiosity and to a much lesser degree surprise.

The emotion of interest does have its own facial expression, of which the most prominent component is having dilated pupils.

Curiosity

Curiosity (from Latin *curiosus* "careful, diligent, curious," akin to *cura* "care") is a quality related to inquisitive thinking such as exploration, investigation, and learning, evident by observation in human and many animal species. The term can also be used to denote the behaviour itself being caused by the emotion of curiosity. As this emotion represents a thirst for knowledge, curiosity is a major driving force behind scientific research and other disciplines of human study.

Although many living beings have an innate capability of curiosity, it should not be categorized as an instinct because it is not a fixed action pattern; rather it is an innate basic emotion because, while curiosity can be expressed in many ways, the expression of an instinct is typically more fixed and less flexible. Curiosity is common to human beings at all ages from infancy through adulthood, and is easy to observe in many other animal species. These include apes, cats, and rodents.

Brain

Although the phenomenon of curiosity is widely regarded, its neural correlates still remain relatively unknown. However, recent studies have provided insight into the neurological mechanisms that may be associated with curiosity, such as learning, memory, and motivation. Such research aims to transition the study of curiosity from a speculative realm to one of more scientific credibility. Various theories have been proposed in order to elucidate the mechanism of curiosity:

Curiosity-drive Model

The curiosity-drive model states that experiences that are novel and complex create a sensation of uncertainty in the brain, a sensation perceived to be unpleasant. Curiosity acts as a means in which to dispel this uncertainty. By exhibiting curious and exploratory behaviour, organisms are able to learn more about the novel stimulus and thus reduce the state of uncertainty in the brain. However, this model does not account for the observation that organisms display curiosity even in the absence of exciting and new stimuli. This type of exploratory behaviour is common in many species. Take the example of a human toddler who, if bored in his current situation devoid of arousing stimuli, will walk about until something interesting is found. The observation of curiosity even in the absence of novel stimuli pinpoints one of the major shortcomings in the curiosity-drive model.

Optimal Arousal Model

The optimal-arousal model of curiosity posits that the brain aims to maintain an optimal level of arousal. If the stimulus is too intensely arousing, a “back-away” type behaviour is engaged. In contrast, if the environment is boring and lacks exciting stimuli, exploratory behaviour will be engaged until something optimally arousing is encountered. In essence, the brain is searching for the perfect balance of arousal states. This model aptly addresses the observation that organisms display curiosity even in the absence of novel and exciting stimuli. While this theory addresses some discrepancies in the curiosity-drive theory, it is not without fault. If there is an ideal state of curiosity that should be maintained in the brain, then gaining new knowledge to eliminate that state of curiosity would be considered counter-productive.

Integration of Reward Pathway

Taking into account the shortcomings of both curiosity-drive and optimal-arousal models, there have been attempts to integrate the neurological aspects of reward, wanting, and liking into a more comprehensive theory for curiosity, one that is explained by biological processes. The act of wanting new information involves mesolimbic dopamine activation, which assigns an intrinsic value to that new information that the brain then interprets as a reward. This is the neurobiology that motivates exploratory behaviour. In addition, opioid activity in the nucleus accumbens evaluates stimuli and attaches an immediate value to the novel object, a sensation known as "liking". This liking stimulates pleasure. The chemical processes of both wanting and liking play a role in activating the reward system of the brain, and perhaps in curious tendencies as well.

Neurological Aspects

Due to the complexity of the subject, focusing on specific neural processes within curiosity can help in better understanding the phenomenon of curiosity as a whole. The following neural aspects can be thought of as essential sub-functions of curiosity:

Attention

Attention is the cognitive process by which one can selectively focus and concentrate on particular stimuli in the surrounding environment. There may be many stimuli in the surrounding area, but as there are limited cognitive and sensory resources, attention allows the brain to better focus on what it perceives to be the most important or relevant of these stimuli. Scientists can measure the amount of attention an individual devotes to a stimulus by tracking eye movements. Organisms focus their eyes on stimuli that are particularly stimulating or engaging; the more attention a stimulus garners, the more frequent the eye will be directed towards that stimulus. Normal individuals will look at new stimuli at least two to three times more often than familiar or repetitive stimuli. Exciting or novel stimuli demand more attention than stimuli perceived as boring.

Motivation and Reward

The drive to learn new information or perform some action is often initiated by the anticipation of reward (an emotional sensation of relief and happiness). In this way, the concepts of motivation and reward are intrinsically tied to the phenomenon of curiosity.

Reward can be defined as an effect of some action that positively reinforces that behaviour. Feelings of pleasure and satisfaction are often associated with reward.

There are many areas in the brain used to process reward, such as the nucleus accumbens, the substantia nigra, the striata and the ventral tegmental area (VTA). These structures together form the reward pathway.

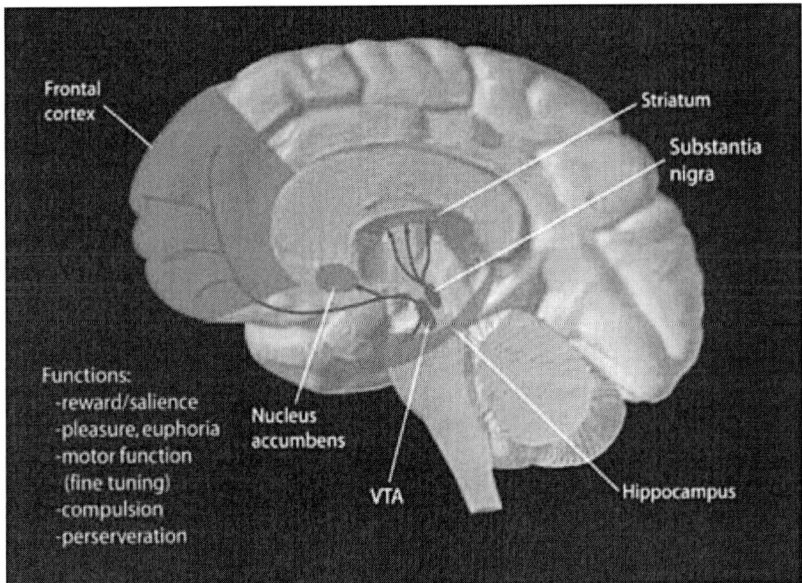

Figure: *Dopamine Pathway in the Brain*

There are many prominent neurotransmitters released in the activation of the reward pathway, the most relevant of which include dopamine, serotonin and opioid-derived chemicals. Recent studies have shown that dopamine may be important for the process of curiosity, most particularly in assigning and retaining reward values for information gained.

Midbrain dopamine neurons in monkeys are activated when determining the value of stimuli. There is some level of dopamine neuron activation when the reward of a familiar stimulus is already known, but perhaps more interestingly, there is a higher dopamine release when the reward is unknown and the stimulus is novel. Additionally, reward values were better retained (a function of both reward and memory) in monkeys that exhibited more curious behaviour. Such studies further implicate the reward pathway in curious behaviour.

Personality and Vocational Development

Numerous companies have discovered that increasing the diversity of their workforce pays off in improved performance, happier customers, and more satisfied employees. Consider Wal-Mart. "Much of Wal-Mart's substantial growth has come in urban areas, prompting the retailer to

diversify its humongous 800,000 workforce to capitalize on local talent pools

and do what it does best: sell. Catering to minority customers is far more effective when a company addresses the distinctions that drive purchasing decisions among various ethnic groups. So putting more people of colour on the sales floor—and in executive positions—is really a no-brainer in this company."

Now consider the role Glen Toney plays at Applied Materials, a $4 billion manufacturer of semiconductor equipment. A 20-year employee of the company and group vice president of corporate affairs, Toney mentors several of the company's minority employees and keeps top executives informed about promising minority workers. He notes that "people who come aboard here have to move faster than they ever have before, and the organization is complex and can be

frustrating." The fatherly role Toney and others play helps explain the company's reputation in the Silicon Valley as a good place for people of colour to work.

Toyota tries to locate highly competent minority candidates. A member of the minority advisory board commented, "They'll go outside the automobile industry to get somebody who is energetic and shows promise and wants to become an automobile dealer. Then that person will take an awful lot of schooling and training." This enthusiasm about minority employees attracts many minority customers who recognize a company's reputation as being minority-friendly.

The Diverse Workplace

Demographics, competition for talent, marketplace demands, and the changing environment call for a diverse workforce. This workforce includes (and treats equally) men and women, employees with differing ethnic backgrounds, younger and older workers, physically challenged employees, and other workers who differ from the dominant group of white, male employees in the United States. By bringing a greater pool of talent to the workplace, diversity often results in better decision making, an increased understanding of customers' needs, and a greater staffing ability. Changes in the workplace have made cultural ethnocentrism, the belief in the preeminence of one's own culture, dysfunctional in a global economy. Managers in the United States have rejected cultural ethnocentrism for the following reasons:

respect for individual and cultural differences; a legal system that values equal opportunity and nondiscrimination in the workplace; a global economy that markets goods and services to diverse cultures; belief in the benefits of hiring workers that resemble their customers; and an already-changing workforce.

Women in the Workplace

A dramatic increase in the numbers and percentage of women in the workplace has occurred. This change has resulted from equal employment and affirmative action legislation, the feminist movement, and economic realities. Even today, women still earn less than their male counterparts. For example, full-time working women's earnings were 76 percent of men's earnings in 1998. White workers, middle-aged workers, older workers, and those with only a high school education experienced the greatest gender earnings wage gap. Earnings of women with college degrees increased by close to 22 percent in the past two decades. This improvement contributed in part to an increase in the earnings differences between white women and black and Hispanic women in the same time period.

As their representation has increased, women continue to experience unique concerns and problems. Women's lives differ from men's because they have responsibility for child bearing and generally assume primary responsibility for child rearing. Women more often than men choose to reduce their work commitment to part-time or conduct their careers in a serial fashion, spending time as a full-time wife and mother before reentering the workplace. In one study, part-time work was associated with less interference between work and family responsibilities, better time management ability, and greater life satisfaction for women. In a different, three-year study of 1,000 female managers by Catalyst, a New York research firm that focuses on women's issues, the women who worked part-time said they were happier and more productive than when they worked full-time. Part-time work generally allows women to better balance work and family needs. Yet part-time work can also slow a person's career advancement and result in lower salaries.

The Glass Ceiling May Hinder Women's Advancement.

This invisible barrier to movement into top management results from discrimination in the workplace, the inability of women and minorities to penetrate the "old boys' network," and the tendency of executives to promote others like themselves. While the number of top women business leaders has increased, their movement onto boards of directors and top executive positions remains stalled. For example, the chemical industry has few women in top-level positions, and women represent less than 10 percent of board seats in a survey of 48 companies.

Sex role stereotyping is more problematic in firms with relatively low proportions of senior women.

While the European workforce includes 41 percent women, they hold only 29 percent of management jobs, less than two percent of senior management jobs, and only one percent of board seats.

Women earn up to 40 percent less in manufacturing jobs and 35 percent less in service jobs. The slow progress results from lack of child care, as well as women's unwillingness to ask for flexibility.

Women hold only 14 percent of international management assignments, primarily because companies have been unwilling to send them overseas. Myths that women do not want to be international managers and that foreigners may be prejudiced against women expatriate managers have been shown to be untrue. The senior manager of human resources in Asia for Cisco Systems argues that Western women are generally well received in other countries because they're not expected to conform to the same standards as local women and so can function more as they would in the same job in the United States. Women's desire and ability to do high-quality work, as well as support from senior management, further bolster their position abroad. Companies can increase the likelihood that high-potential women will accept overseas assignments in a number of ways. First, they can help them break through the glass ceiling and assume top-level management positions. Second, they can create career development programmes that include international assignments. Third, they can develop a systematic way to identify potential expatriates and convince them to seek international assignments. Fourth, top executives can make sure women receive pre-departure cross-cultural training. Fifth, they can provide support that helps women address family needs, such as child care and relocation for their spouses. Finally, they can publicize successful women expatriates.

Race in the Workplace

The percentage of African Americans in the workplace has increased significantly in the past 25 years, due in large part to affirmative action requirements.

Now African Americans have assumed more jobs in the executive suite. Lloyd Ward, for example, who began his life in a 400-square-foot house with no running water, rose to become CEO of Maytag Appliances after successful stints at Procter & Gamble and Pepsico. Ward notes, "There are many who are systematically excluded. [But] the oppressed have to overcome the prejudices of society. Knock on the door, pull on the handle, and, if you have to, dismantle the hinge."

Race combined with gender can create a particularly potent barrier that prevents women of colour from advancing into executive positions. Some African American women have made it to the upper echelons of power and influence. They work for companies such as American Express, Kraft Foods, IBM, and Xerox, and hold executive positions such as president, chief executive, executive vice president, and vice president. Reducing stereotypes and promoting workers on the basis of ability and demonstrated competence presents a major challenge for managers. The Corporate Few, an informal network of African American employees initiated in 1971, mentors young African Americans. Personality refers to a set of distinctive personal characteristics, including motives, emotions, values, interests, attitudes, and competencies. How would you describe Glen Toney's personality? We might describe him as extroverted and competitive.

We might describe him as having a Type A personality or being high in self-efficacy. His heredity and his social, cultural, and family environments likely influenced his personality. His personality in turn influences the way he acts. For example, his personality might cause him to naturally set challenging goals and rely on his relationships with others to achieve them. How would you describe the personality of other employees of Applied Materials? The personalities of top executives can help explain dysfunctional organizations.

For example, an executive who believes that no one can be trusted often creates an organization in which secrecy and guardedness characterize the culture. Or a manager whose personality reflects a need for control will often create an organization that relies too much on formal controls and direct supervision to accomplish the organizational goals. An attempted merger between SmithKline

Beecham and Glaxo Wellcome collapsed the first time in part because of a clash between the charismatic CEO of SmithKline and the strong-willed top executive of Glaxo Wellcome over who should run the new company. Now they have given the leadership of the combined company to a third person, characterized as a patient, highly disciplined executive who can provide calming and authoritative leadership.

Measuring Personality

Trained and certified professionals generally assess personality in three ways: Personality inventories require the person to answer questions that describe the respondent's personality.

Projective tests require the person to describe what she sees in a picture or relatively ambiguous stimulus, such as an inkblot. A detailed scoring protocol places the person along numerous personality dimensions.

Simulations, role-playing exercises, and stress interviews require the person to behave in specific situations. An observation and scoring protocol categorizes the person along dimensions such as adaptability, assertiveness, or dominance.

Managers might use information collected from these instruments as part of the pre-employment screening process or promotion decisions. A 1997 survey by the Society for Human Resources Management indicated that 22 percent of U.S. companies use personality tests to screen candidates. For example, companies use the 50-adjective Predictive Index to help determine the most suitable type of work for potential and current employees. Others use the Sales Success Predictor to measure confidence, aggressiveness, initiative, and creativity for potential salespeople.

After administering a test to help understand an employee's personality, the manager can examine how personality affects the worker's behaviour. Will the employee likely work well on a team? Does the employee have a drive to succeed, demonstrate compatibility with others, and have positive feelings of self-worth?

The manager can then adjust the work situation to better match workers' personalities and hence obtain better outcomes. For example, BellSouth and TManage have agreed to sell Team Telework Connections, which helps set up telecommuting programmes. The package includes personality tests that can help determine whether employees are suitable for telecommuting.

Personality Traits and Attributes

Psychological research has identified many traits and attributes, some measured by the previously mentioned instruments, that compose a person's personality. Personality traits are distinguishing qualities or characteristics that are the embodiment of an individual's. They are your habitual patterns of behaviour, temperament and emotion.

Skills, on the other hand, are the learned capacity to carry out specific tasks. They are competences or the talents to do things. These proficiencies can include critical thinking, manual, negotiation, outdoor, presentation, or technological. Typically, skills are special abilities that are acquired through training and experience.

The building block of successful career development is comprised of four components: skills, values, interests and personality traits. I have been a practicing career counsellor for a long-time, and I have found an abundance of personality traits that are characteristic of successful people. However, I the following is my top 10 list. Successful people tend to be/have:

1. *Attitude* – The capacity to stay optimistic and positive. The #1 quality for career success is "Championship Thinking."
2. *Enthusiastic* – The possession of intense and eager interest in a subject or cause. It is an energy that often inspires others.
3. *Ethical* – The quality of having and living by a code of sound moral principles.
4. *Goal Focused* – The ability to have clarity on the objectives that you strive for in your personal and professional life.
5. *Listener* – The capacity to suspend your own agenda and deliberately and empathically allow others to be heard.
6. *Networked* – A well developed circle of influence of interconnected positive relationships.
7. *Persistent* – The ability to endure in the face of adversity. It is a patient and relenting effort to achieve despite difficulties.
8. *Self-Aware* – The understanding and knowledge of who you are including your skills, values, interests, behaviours and character.
9. *Self-Confident* – The firm belief in your abilities. Seek professional help if this is an area of weakness – it will be worth it.

10. *Self-Discipline* – The ability to control and restrain impulses. Energy then can be focused and channelled toward your ambitions.

It is impossible to limit the list to just 10, and so here are 25 more that represent my second tier:

1. Adaptive
2. Analytical Mind
3. Articulate
4. Balanced
5. Collaborative
6. Committed
7. Courageous
8. Creative
9. Decisive
10. Detail-Oriented
11. Emotionally Competent
12. Friendly
13. Hard Working
14. Humorous
15. Intelligent
16. Organized
17. Prepared
18. Productive
19. Relationship-Oriented
20. Responsible
21. Sincere
22. Self-Sacrificing
23. Trustworthy
24. Visionary
25. Wise.

Your list may differ and certainly, the list of personality traits could be much longer. As a strengths-based career counsellor. If you need assistance, ask three people that you know and trust what they perceive to be your best characteristics. This will help you get clarity on what you have to offer an employer. As a result you will be able to better answer such important questions as, "Why should we hire you?" or "How would you describe yourself?" The right combination of personality traits can greatly assist an individual on the road to success.

Economic Factors in Vocational Development

Informed and Considered Career Decisions

Informed and considered career decisions are the product of a career development process that includes creating awareness of options, exploring possible career pathways, reviewing available information, clarifying interests, values, and skills through assessment, reflecting upon experiences, relating education and training options to occupational goals, experimenting through work sampling, volunteering, or employment, consulting with knowledgeable people in the field of interest, formulating plans for education, training, career entry, and retraining, making decisions and refining plans, implementing and adapting plans, and applying the career development process throughout the lifespan.

Informed and considered career decisions result in improved matches between people and their work. Such matching manifests itself in improved utilization of education and training resources, higher levels of worker satisfaction, preferred patterns of employment stability and mobility, increased income and benefits, and many attendant benefits to families and communities.

Career guidance professionals may facilitate the career development process, or individuals may engage in the process on their own. Not all people will engage in all steps, and the sequence may vary; but however obtained, informed and considered career decisions represent a match of person and work in which the individual's skills, interests, values, beliefs, and purposes fit, align with, inform, and contribute to work, and work contributes to the individual's well-being and life goals.

For students, career information is an essential part of a comprehensive guidance process that extends throughout school years.

The career planning process was once thought to be completed during youth or young adulthood. With a changing nature of employment and higher expectations of individuals for quality in their relationship with work, a need has emerged for career development processes to take place throughout one's life. Indeed, experts such as

Savickas (1999) and Jarvis (2003) assert that career self management is fundamental to success in the contemporary economy, which is characterized by rapid changes in the workplace, globalization, contingent work, international competition, and jobs that increasingly blur roles, functions, and responsibilities in accord with project needs. Career self management is the internalization of career development processes that enable an individual to navigate and prosper in a work world in which one's relationship to employment is in a state of flux, in which changing jobs and employers is the norm. In this challenging work world (liberating for some and terrifying for others), one's ability to work is mediated by the degree to which one can self market, self manage, align skills with work requirements, and satisfy clients and customers. In short, career self management rests squarely on the individual's ability to make informed and considered career decisions.

For many workers, changing occupational structures are thrusting them into situations that require career decision making. The Bureau of Labour Statistics estimates that there are 10.2 million contract workers in the U.S. (Washington Post, 2000), and millions more are caught in the decline of manufacturing and the shift to a knowledge economy. Even among employed Americans, there is little doubt that they would better inform themselves about career options if they were starting over (Hoyt and Lester, 1995).

Fully 70 percent indicated they would seek more and better information before entering a career. And there is little doubt that the employment structures of the past in which one signed on with an employer for a lengthy stint provide fewer and fewer Americans with that type of employment relationship. The most recent round of manufacturing job losses, which may represent structural changes in the U.S. economy, has left millions of Americans with uncertain futures as they search for pathways to re-employment, new careers, or survival without a traditional job. Whether employed or out of work, it is fair to say that all Americans will confront the question, "What work is right for me?" multiple times, if not continuously, throughout their work lives.

Information, Systems, Processes, and Networks:

Facilitating Informed and Considered Career Decisions Career information is part of a nexus of products, services, and processes that facilitate informed and considered career decisions.

Career information is the intelligence that guides workers (and the professionals who advise them) in the analytical process of examining, comprehending, and making decisions about the world of work. Career information comprises occupational information, industry information, education and training information, financial aid information, and career development process information. Career information is an essential component of career information systems, career guidance, and career education. It is important to distinguish between career information and data such as labour market information, occupational data, and economic data. Career information developers convert these data into products understandable by and developmentally appropriate for intended audiences. Career information renders labour market information, occupational data, and economic data understandable and meaningful in the context of individual career development.

Career information makes possible systems that support career development and processes such as career guidance and career education. Career information is absolutely the one tool upon which nearly every step in the process of making informed and considered career decisions depends.

Career Information Systems

Comprehensive career information systems, termed career information delivery systems, integrate information components with assessments, searching features, and other components.

Career information delivery systems add value to career information by relating and meaningfully integrating components in order to provide end users with personally tailored information. For example, some systems enable users to identify their strongest work skills in order to find occupations that demand these skills. In this way, a user can find work that allows the transfer of accumulated skills and expertise. Many systems provide assessments of work-related interests that enable users to explore occupations that match their particular patterns of interests. Career information delivery systems typically relate occupational information to education and training information; users can easily determine the preparation requirements for an occupation and can find education and training providers.

Career Information Processes

Career information processes include career counselling, career guidance, career consulting, and career education. Increasingly, there are sophisticated resources that enable individuals to make informed and considered career decisions through career development processes delivered via the World Wide Web.

Particularly relevant to this discussion:

1. The value added to career information through the many ways in which information is delivered, contextualized, and made meaningful by counsellors, teachers, and others, and
2. The degree to which individuals grow and develop, internalize career development processes, and become life-long career self-managers (and sometimes teachers of others).

Career interventions mediated by counsellors have substantially stronger effects than unmediated career interventions. Whiston, Sexton, and Lasoff and Whiston, Brecheisen, and Stephens offer strong support for career interventions that are delivered by counsellors. However, unmediated career information and services can extend to vast audiences and can provide a service to people who don't have access to the services of a career professional. Several studies have found that career classes, workshops, and structured groups are useful interventions that produce a variety of documented outcomes.

Ogle (2001) found that lower student-counsellor ratios resulted in increased college-going rates for high school graduates, an effect that persists when taking into account socio-economic and demographic differences.

Increasing the amount of time that students spend talking with counsellors and teachers about students' plans is associated with increased achievement in mathematics, science, and reading.

Career Information Networks

Career information networks derive from government, business, and nonprofit and professional organizations. In addition to the structures of state and federal government, career information networks form around specific career information systems or products such as Choices (Bridges), the Coordinated Occupational Information Network (Coin, Inc.), SIGI Plus (Education Testing Service), the Career Information System (University of Oregon), and ACT Discover (ACT). With the common interest of improving career information products and services, these networks provide professional oversight and bring knowledge of end users' experiences with their respective products and services.

Professional organizations that embrace career information and career development include the National Career Development Association, the Association of Computer-based Systems for Career Information, the Career Education

Association, and the American School Counsellor Association. Functioning independently, but often in concert, the career information networks strengthen career information and career development through professional development and the establishment of professional and ethical standards, through audience analyses and needs assessments, through guidance for professionals in what constitutes developmentally appropriate career development, and through research sponsorship and dissemination. In sum, the networks create a professional culture around career information and career development. It is in the context of this culture that the value of career information is magnified exponentially.

Often, government investments in career interventions are viewed as costs to be justified by measurable macroeconomic returns: increased employment, improved educational attainment or achievement, gains in income, etc. Herr points out that career development professionals are often viewed as consumers of such investments, when, in fact, they are also producers. Career development professionals take career information and embed it into career information systems, and into career information processes such as career education, career guidance, and career counselling services.

Career networks add further value through improving practice. Any cost/benefit analysis of career information and services must consider the value added to public and private investments by the array of career development professionals who create information systems, processes, and networks that facilitate informed and considered career decisions.

Measurement Issues

Career information is embedded in systems, processes, and networks. As the complexity of its context grows, the value and effect of career information also grows. The amount of return on investment is very difficult to measure. How much value accrues to a ten-dollar wrench in the hands of an experienced mechanic? In the hands of an experienced mechanic at a top-notch repair shop? In the hands of an experienced mechanic at a top-notch repair shop that is part of an international network of technical support? Do you count the value of every car the mechanic repairs? The engine damage prevented? The value of jobs kept because of reliable transportation?

As with most social phenomena, it is neither possible to grasp all of the inputs of the career development process nor all of the outputs. It may not be possible to generalize returns from one audience to another. The number and intensity of interventions vary as do the professionals who apply the interventions.

Although there is considerable outcome research to review, studies often focus narrowly on specific audiences and specific outcomes. Much research is concentrated on high school and college students. Even so, a rich tapestry of professional research reveals that career development processes produce intended outcomes in direct relation to the quality, number, and frequency of interventions. These outcomes contribute to informed and considered career decisions.

. Dykeman et al. (2003) posit that career interventions lead to increased academic efficacy and motivation, two variables that are known to be related to improved academic achievement. In this study, "academic planning counselling" was found to have a positive influence upon mathematics achievement. The authors speculate that mathematics is particularly susceptible to influence, because counsellors can help students understand how mathematics relates to their lives and future plans.

Improved Preparation and Participation in Postsecondary Education

Several factors influence postsecondary participation:

- preparing academically through a rigorous programme of advanced coursework,
- having intentions for higher levels of education,
- having expectations that one can achieve at higher levels of education,
- participating in a career planning process that articulates goals, steps, and benchmarks,
- receiving supportive guidance,
- having postsecondary information about institutions, majors, financial aid, the college applications process, and support services available,
- getting good grades, and
- being satisfied with the school experience.

Many career interventions address the factors listed above. The National [United Kingdom] Institute for Careers Education Counselling reports various studies that indicated positive effects of career education on student intentions for and participation in higher education.

Lower Unemployment Rates and Shorter Periods of Unemployment

People who make informed and considered career decisions complete higher levels of education. A correlate of educational attainment is lower rates of unemployment.

Veum and Weiss (1993) reported that (for workers ages 18-27) the duration and frequency of unemployment is a direct function of thelevel of education - the higher the level of education, the fewer bouts of unemployment and the shorter the duration of unemployment.

Allotments for unemployment compensation on a benefits for housing assistance, food, and re-employment increase as a function of unemployment.

Mayston states that career guidance plays a valuable role by providing information about the suitability and availability of career opportunities. Derivative of this increase in human capital are reductions in unemployment and in employment security costs to employers. Entrants to the labour market face many challenges (high skill requirements, scarcity of jobs, preference for experienced workers, competition from unemployed workers, etc.). A career plan may be the best strategy for successfully engaging young people with work that has the greatest likelihood of success, satisfaction, and (within the limits of a volatile employment context) stability. Such a plan derives its effectiveness from a thorough examination of career information, including consideration of experience and preparation requirements and reflection upon the many internal and external factors that mediate appropriateness or fit.

Lower Costs of Worker Turnover

Informed and considered career decisions result in better person-work fit, increased job satisfaction, and diminished chances of occupational mismatch. Having learned about, prepared for, and experienced an occupation prior to committing to it, the employee who has skills to make informed and considered career decisions will bring to the workplace much knowledge that informs, guides, and helps the employee to anticipate work requirements, expectations, and the culture of the particular work environment.

Younger employees change jobs and employers with great frequency. Most workers have had between six and eight jobsby age 27. The cost of training and orienting employees, the lost productivity of vacant or poorly served positions, and the many costs attendant to an individual's loss of employment create a strong motivating force for reducing employee turnover.

Lower Health Care Costs

A satisfying career in which one finds achievement, enjoyment, and meaning contrasts sharply with the occupational mismatch that leads to job stress, frustration, and, sometimes, job loss or even violence. As mentioned earlier, Herr (1998) lists the many health consequences of job stress or job loss: physiological, psychological, emotional, and behavioural problems (problems that extend beyond the worker to families, friends, and communities).

Although it is impossible for every worker to be blissfully employed, many workers spend numerous years working before finding their niche. Making it possible for more individuals to make informed and considered career decisions could shorten the time (and the attendant health consequences) of occupational mismatch.

By increasing the proportion of employees well-matched to their work, employers would save on health care costs, and families would realize both tangible and intangible benefits.

If less money were required for 'vocationogenic' illness, more money would be available for the unavoidable health issues faced by workers and their families.

Lower incarceration and criminal justice costs

Reduced unemployment and job stress coupled with increased achievement and self esteem would lead to fewer property crimes and would reduce the incidence of workplace violence. A one-percent reduction in crime would reduce the prison population and would save over one and one-half billion dollars per year (Bureau of Justice Statistics, not dated) for direct costs of criminal justice, not including the savings from reduced social work, police, and social welfare costs.

Increased Worker Productivity

People who make informed and considered career decisions make committed and engaged workers. People who make informed and considered career decisions have greater ownership of their work roles, persist in the face of adversity, take initiative, and invest in their ongoing professional development. They are better collaborators, more likely to get along with their co-workers and supervisors, and more likely to add value to whatever enterprise in which they engage. All of these qualities add up to increased productivity.

Disabilities in Vocational Development

The current high rates of unemployment and underemployment of individuals with disabilities is evidence that traditional approaches to career development and transitions planning have not adequately met the needs of persons with disabilities. An individual's family and significant others have been recognized as having major impact on career development, although the ongoing dynamics of family influence on career development are not fully understood. Currently, there is a lack of a conceptual framework to guide professionals in developing programmes to utilize the family as a resource in the career development of individuals with disabilities.

Career Planning

Supervisors should discuss career expectations with each employee, including an evaluation of the employee's interest, talents and skills in relation to the requirements of available jobs. If an employee's career goals seem unachievable, the supervisor should provide constructive feedback and try to reach an agreement with the employee on appropriate goals and the path to achieving them. However, the supervisor should not assume an employee's disability will be a barrier.

Team Building

Team building opportunities give employees chances to solve problems and develop solid working relationships with co-workers. Supervisors should ensure that employees have leadership opportunities and are assigned to special projects, planning sessions, off-site projects, and assignments requiring travel. Do not make career development decisions for an employee based on limiting concepts or stereotypes about that employee.

Networking

Employees should be included in both formal work groups and informal employee gatherings. People with disabilities enjoy the same types of social and recreational activities as employees without disabilities. Often, important business may be discussed at these events and interpersonal relationships are developed. All employees should be given the opportunity to participate. It is critical to arrange events in accessible facilities and arrange transportation to accommodate staff with disabilities.

Mentoring

Mentoring individuals builds human capital. Mentoring experiences prepare individuals for advancement by strengthening their skills and providing them with confidence. Individuals with disabilities continue to face attitudinal barriers in employment.

The mentoring process can help break down employment barriers by encouraging individuals to take a more active role in planning and pursuing their careers.

Employees with Disabilities should be encouraged to find mentors, whether or not the mentor has a disability. Mentors provide many benefits such as:

- Broadened perspectives about the transferability of skills and interest, as well as future career directions to consider.
- Motivation to take calculated risks.
- Advice on the "politics" of dealing with human relationships within the organization.
- Coaching on technical, interpersonal, and management skills.
- Encouragement.
- Networking contacts, references, and introductions.

Training

The organization should ensure that training opportunities are available to employees with disabilities. Formal classes must be held in accessible facilities.

Materials should be available in large print for persons who are visually impaired, interpreters should be provided for participants who are hearing-impaired, and other necessary accommodations made. Employees with disabilities should request any such accommodations.

Self-Development

All employees must take responsibility for their own career development. Employees should continually seek out new education, training and information. They should keep up on the latest information in the field, network and volunteer for new assignments.

The synthesizing process

Children and youth progress through a career development process as they mature. It consists of four stages: Career Awareness, Career Exploration, Career Preparation, and Career Placement. Adults also continue to grow and develop in their careers as they age, albeit at a slower rate than children. Adults usually enter the final development process (the career placement stage) in the latter stages of their secondary or post-secondary educational experiences. They then gradually progress through an additional two stages: Career Maintenance and Career Mentoring. However, adults who acquire a disability (e.g. adventitiously blinded adults) may need to cycle back through some of the stages of the career development process. This is because they initially progressed through the process as fully sighted people and may have many of the same misperceptions as the general public about what a person can do with limited or no sight.

Following the acquisition of disability-specific skills, it's important for adults who lose vision to re-assess themselves in terms of the career development process. They will need time, in much the same way that children and adolescents need time, to move through the six stages. The difference is that adventitiously blinded adults will not need as much time to go through the first four stages of the process as children do.

The Six Stages of the Career Development Process

Career Awareness: Children experience the career awareness stage as they learn about themselves and what they enjoy doing (interests), what they can do particularly well (abilities), and learn what's important to them (values or beliefs).

It's during the career awareness stage that children also learn about the world of work: what jobs are available in the community, what jobs their parents and other significant adults in their lives are doing, and what tasks are inherent to these different types of jobs. For children who are blind or partially sighted, it's important to let them explore tools, materials, and activities associated with domestic chores and to give them responsibilities when they are old enough to do tasks around the house. It's also important to describe what others are doing outside of their visual or tactual range – what tasks they are performing, what they are wearing, what tools they are using, etc. – so that they can learn about jobs and job tasks though this kind of casual or "incidental" exposure.

Career Exploration: The next stage is career exploration and this is when children begin to investigate the careers that are of interest to them. They learn the skills that are required and how to develop their knowledge, skills, and abilities to enter career fields that appeal to them.

They read biographies or autobiographies of famous people and learn about their careers, watch movies or television shows with characters performing in different jobs, observe adults doing things that they'd like to be doing (e.g., performing music or competing in athletics), and ask adults questions about jobs of interest and the careers associated with them. During the career exploration stage, children are trying to sort the roles they see adults playing and determine which of those roles might suit them.

This is the time that they explore their talents and determine how others are using similar skills and abilities in careers. It's important that children actively engage in community-based functions such as field trips or "take your child to work" days to encourage them to investigate topics and tasks related to career opportunities. They need to attend performances in areas of interest, participate in recitals and competitions, or join teams to see how their performance compares to their same-aged peers.

Career Preparation: In the career preparation stage, children and youth gather the knowledge they will need to perform in their careers, including the basic literacy skills necessary to function in modern society and work successfully in an information age. In addition, they continue to refine their basic work competencies such as learning different organizational techniques and expected work behaviours such as following instructions.

During the career preparation stage, they also refine their skills and abilities through participation in school and community activities; as well as, at home with chores as they assume more and more responsibility with age.

All children have areas of innate ability. It's during the career preparation stage that they determine which of their natural abilities or talents they want to strengthen through practice and training to a point that they can compete with others whose talents are comparable. It's during this stage that adolescents decide whether to prepare for further academic training following their secondary school programmes, pursue vocational skills training, or go to work.

Through engagement at school, chores at home and activities in the community, such as volunteer experiences, youth develop skills that will transfer to future work environments and prepare them for their careers.

Career Placement: Career placement is the stage that is most often experienced during late adolescence and early adulthood, when young adults land their first job outside of their homes for pay. They typically work at a variety of jobs, "trying them on for size". It's through placement into jobs that young people learn what employers expect of them, how to be responsible and contributing members of society, as well as the value of doing work for remuneration (whether it's money or the more subtle benefits received through apprenticing such as skill development and gaining experience).

They also have the opportunity through such engagement to secure references from people outside of their immediate families who can vouch for their ability to perform on a job. This access to prospective references is a critical factor for youth with disabilities as employers tend to pay more attention to references from other employers than to those received from friends and family.

Career Maintenance: The career maintenance stage follows the successful landing of a job. During this stage, the worker settles into a pattern, becoming comfortable with job duties and co-workers and finding a balance between work and play. Adults who successfully manage their careers typically map out where they'd like to be over time and strive to achieve those goals.

The skills required to maintain employment are largely social (learning to get along with co-workers, customers or clients) and, to a lesser degree, vocational (learning the knowledge and work-related skills to perform well and consistently meet productivity standards). Learning social skills is critical for individuals because if their co-workers, customers or clients like them, they will help them keep their jobs – if they don't, they will work against them, either overtly or covertly, and maintaining employment will be a challenge.

While adults may change jobs a number of times over the course of their working lives, it's imperative that those changes be as positive as possible (moving to a new job because of an improved opportunity, a chance to assume more responsibility, or relocating to a new community). To maintain a career, it's important to consider how jobs people have had and are doing relate to their overall career objectives and goals.

If an individual's job doesn't connect to their long-term career goals, it's like starting over with each move to a new job. If individuals must re-career due to downsizing or an injury or illness, they need to be prepared to discuss how the work they've performed previously has transferability to their new career goals.

Career Mentoring: When adults near the end of their working lives, they often have the opportunity to mentor other workers and guide them in their career development process. This career mentoring stage can occur while an individual is still working or following retirement. The career mentoring stage is a time to prepare young people or people new to employment to the expectations and demands of a career field.

It's in the career mentoring stage where mature workers have an opportunity to share what they've learned that has enabled them to be successful in their jobs and set the stage for others to follow suit. Career mentoring may be thought of as succession planning: current workers teach those who will take their positions in the future.

Vocational Adjustment and General Adjustment.

When deciding on a career direction, consider whether your disability will affect your capacity to work in the career(s) you are interested in. The challenge in thinking about the effect of your disability on your future work life is to balance a realistic approach with a confidence that people with disability can and do work successfully in a wide range of fields. The effects of your disability should and need not be an unnecessary barrier to working in your dream career.

Here are some strategies for thinking about potential careers as a graduate with disability:

- Don't assume from initial information about the industry that you couldn't perform the work. Ask specific questions and seek advice. You might be surprised by the workplace adjustments that are possible and effective.
- Do a 'reality test' on whether work in your selected career can be adjusted to accommodate the effects of your disability in the workplace. Find out as much as possible about the daily work tasks usually involved in the industry and the job requirements. Think practically through the day to day realities of the tasks you would need to perform and the other requirements you would have to meet.

- Have a broad understanding of your right to workplace adjustments under anti-discrimination legislation and therefore what you can and should expect an employer to do to accommodate the effects of your disability at work.

What are Some Examples of Workplace Adjustments?

Examples of reasonable adjustments or workplace adjustments include:

- changes to recruitment and interview procedures (e.g. making the interview questions available in different formats: plain English, electronic, large print)
- changes to the work environment (e.g. making the work areas and facilities accessible to a worker in a wheelchair)
- changes to job design, work schedules or other work practices (e.g. flexibility with leave arrangements to enable a worker to attend medical appointments)
- changes to equipment (e.g. installing visual fire alarms for deaf workers)
- providing training or other help (e.g. extending training time for workers with a learning disability or intellectual disability)
- changing communication systems or information provided (e.g. having information available in written form and not just spoken at meetings)
- flexibility around hours of work (e.g. starting and finishing work later to enable a worker to work at the best time when their medication does not impact on the job).

7

Skill Development and Vocational Training

The foundations of growth in any economy are always based on the skills and knowledge of the human resources. This is a critical element to addressing the challenges and opportunities for growth in this highly competitive and globalised world. As India moves rapidly towards achieving ambitious economic and social targets, engaging the human resources for skills development will be critical for ensuring success as a knowledge economy.

For India the challenge magnifies due to unprecedented issues of scalability i.e. reaching out to 500 million by 2022 coupled with multiple challenges in implementation. Important here is to combine the efforts connect the dots and map the implementation frameworks to the strategic plans, especially when the entire country debates on planning and executing the 12th Five Year plan where skills development has been positioned as an obvious and urgent agenda cutting across all sectors. In light of this it is absolutely essential for all stakeholders to sit together, discuss, and debate the ambitions, challenges and solutions.

Skill Development

A skill is the learned ability to carry out a task with pre-determined results often within a given amount of time, energy, or both. In other words the abilities that one possesses. Skills can often be divided into domain-general and domain-specific skills. For example, in the domain of work, some general skills would include time management, teamwork and leadership, self motivation and others, whereas domain-specific skills would be useful only for a certain job. Skill usually requires certain environmental stimuli and situations to assess the level of skill being shown and used.

People need a broad range of skills in order to contribute to a modern economy. A joint ASTD and U.S. Department of Labour study showed that through technology, the workplace is changing, and identified 16 basic skills that employees must have to be able to change with it.

Labour Skills

Skilled workers have long had historical import as masons, carpenters, blacksmiths, bakers, brewers, coopers, printers and other occupations that are economically productive. Skilled workers were often politically active through their craft guilds.

Relative Supply of Skilled Labour

Education is an important factor in increasing skill level. The increase in number of people attending high schools and colleges contribute to the increase in the supply of skilled labour. Mass education, however, is not the only factor. Immigration is also a big contributor. Immigrants created a bimodal skill distribution, where most immigrants were either low skill or high skill workers. There were few who were in between.

Historical Reference - In the United States such factors have caused an overall increase in the supply of skilled labour during the 20th century. The shift from unskilled to skilled labour can be attributed to increases in human capital, or in other words increasing the efficiency of humans through investment in knowledge. The American boom in public education, specifically high schools, congruently increased the level of human capital and total factor productivity.

Relative Demand of Skilled Labour

One of the factors that increases the relative demand for skilled labour is attributed to the introduction of computers. In order to operate computers, workers must build up their human capital in order to learn how such a piece of machinery works.

Thus, there is an increase in the demand for skilled labour. In addition to the technological change of computers, the introduction of electricity also replaces man power (unskilled labour) which, in turn, also shifts out the demand curve.

Technology, however, is not the only factor. Trade and the effects of globalization also play a role in affecting the relative demand of skilled labour. One case includes a developed country purchasing imports from a developing country, which in turn replaces products made with domestic low-skilled labour. This, in turn, decreased the demand for low-skilled workers. Both of these factors, thus, increase the wages of highly skilled workers.

Life Skills

Life skills are problem solving behaviours used appropriately and responsibly in the management of personal affairs. They are a set of human skills acquired via teaching or direct experience that are used to handle problems and questions commonly encountered in daily human life. The subject varies greatly depending on societal norms and community expectations.

Enumeration and Categorization

UNICEF states "there is no definitive list" of life skills but enumerates many "psychosocial and interpersonal skills generally considered important." It asserts life skills are a synthesis: "many skills are used simultaneously in practice. For example, decision-making often involves critical thinking ("what are my options?") and values clarification ("what is important to me?"). Ultimately, the interplay between the skills is what produces powerful behavioural outcomes, especially where this approach is supported by other strategies..."

Life skills can vary from financial literacy, substance abuse prevention, to therapeutic techniques to deal with disabilities, such as autism. Life skills curricula designed for K-12 often emphasizes communications and practical skills needed for successful independent living for developmental disabilities/special education students with an Individualized Education Programme (IEP). However, some programmes are for general populations, such as the Overcoming Obstacles programme for middle schools and high schools.

Parenting 2.0 (P2.0), LinkedIn's largest parenting group with more than 2,700 members (as of March, 2013), defines Life Skills as all the non-academic foundational skills human beings learn and use to thrive individually and live optimally in community with others. P2.0's founder, Marlaine Paulsen Cover created a Life Skills Report Card that lists five basic skills categories:

- Personal care
- Organization
- Respect for self and others
- Communication
- Social skills and proposes that life skills should be considered as important as academic skills.

Parenting

Life skills are often taught in the domain of parenting, either indirectly through the observation and experience of the child, or directly with the purpose of teaching a specific skill. Yet skills for dealing with pregnancy and parenting can be considered and taught as a set of life skills of themselves. Teaching these parenting life skills can also coincide with additional life skills development of the child. Many life skills programmes are offered when traditional family structures and healthy relationships have broken down, whether due to parental lapses, divorce or due to issues with the children (such as substance abuse or other risky behaviour). For example, the International Labour Organization is teaching life skills to ex-child labourers and risk children in Indonesia to help them avoid the worst forms of child labour.

Youth: behaviour Prevention vs. Positive Development

While certain life skills programmes focus on teaching the prevention of certain behaviours the Search Institute has found those programmes can be relatively ineffective. Based upon their research The Family and Youth Services Bureau, a division of the U.S. Department of Health and Human Services advocates the theory of Positive Youth Development as a replacement for the less effective prevention programmes. Positive Youth Development, or PYD as it's come to be known as, focuses on the strengths of an individual as opposed to the older methods which tend to focus on the "potential" weaknesses that have yet to be shown. The Family and Youth Services Bureau has found that individuals who developed life skills in a positive, rather than preventive, manner feel a greater sense of competence, usefulness, power, and belonging.

Life Skill Development in Adults

Beyond the K-12 domain, other life skills programmes are focused on social welfare and social work programmes, such as Casey Life Skills. This programme covers diverse topics: career planning, communication, daily living, home life, housing and money management, self care, social relationships, work and study skills, work life, pregnancy and parenting.

People Skills

According to the *Portland Business Journal*, people skills are described as:

- understanding ourselves and moderating our responses
- talking effectively and empathizing accurately
- building relationships of trust, respect and productive interactions.

A British definition is "the ability to communicate effectively with people in a friendly way, especially in business." The term is not listed yet in major US dictionaries.

The term people skills is used to include both psychological skills and social skills, but is less inclusive than life skills.

Guidelines relating to what later generations eventually dubbed "people skills" have been recorded from very early times. Two examples of early human guidelines appear in the Old Testament. Leviticus 19:18 advises: "Do not seek revenge or bear a grudge against your people, but love your neighbour as yourself"; and Solomon's wisdom in Proverbs 15:1 includes: "A gentle answer turns away wrath, but a harsh word stirs up anger." However the Bible also condemns 'flattery' (Psalms 5:9).

Human-relations studies became a movement in the 1920s, as companies became more interested in the "soft skills" and interpersonal skills of employees. In organizations, improving people skills became a specialized role of the corporate trainer. By the mid-1930s, Dale Carnegie popularized people skills in *How to Win Friends and Influence People* and *How to Stop Worrying and Start Living* throughout the United States of America and later throughout the world.

In the 1960s, US schools introduced people-skills topics and methods—often as a way to promote better self-esteem, communication and social interaction. These encompassed psychologist Thomas Gordon's "Effectiveness Training" variations as well as many other training programmes. (By the 1980s, "traditional education" and a "back-to-basics" three-Rs emphasis largely pushed these programmes aside, with notable exceptions.) By 1974 the actual term "people skills" had come into use.

Educational Importance/impact

A significant portion of the deaths in the United States can be attributed to psychosocial deficits in people skills for stress management and supportive social connection. Business, labour and government authorities agree that wide-ranging people skills are necessary for 20th-century work success in the SCANS report. At least one foundation, Alliances for Psychosocial Advancements in Learning (APAL), has made support of SCANS-related people skills a major priority.

UNESCO research found that young people who develop speaking/listening skills and getting to know others have improved self-awareness, social-emotional adjustment and classroom behaviour; self-destructive and violent behaviour also were decreased. The Collaborative for Academic Social and Emotional Learning (CASEL) has identified 22 programmes in the US that are especially comprehensive in social-emotional learning coverage and effective in documented impacts.

Life Skills-based Education

Life skills have been defined by the World Health Organization (WHO) as "abilities for adaptive and positive behaviour that enable individuals to deal effectively with the demands and challenges of everyday life". They represent the psycho-social skills that determine valued behaviour and include reflective skills such as problem-solving and critical thinking, to personal skills such as self-awareness, and to interpersonal skills. Practicing life skills leads to qualities such as self-esteem, sociability and tolerance, to action competencies to take action and generate change, and to capabilities to have the freedom to decide what to do and who to be. Life skills are thus distinctly different from physical or perceptual motor skills, such as practical or health skills, as well as from livelihood skills, such as crafts, money management and entrepreneurial skills . Health and livelihood education however, can be designed to be complementary to life skills education, and vice versa.

Life Skills-Based Education (LSBE) has a long history of supporting child development and health promotionin many parts In 1986, the Ottawa Charter for Health Promotion recognized life skills in terms of making better health choices. The 1989 Convention on the Rights of the Child (CRC) linked life skills to education by stating that education should be directed towards the development of the child's fullest potential. The 1990 Jomtien Declaration on Education for All took this vision further and included life skills among essential learning tools for survival, capacity development and quality of life. The 2000 Dakar World Education Conference took a position that all young people and adults have the human right to benefit from "an education that includes learning to know, to do, to live together and to be", and included life skills in two out of the six EFA Goals.

Life skills-based education is now recognized as a methodology to address a variety of issues of child and youth development and thematic responses including as expressed in UNGASS on HIV/AIDS (2001), UNGASS on Children (2002), World Youth Report (2003), World Programme for Human Rights Education (2004), UN Decade on Education for Sustainable Development (2005), UN Secretary General's Study on Violence Against Children (2006), 51st Commission on the Status of Women (2007), and the World Development Report (2007).

Expected learning outcomes include a combination of knowledge, values, attitudes and skills with a particular emphasis on those skills that related to critical thinking and problem solving, self-management and communication and inter-personal skills.

Social Skills

Social skill is any skill facilitating interaction and communication with others. Social rules and relations are created, communicated, and changed in verbal and nonverbal ways. The process of learning such skills is called socialization.

Interpersonal skills are sometimes also referred to as people skills or communication skills. Interpersonal skills are the skills a person uses to communicate and interact with others. They include persuasion, active listening, delegation, and leadership.

The term "interpersonal skills" is used often in business contexts to refer to the measure of a person's ability to operate within business organizations through social communication and interactions. Interpersonal skills are how people relate to one another.

Causes of Deficits

Alcohol

Social skills are significantly impaired in people suffering from alcoholism due to the neurotoxic effects of alcohol on the brain, especially the prefrontal cortex area of the brain. The social skills that are impaired by alcohol abuse include impairments in perceiving facial emotions, prosody perception problems and theory of mind deficits; the ability to understand humour is also impaired in alcohol abusers. Impairments in social skills also occur in individuals who suffer from fetal alcohol spectrum disorders; these deficits persist throughout affected people's lives and may worsen over time due to the effects of ageing on the brain.

ADHD

Approximately half of ADHD children and adolescents will experience peer rejection compared to 10-15 percent of non-ADHD children. Adolescents with ADHD are less likely to develop close friendships, although it might be easier by the time adolescents age into adulthood and enter the workplace. Difficulties in sustaining romantic relationships may also occur in high school and college aged individuals with ADHD.

Training in social skills, behavioural modification and medication may have some limited beneficial effects; the most important factor in reducing emergence of later psychopathology is the ADHD individual forming friendships with people who are not involved in devient/delinquent activities and do not have other disabilities or symptoms similar to ADHD. Poor peer relationships can contribute to major depression, criminality, school failure, and substance use disorders. Adolescents with ADHD are more likely to find it difficult in making and keeping friends due to their attentional deficits causing impairments in processing verbal and nonverbal language which is important for social skills and adolescent interaction; this may result in such adolescents being regarded by their peers as immature or as losers. Romantic relationships are usually difficult in the adolescent and college age because of the lack of attention of non verbal cues such as flirting gestures, tone of voice, which may include misinterpretation if whether the person is romantically attracted to that person, along with the impulsiveness of "jumping into" relationships.

Autism

People with autistic spectrum disorders such as Asperger's Syndrome generally have difficulty with social skills. This is most likely the result of the lack of theory of mind, which enables the person to understand other people's emotions. Many people in the spectrum have many social idiosyncracies such as obsessive interests and routines, lack of eye contact, one sided conversations, abnormal body language and non-verbal communication.

In behaviour therapy

To behaviourists, social skills are learned behaviour that allow people to achieve social reinforcement. According to Schneider & Byrne (1985), who conducted a meta-analysis of social skills training procedures (51 studies), operant conditioning procedures for training social skills had the largest effect size, followed by modelling, coaching, and social cognitive techniques.

Behaviour analysts prefer to use the term behavioural skills to social skills. Behavioural skills training to build social and other skills is used with a variety of populations including in packages to treat addictions as in the community reinforcement and family training approach.

Training of behavioural skills is also used for people who suffer from borderline personality disorder, depression, and developmental disabilities. Typically behaviourists try to develop what are considered cusp skills, which are critical skills to open access to a variety of environments.

The rationale for this type of an approach to treatment is that people meet a variety of social problems and can reduce the stress and punishment from the encounter as well as increase their reinforcement by having the correct skills.

> *"Social skills can be measured on about how you treat other people and how you react to them. It's a matter of dealing with the people around you. Different tests will help you to provide and tell what kind of personality you have towards others. If you are in doubt of your behaviour, then you may be in touched with this kind of test. This would not help you totally, but this would serve as your guide in handling your personality towards the people whom you're reacting with." (Ledesma, 2009)*

Controversies

The concept of social skills has been questioned. The question is whether one response is needed or whether any response tailored in a context will meet the requirements. Romanczyk laid out a model of social acquisition for children with autism.

Soft Skills

Soft skills is a sociological term relating to a person's "EQ" (Emotional Intelligence Quotient), the cluster of personality traits, social graces, communication, language, personal habits, friendliness, and optimism that characterize relationships with other people. Soft skills complement hard skills which are the occupational requirements of a job and many other activities. Soft skills are personal attributes that enhance an individual's interactions, job performance and career prospects. Unlike hard skills, which are about a person's skill set and ability to perform a certain type of task or activity, soft skills relate to a person's ability to interact effectively with coworkers and customers and are broadly applicable both in and outside the workplace.

A person's soft skill EQ is an important part of their individual contribution to the success of an organization. Particularly those organizations dealing with customers face-to-face are generally more successful, if they train their staff to use these skills. Screening or training for personal habits or traits such as dependability and conscientiousness can yield significant return on investment for an organization. For this reason, soft skills are increasingly sought out by employers in addition to standard qualifications.

It has been suggested that in a number of professions, soft skills may be more important over the long term than occupational skills. The legal profession is one example where the ability to deal with people effectively and politely, more than their mere occupational skills, can determine the professional success of a lawyer.

Soft Skills are *behavioural* competencies. Also known as *Interpersonal Skills,* or *people skills,* they include proficiencies such as communication skills, conflict resolution and negotiation, personal effectiveness, creative problem solving, strategic thinking, team building, influencing skills and selling skills, to name a few.

Hard Skills

Hard skills are any skills relating to a specific task or situation. These skills are easily quantifiable unlike Soft skills which are related to one's personality.

Division of Labour

The division of labour is the specialisation of cooperating individuals who perform specific tasks and roles. Historically, an increasingly complex *division of labour* is associated with the growth of total output and trade, the rise of capitalism, and of the complexity of industrialised processes. The concept and implementation of division of labour has been observed in ancient Sumerian (Mesopotamian) culture, where assignment of jobs in some cities coincided with an increase in trade and economic interdependence. In addition to trade and economic interdependence, division of labour generally increases both producer and individual worker productivity.

In contrast to *division of labour*, division of work refers to the division of a large task, contract, or project into smaller tasks — each with a separate schedule within the overall project schedule. *Division of labour*, instead, refers to the allocation of tasks to individuals or organisations according to the skills and/or equipment those people or organisations possess. Often *division of labour* and division of work are both part of the economic activity within an industrial nation or organisation.

Global Division of Labour

There exist, as yet, few comprehensive studies of the global division of labour (an intellectual challenge for researchers), although the ILO and national statistical offices can provide plenty of data on request for those who wish to try.

In one study, Deon Filmer estimated that 2,474 million people participated in the global non-domestic labour force in the mid-1990s. Of these,

- around 15%, or 379 million people, worked in industry,
- a third, or 800 million worked in services, and
- over 40%, or 1,074 million, in agriculture.

The majority of workers in industry and services were wage & salary earners - 58 percent of the industrial workforce and 65 percent of the services workforce. But a big portion were self-employed or involved in family labour. Filmer suggests the total of employees worldwide in the 1990s was about 880 million, compared with around a billion working on own account on the land (mainly peasants), and some 480 million working on own account in industry and services. The 2007 ILO Global Employment Trends Report indicated that services have surpassed agriculture for the first time in human history: "In 2006 the service sector's share of global employment overtook agriculture for the first time, increasing from 39.5 per cent to 40 per cent. Agriculture decreased from 39.7 per cent to 38.7 per cent. The industry sector accounted for 21.3 per cent of total employment."

Globalization

The issue reaches its broadest scope in the controversies about globalization, which is often interpreted as a euphemism for the expansion of world trade based on comparative advantage. This would mean that countries specialise in the work they can do at the lowest cost. Critics however allege that international specialisation cannot be explained sufficiently in terms of "the work nations do best", rather this specialisation is guided more by commercial criteria, which favour some countries over others.

The OECD Recently Advised (28 June 2005) That: Efficient policies to encourage employment and combat unemployment are essential if countries are to reap the full benefits of globalization and avoid a backlash against open trade... Job losses in some sectors, along with new job opportunities in other sectors, are an inevitable accompaniment of the process of globalization... The challenge is to ensure that the adjustment process involved in matching available workers with new job openings works as smoothly as possible.

Modern Debates

In the modern world, those specialists most preoccupied in their work with theorizing about the division of labour are those involved in management and organization. In view of the global extremities of the division of labour, the question is often raised about what division of labour would be most ideal, beautiful, efficient and just.

It is widely accepted that the division of labour is to a great extent inevitable, simply because no one can do all tasks at once. Labour hierarchy is a very common feature of the modern workplace structure, but of course the way these hierarchies are structured can be influenced by a variety of different factors.

It is often agreed that the most equitable principle in allocating people within hierarchies is that of true (or proven) competency or ability. This important Western concept of meritocracy could be read as an explanation or as a justification of why a division of labour is the way it is.

In general, in capitalist economies, such things are not decided consciously. Different people try different things, and that which is most effective cost-wise (produces the most and best output with the least input) will generally be adopted. Often techniques that work in one place or time do not work as well in another. This does not present a problem, as the only requirement of a capitalist system is that you turn a profit.

Sexual Division of Labour

The clearest exposition of the principles of sexual division of labour across the full range of human societies can be summarized by a large number of logically complementary implicational constraints of the following form: if women of childbearing ages in a given community tend to do X (e.g., preparing soil for planting) they will also do Y (e.g., the planting) while for men the logical reversal in this example would be that if men plant they will prepare the soil. The 'Cross Cultural Analysis of the *Sexual Division of Labour* by White, Brudner and Burton (1977, public domain), using statistical entailment analysis, shows that tasks more frequently chosen by women in these order relations are those more convenient in relation to childrearing. This type of finding has been replicated in a variety of studies, including modern industrial economies.

These entailments do not restrict how much work for any given task could be done by men (e.g., in cooking) or by women (e.g., in clearing forests) but are only least-effort or role-consistent tendencies. To the extent that women clear forests for agriculture, for example, they tend to do the entire agricultural sequence of tasks on those clearings. In theory, these types of constraints could be removed by provisions of child care, but ethnographic examples are lacking.

New International Division of Labour

In economics the new international division of labour (NIDL) is an outcome of globalization. The term was coined by theorists seeking to explain the spatial shift of manufacturing industries from advanced capitalist countries to developing countries—an ongoing geographic reorganization of production, which finds its origins in ideas about a global division of labour. It is a spatial division of labour which occurs when the process of production is no longer confined to national economies. Under the "old" international division of labour, until around 1970, underdeveloped areas were incorporated into the world economy principally as suppliers of minerals and agricultural commodities. However, as developing economies are merged into the world economy, more production takes place in these economies.

This has led to a trend of transference, or what is also known as the "global industrial shift", in which production processes are relocated from developed countries (the USA, Europe and Japan) to developing countries in Asia (for example China, Vietnam and India) and Latin America. This is because companies search for the cheapest locations to manufacture and assemble components, so low-cost labour-intensive parts of the manufacturing process are shifted to the developing world where costs are substantially lower. Companies do so by taking advantage of transportation and communications technology, as well as fragmentation and locational flexibility of production. From 1953 to the late 1990s, the industrialized economies' share of world manufacturing output declined from 95% to 77%, and the developing economies' share more than quadrupled from 5% to 23%.

The resultant division of labour across continents closely follows the North–South socio-economic and political divide wherein the North—with one quarter of the world population—controls four fifths of the world income while the South—with three quarters of the world populations—has access to one fifth of the world income.

Vocational Development in 21st Century

The symbolism of the new millennium is particularly portentous for the career guidance profession. The profession is essentially a twentieth century creation. It was at the turn of this century that the first vocational guidance bureaux began to appear both in the USA andin Europe, and that the first major book in the field –Frank Parsons' posthumous classic,

Choosing a Vocation –was published. In historical terms, if one looks at it from a detached viewpoint, career guidance was a classic product of the late industrial era. It was at that point, where the traditional mechanisms of role allocation within social classes ceased to be sufficient to cope with the pace of economic and industrial change, that formal guidance services began to be developed to supplement them. The role of such services was to provide more formal and more flexible role allocation. Their methods reflected this role.

Within the industrial era, the field has been only weakly professionalised. Both here and in other countries, many of its practitioners are members of other professional groups –teachers, psychologists, labour market administrators. It is only a fairly small residual group who define themselves primarily as careers advisers or career counsellors. They include many worthy and dedicated individuals, but their work on the whole has remained undervalued. This is partly because the shape of people's careers has been largely dictated by selective organisational processes within the education and employment systems. The role of guidance has been to supplement and to lubricate these processes.

The Traditional Concept of Career

The traditional concept of career has been concerned with progression up an ordered hierarchy within an organisation or profession. If you ask most people what they understand by career, this is still the conception they hold. It is an essentially bureaucratic conception: neat and orderly. It is not without virtue. It provides order for individuals, giving them a secure basis for their lives. It provides order for society, because it ties individuals into social structures, rewarding them for their investment in those structures. It is meritocratic, allowing individuals to be promoted according to their abilities and achievements rather than the accidents of birth. It permits individual choice, particularly in choosing the particular ladder which the individual seeks to climb. It therefore requires careers advisers to help individuals in making these initial choices. Thereafter, however, the system requires little further lubrication from such advisers: it works of its own accord.

Our educational system, we should note, is still based on this model. It is heavily front-loaded. It is expected to select out and process young people, so that they emerge ready to set foot on their appointed ladder. The apparatus of course choices is part of this process. Careers advisers and teachers involved in guidance roles are its technicians. They may not like to think of themselves in this way, but in structural terms that is what they are: technicians, lubricating the system.

But this model is fragmenting –fast. It less and less describes the real world. There are fewer ladders around, and those that survive look less and less secure. The reason is the pace of change. Bureaucracies work well in a relatively static world, but they struggle to cope with change. And change is now endemic: particularly economic change, stemming from the globalisation of markets; and technological change, stemming from the pervasive impact of information and communication technologies. The result is that all organisations have to be prepared to change much more regularly and much more rapidly than ever before. They are therefore seeking more compact, more fluid and more flexible forms. Accordingly, they are less and less prepared to make long-term commitments to individuals. The orderly pathways are disappearing: as Robin Linnecar graphically put it, it's now more like crazy paving, which individuals are having to lay for themselves.

The effect can feel like anarchy, as the familiar landmarks disappear. Rifkin talks about the end of work; Bridges talks about the end of jobs. It is easy, too, to find people who talk about the end of career. Work has a critical role within all religions, as a way of making sense of our time on earth. But the structures through which it is organised are made by people, and they change. They took very different forms in pre-industrial eras than in the industrial era, and they are clearly going to take very different forms again in the post-industrial era into which we are now moving.

These new forms could be much creative, offering much more scope for the realisation of untapped human potential, than the models we have had hitherto. But only if we can find the concepts and the structures which will release this potential. I believe that a re-cast concept of career has a critical role to play in this respect.

The New Concept of Career

"Career", in my view, now needs to be redefined. Like many good words in the English language, it is richly ambiguous. It can describe neat progression up a hierarchy; but we also refer to "careering about". We need to redefine it as the individual's lifelong progression in learning and in work. Learning embraces all forms of learning: not only formal education, but training, and informal learning too. Work embraces all forms of work: not only employment, but self-employment, and unpaid work within the home and community as well. The challenge is the notion of "progression". Progression can take place laterally as well as vertically: it can incorporate elements of "careering about". But it retains the sense of development, of moving forward: career is more than mere biography. Learning is the key to progression in work. Our task is to help all individuals to interweave the two, on a lifelong basis.

This task is big business: indeed, it lies at the heart of the challenges with which governments are grappling as we approach the new millennium. The public debates are conducted largely in code. The key phrases used are three-fold: the need for labour market flexibility, for a skills revolution, and for avoiding social exclusion. We need labour-market flexibility in order to respond to change. We need a skills revolution –a raising of the skills of all our people –in order to be competitive in world markets. And we need to avoid social exclusion –marginalising particular groups of people –both because it is morally wrong and because it is enormously expensive in terms of its impact on drug usage, crime, and violence, which reduce the quality of life for all of us. The trouble is that the three goals tend to drive in different directions. Flexibility easily means increasing gaps between the work-rich and the work-poor: between those who can make it big, and those who are left to fight for survival. This increases social exclusion; it also means that many of those trying to make out on the edge of the labour market have no opportunity to enhance their skills.

"Lifelong learning" is now a widely-heard mantra. What the use of the word "career" does is to link lifelong learning to work, to add the element of progression, and to ground both firmly in the individual. But for people to understand the new concept, and to see it as applying to all, requires major changes in their mind-set. Certainly in the UK, many people are locked into the old concept, seeing "career" as describing the past rather than the future, as applying to "them" rather than to "us". Those involved in career guidance need to be at the forefront of efforts to change the mind-set. And that requires an active involvement in public policy.

Policy used to be about structures and systems: about setting up government interventions administered by government bureaucracies. Now, increasingly, it is about enabling processes: about working with, and seeking to influence, the enterprise and energies of many other people and organisations. It is about ensuring that public interests are met, as far as possible, through private actions, but influencing these actions to ensure that they collectively meet the long-term interests of all, rather than the short-term interests of the few. That is why words like "partnerships" are nowadays rife in public-policy documents. Career guidance services need to be parts of these partnerships, bringing their distinctive expertise to the table.

One of the powerful elements careers advisers bring with them is their understanding of the importance of so-called "soft" interventions which work through people rather than on them. All their professional activities are interventions of this kind. Just as employers are becoming increasingly aware of the importance of soft process skills alongside hard technical skills, so policy-makers need to become more aware of the power and significance of soft policy interventions. Most policy-makers still find it difficult to get hold of them: they tend to be locked into structural mind-sets, into system-think rather than person-think. The career guidance profession can help them to adapt to the softer ways of thinking. And in doing so, it can help them to understand the importance of its own work as soft policy interventions.

This is critical for the profession, because without policy attention and support, its work looks vulnerable. Viewed from a distance, much of it seems very much like a relic from the late industrial era. In all countries, career guidance systems are still heavily concentrated around the exit point from full-time education into the world of work. Their information systems, whatever they call them, still tend to be occupational systems rather than career systems. They describe a world of work ordered neatly into occupations and organisations, with neatly-defined entry points framed in terms of educational qualifications. We all know that the world of work is much more complex and dynamic than this more messy, in fact –but in seeking to tidy it up to make it comprehensible, the profession tends to fall back on the old models.

The risk is that what it is left with is a fading role within a fading structure. Schools, in particular, look more and more like industrial-era remnants. We still herd pupils into schools, just as we used to herd workers into factories. Attendance is mandatory: no "hot desks" here. Information is transmitted by teacher to pupil, rather than building systems around the power of information technology. Motivation is based extrinsically on gaining access to pieces of paper which provide passports to enter the world of work. Careers advisers are gatekeepers, checking the visas.

The profession needs therefore to get serious about promoting what it can offer, and to ensure that it is based on a cutting edge understanding of the transformations that are taking place in the world of work. In my view, it has a critical role to play in helping both individuals and organisations to adapt to the transformations. In this sense, it is an agent of change not in a naively radical 1960s sense but in dancing with the rhythms of historical change. In schools, for example, it should be at the forefront of helping schools to think through the implications of the new world of work for their structures and their curriculum. It also needs to ensure that young people when they emerge from schools are equipped with the career management skills which will enable them to construct their careers. This is a far more demanding role than just slotting them into university or college courses. It needs to start in primary school, not at the end of secondary school. It is essentially about learning, and learning accordingly now needs to be at the heart of career development theories.

Today more than ever, hostile markets, reorganizations and mergers, a maturing workforce, and flattened career and leadership ladders threaten the existence of organizations. Issues of recruitment and retention have moved from backrooms to boardrooms. Human assets drive the locomotive of business success and we are in a full-throttle, knowledge economy. The stronger our people, the stronger our corporations. "It is the dedication, motivation, knowledge and skill sets of individuals that make a tremendous difference in the organization."

Vocational Development programmes help connect personal passion with meaningful and important work that drives organizations. In a study of 1500 companies, Lowell Bryan and Claudia Joyce found that companies with a large percentage of employees who are engaged in problem solving rather than repetitive work are delivering enormous profits. They found that "profit-per-employee" in thinking-intensive organizations was $30,000 more than competitors in the same industry. The authors extrapolate that a hundred thousand of such employees could potentially deliver tens of billions of dollars in increased revenues by effectively mobilizing knowledge and skills. They assert that organizations that fail to fully develop human assets are in jeopardy of losing competitive advantage. Bryan and Joyce.

The Purpose and Importance of Vocational Development Programmes

Vocational Development is a two-way street between organizations and employees. Managers are the communication links and coaches. Companies and employees must be able to bend and not break in the face of economic storms. Successful organizations have flexible employees who are ready to meet the changing needs of the economy. Organizations need to communicate the mission, strategies, pressing problems and engage employees in meaningful work in this changing global environment. Careers are fluid. People may work anywhere at anytime, but to be productive and effective, they need to be grounded in knowledge of the industry, and in the core technologies and local cultures. We have been designing and implementing CD Programmes for over twenty years – the precursor of talent management systems. The purpose of these programmes today is the same as twenty years ago.

Roles and Responsibilities

Successful CD programmes assure that each player fulfills their role and responsibilities.

Employees: Individual employees are responsible for initiating their own career planning by communicating their value and contribution to the organization, and by assessing their current job satisfaction. It is up to employees to identify their skills, values, and interests; discuss their expectations with their managers; and seek out information about career options.

Peter Drucker believes that, "Success in the knowledge economy comes to those who know themselves - their strengths, their values and how they best perform." He asserts that workers need to recognize who they are, identifying their strengths and recognizing their values. Workers must be aware of their vision and the optimum role they play to achieve productivity and success. "Organizations need to understand the abilities and skills of employees and help them play the most effective roles possible." Peter Drucker.

Leaders and Managers: Managers are a critical link in the career development of their employees. While not expected to be career development experts, leaders and managers can provide vital support for employee career planning. They should encourage employees to take responsibilities for their careers, support them in their realistic personal assessments and provide them with clear and honest feedback about current performance and its implications for future development. They should communicate the formal and informal politics of the organization culture, provide exposure for employees, and connect them with appropriate resources.

Leaders, managers and experts play central roles in identifying the natural strengths of their people while directing their teams to work in a zone of passion and zeal. Through Town Meetings, strategy sessions, business round-tables, and task teams, leaders and managers can design work experiences and stretch assignments that assure individuals are challenged and connecting with critical people in the critical knowledge areas.

Organizations: Organizations are responsible for providing key information on organizational mission, policies, and future directions as well as on current options and possibilities. Organizations provide tools and support for employee self-assessment, training, education, and development. Leaders and rewards systems need to reinforce managers' roles in career development. Existing HR systems and policies as well as new systems can be integrated to create a universal talent management architecture that addresses specific target groups and business needs.

Valerie Matthews writes that over a twenty year span, she had witnessed "Career development programmes that included performance management, employment development, career planning, management assessment, internal staffing, external recruitment, succession planning, high potential resource management and career transition programmes." She states that "The programmes were intended to support the development of all employees and promote retention of key resources. The ultimate objective was to ensure and sustain a supply of qualified resources for positions at all levels." In the battle to retain high levels of knowledge and skill, she reportedly saw one programme after another implode causing disastrous casualties and resulting in costly replacement of many valuable employees. The greatest losses were the skills and knowledge that walked out the door with them. Valerie Matthews.

Career Development Programmes that work build a common language and philosophy that guide leaders, managers and employees to achieve the mission and strategy that run the organization. Know-how, know-why, and know-who are about human assets. Career Development is part and parcel of working in the knowledge economy. Mentors, managers and leaders in the industry guide careers into learning areas that grow the business.

Benefits of Career Development Programmes

The importance of Career Development Programmes cannot be underestimated. In the past thirty years, hundreds of organizations have developed programmes and tools to enhance careers. The tools continue to change, but the basic principles set out in our book, "Designing Career Development Systems," remain sound and successful. Farren et als. Businesses have achieved robust success utilizing the ABC's of Career Development Systems.

Programmes start small but are designed to move enterprise-wide and provide the following benefits:

- Provide a common framework and language for career development and talent management.
- Build an engaging partnership between employees, managers and the organization.

- Shift responsibility for career planning and professional development to individual contributors. Drive individual accountability.
- Highlight existing resources, programmes and HR processes.
- Showcase career mobility and advancement options – not just when jobs are open.
- Provide a process for individual development.
- Increase bench strength in key professions and positions.
- Increase skill development and knowledge in core functional areas.
- Increase the quality and frequency of individual career development and performance discussions.
- Increase confidence and skill for managers to host effective career and development discussions.
- Increase employee engagement, satisfaction and retention.

Business Needs and Drivers of Career Development Programmes

The specific drivers of Career Development Programmes have changed over the past twenty years. In the beginning we were developing career planning frameworks and tools that worked in large organizations and provided training and education to employees and managers. In the early days, our primary purpose was to clarify the roles of the organization, managers and employees and build support structures for the organization that maximized passion and talent. We partnered to assure a common language and framework that would support retention and mobility and that would help mangers assure "right people in the right places." Putting career development in the hand of individuals rather than vocational counsellors was a breakthrough. Skilling managers in career discussions rather than performance discussions was a challenge. Making succession planning criteria, career paths and strategic organization information available to all broke the previous parental mindset. And some of these breakthroughs are still needed in many organizations. Linking Career Development Programmes to strategic business needs and issues has been a constant in our consulting practice throughout these twenty years.

Different Business Needs and Drivers in the Organizations

Retention in a Downsizing Environment: A Telecommunications Company understands the business need for retaining talent during times of change and potential downsizings. Toward that end, the company offers a wealth of career development tools and resources to both employees and managers. Using a robust web portal, career assessment tools and career options information is available 24/7. Key business drivers include retention, employee engagement, and the need to continuously build and grow internal talent and bench strength.

Employer of Choice - Brand Recognition

A Financial Services Company knows the importance of brand recognition to customers as well as employees. Being an "employer is a strategic goal of this company. As the battle for talent is waged, this organization provides career information, tools, and resources to all employees. Managers have learned to highlight career mobility and redeployment options in their development discussions as the company grows, downsizes, and rightsizes. The company even provides assessments tools on the "careers" section of their internet site so that potential employee candidates can see "where they best fit in" to the talent required to keep the company a leader in their industry.

Succession Planning

A National Association seeks to enhance the depth and consistency for succession planning with the top two levels of the organization. They've built a common framework and approach for discussing and evaluating talent. The top hundred leaders are participating in coaching sessions to become more skilled in having career discussions with their colleagues. The organization implements a talent building framework in order to address their issues.

Retention of Key Talent

A Technology Company has been losing key talent in one of their primary professional disciplines. In order to highlight career opportunities and progression, the company built a robust leadership and technical competency model linked to development experiences and training. As a first step, the company introduced this information to potential employees through a career development programme with rich assessment tools. Managers of the high potential individuals are also introduced to this information in tandem with skill building components on how to host engaging and effective career and professional development discussions.

Merger Preparation

A Large Energy Company prepares for a merger with a large utility company. Given the anticipated changes and need for proactive integration, the organization built the foundation for career information and professional development opportunities throughout the business, using a web-based career portal. The company engaged individuals to drive their careers during the change and increased managers' effectiveness to coach and guide their people.

Downsizing Preparation

A Government Agency prepared for downsizing given the reduction in the production of their product. Other government agencies in the area struggle to find qualified talent for growing roles. In order to support employees to redeploy to other government agencies, the organization built a career services centre that included career workshops, individual web-based assessments, and career counselling services to support employees with job search and transition.

Each of these examples were driven by differing needs. Solutions were designed to fit the unique culture and existing Human Resource systems and were carefully crafted to maximize the roles of all stakeholders, organizational systems, and leadership.

In each case, the underlying driver was to assure a talent pool ready to take on present and future challenges. Survey after survey reveal that large corporations are not developing vital leadership skills. The Wall Street Journal reported that "Some 60% of companies have no succession planning of any kind, according to a survey of several thousand members of the Society of Human Resources Management."

Finding the right solutions to business challenges and entrenched cultures generally requires a consultative approach. The best engagement strategy is a carefully woven fabric blending employee's aspirations with the future needs of the organization. There are many ways to assure the passion and productivity that come from a good career fit between the individual and the organization.

Design Principles

Needs might vary but several Career Development design principles remain the same.

Provide Critical Organization Information – people can't plan in a vacuum. What are some of the products, services, breakthroughs that will be critical for the future? What trends in the industry and organization will most impact talent requirements in the near future? What professions, trades or functional areas are key to achieving mission and strategies? What innovations/changes would make the organization more successful? What positions/business units are growing? Shrinking? What have been typical career paths? What are the functional competencies required for success? When all people are seeing and discussing similar information, there will be a coalescence of opportunities, learning and breakthroughs of knowledge.

Involve Key Stakeholders – people are responsible for their own destinies. Developing and implementing a career development programme involves change. The people most closely affected are the experts. Leaders need to be involved and engaged along the way. Awareness and education takes time. Create advisory groups, implementation teams, pilot groups, manager champions to consult to design and development. Start small but work with the most influential people to guarantee a lasting change.

Use Multiple Delivery Methods – people learn in different ways. The most successful programmes have combined career web portals for information and self-assessment, workshops, virtual seminars, career resource centres and/or career coaches. Integrate with existing HR systems and websites. Leverage existing programmes and add career development modules to performance management, on-boarding, career pathing, leadership development, succession planning, etc..

Customize to Your Unique Culture – assure that the look and feel "fits" your organization. Develop a name or brand that inspires and sets a vision. Determine some uncharacteristic strategies that will get attention and produce real change.

Provide Individual Career Assessment Tools – People are shaky about the current financial and career landscape. Although some customer service jobs are returning to the United States, others are at risk because of the housing and lending industries. As we know, talented people frequently leverage shaky times to improve their careers. Leaders and managers are in a unique position to offer their employees career tools to help them prepare for a recession.

Work in the 21st Century

The nature and structure of careers is changing quickly, and with that evolution, the area of career development has become more important, and more challenging, than ever. The title of Douglas Hall and Associates' recent book on careers, *The Career is Dead-Long Live the Career*, captures some of the uncertainty that exists during this period of transition in career definition. This column includes my observations about the factors that are affecting the nature of careers, some of the ways in which careers are changing, how the practice of career development is changing in response, and some of the things I/O psychologists can contribute in this area.

Why is the Nature of Careers Changing?

There are a number of factors related to changing organizational design and structure that are influencing changes in the nature of careers, including the flattening of organizations, increased reliance on teams, the changing nature of the employment contract, and the trend toward leaner companies.

As organizations become flatter, there are fewer jobs in middle and upper management, and the opportunity for traditional career advancement through "climbing the ladder" decreases. Many organizations that are becoming flatter are also developing an increased reliance on teams.

In some cases, teams are expected to take the place of middle managers, as the team members develop the ability to self-manage. In addition, jobs may be less clearly defined within a team environment, making career planning more difficult for employees used to seeing a linear career path.

The changing employment contract and the drive to be lean are factors that have reduced the stability of a traditional career, as well as affecting morale, loyalty, and employees' expectations. Employees cannot count on long-term commitment from their employer, nor can they necessarily count on their skills being valued in the job market.

How are Careers Changing?

Careers are changing in a number of specific ways. To name a few, people are less likely to remain in one job or area of specialization, effective performance in many jobs requires continuous learning and acquisition of new skills, people are less likely to remain employed by the same company, and the overall responsibility for developing and enhancing careers is shifting more heavily to the employee. These changes create an environment in which employees must reevaluate their capabilities and career plans regularly, and organizations are less likely to cultivate loyalty and commitment. Careers are more likely to be made up of lateral and diagonal moves; employees and employers alike are more likely to take risks when matching people and jobs, and the need for more creativity and dialogue about how to put employees' talents to use is growing. The shift in ownership or responsibility of careers and their development is a significant change. The Career Action Centre (in Palo Alto, CA) characterizes this transition as employees becoming more "career self-resilient" meaning that employees take more responsibility for, and control of, their careers, and develop resilience to the sometimes negative effects of today's world of work. This organization counsels people and organizations to accept the changing definition of careers and learn to succeed within it.

How are these Changes Affecting the Practice of Career Development?

Today's practice of career development is likely to include continued development of creative approaches to skill building, more sophisticated assessment and development tools, links to other human resource systems, and increased clarity around providing value to both employees and the company.

Some of the approaches to skill building that seem to work well within today's organizations include cross-training and job rotation to provide people the opportunity to develop new skills or enhance existing skills in on-the-job situations, and mentoring programmes, which help people develop relationships that can assist their career success and growth.

Traditional mentoring programmes may assign people with more organizational experience and a higher job level as mentors to newer, lower level employees; given the speed with which organizational structures and needs are changing, mentoring programmes may need to take new forms in order to assign mentors who can help employees navigate careers in fast-paced, ever changing organizations.

Assessment and development tools are becoming more sophisticated. Many of the assessment tools include multi-rater feedback, while new development tools structure tailored development plans around on-the-job opportunities in combination with formal learning opportunities.

In addition, many of today's tools are part of integrated human resource software packages. For example, performance management systems with a career development component reinforce the organization's commitment to the development of individuals beyond the requirements of the job. Training and career development are often linked, as well. Employees receiving feedback on a career-related assessment may be directed to particular internal training programmes-all within a single software application.

Most career development programmes can be seen to have a clear dual-focus-individual and organizational. Career development programmes work for individuals by providing support, career planning services, and learning opportunities. The programmes serve the organizations by developing internal talent, supporting succession planning efforts, and working to counter low morale associated with uncertainty and instability.

This last factor, countering low morale, may explain some of the increase in interest paid to career development. As organizations become less willing (and able) to offer job security, they are searching for other ways to show the employees that they are valued, and one of those ways is to support employees in their efforts to become and remain competitive and fully employable-inside or outside of the company. Having the opportunity to develop their skills may help employees develop their self-esteem; in Manuel London's recent book on careers, Brockner and Lee refer to career development as self-affirming.

What Can I/O psychologists Contribute to Career Development?

Our knowledge and skills can inform career development efforts in a number of ways, including: creating assessment methods and development tools, assisting in human resource planning activities, identifying career paths, and conducting high quality programme evaluation. At the core of career development is assessment of individuals' skills and capabilities.

The quality of career advice given is largely dependent on the accuracy and thoroughness of the assessment conducted, and our work in designing assessment tools for skills that are required in today's careers and organizations is critical. Once advice is given, career development programmes usually try to help employees respond to identified developmental needs, through guidance, development tools, or a combination of the two. Our work in the area of skill development and learning can help ensure that when people work to develop their skills, they will be more likely to succeed.

Effective career development programmes are informed by sound human resource planning. Through planning, companies can identify the skills that will be needed in the future, the areas of job growth anticipated, and existing competencies that will no longer be required. A career development programme informed by this type of information can serve employees better by directing them toward areas that the company will need and value, and can serve the organization better by developing internal talent to meet future needs. We can bring our techniques (e.g., future job analysis and work analysis) to human resource planning, and increase the quality of this information.

Another area where our expertise is important is career planning. We can use our knowledge of job design and organizational design to identify logical connections among jobs that can form meaningful career paths. For example, by identifying the skill requirements of multiple job families within a company, we may be able to identify jobs for which a similar requirement profile exists, even if the titles and organizational locations are very different.

Finally, as with any organizational intervention, evaluation of career development programmes is important. The programmes require significant amounts of employee and managerial time, as well as a substantial financial investment in many cases. We can design evaluation processes to learn what is working well, and what is not, to inform the improvement of the programmes and to assist them in delivering the individual and organizational support they are designed to provide.

Changing job Market and State of Education

Economic and social forces have churned up a perfect storm for higher education. Consequently, the university of the future may bear little resemblance to education today.

Economic Globalization and World of Work

Globalization is the process by which markets integrate worldwide. Over the past 60 years, it has accelerated steadily as new technologies and management expertise have reduced transportation and transaction costs and as tariffs and other man-made barriers to international trade have been lowered.

The impact has been stunning. More and more developing countries have been experiencing sustained growth rates of 7-10 percent; 13 countries, including China, have grown by more than 7 percent per year for 25 years or more. Although this was unclear at the outset, the world now finds itself just past the midpoint in a century-long process in which income levels in developing countries have been converging toward those in developed countries. Now, the emerging economies' impact on the global economy and the advanced economies is rising rapidly.

Until about a decade ago, the effects of globalization on the distribution of wealth and jobs were largely benign. On average, advanced economies were growing at a respectable rate of 2.5 percent, and in most of them, the breadth and variety of employment opportunities at various levels of education seemed to be increasing. With external help, even the countries ravaged by World War II recovered. Imported goods became cheaper as emerging markets engaged with the global economy, benefiting consumers in both developed and developing countries.

But as the developing countries became larger and richer, their economic structures changed in response to the forces of comparative advantage: they moved up the value-added chain. Now, developing countries increasingly produce the kind of high-value-added components that 30 years ago were the exclusive purview of advanced economies. This climb is a permanent, irreversible change. With China and India — which together account for almost 40 percent of the world's population — resolutely moving up this ladder, structural economic changes in emerging countries will only have more impact on the rest of the world in the future.

By relocating some parts of international supply chains, globalization has been affecting the price of goods, job patterns, and wages almost everywhere. It is changing the structure of individual economies in ways that affect different groups within those countries differently. In the advanced economies, it is redistributing employment opportunities and incomes.

For most of the postwar period, U.S. policymakers assumed that growth and employment went hand in hand, and the U.S. economy's performance largely confirmed that assumption. But the structural evolution of the global economy today and its effects on the U.S. economy mean that, for the first time, growth and employment in the United States are starting to diverge. The major emerging economies are becoming more competitive in areas in which the U.S. economy has historically been dominant, such as the design and manufacture of semiconductors, pharmaceuticals, and information technology services. At the same time, many job opportunities in the United States are shifting away from the sectors that are experiencing the most growth and to those that are experiencing less. The result is growing disparities in income and employment across the U.S. economy, with highly educated workers enjoying more opportunities and workers with less education facing declining employment prospects and stagnant incomes. The U.S. government must urgently develop a long-term policy to address these distributional effects and their structural underpinnings and restore competitiveness and growth to the U.S. economy.

Jobless in the U.s.

Between 1990 and 2008, the number of employed workers in the United States grew from about 122 million to about 149 million. Of the roughly 27 million jobs created during that period, 98 percent were in the so-called nontradable sector of the economy, the sector that produces goods and services that must be consumed domestically. The largest employers in the U.S. nontradable sector were the government (with 22 million jobs in 2008) and the health-care industry (with 16 million jobs in 2008).

Together, the two industries created ten million new jobs between 1990 and 2008, or just under 40 percent of total additions. (The retail, construction, and hotel and restaurant industries also contributed significantly to job growth.) Meanwhile, employment barely grew in the tradable sector of the U.S. economy, the sector that produces goods and services that can be consumed anywhere, such as manufactured products, engineering, and consulting services. That sector, which accounted for more than 34 million jobs in 1990, grew by a negligible 600,000 jobs between 1990 and 2008.

Dramatic, new labour-saving technologies in information services eliminated some jobs across the whole U.S. economy. But employment in the United States has been affected even more by the fact that many manufacturing activities, principally their lower-value-added components, have been moving to emerging economies.

This trend is causing employment to fall in virtually all of the U.S. manufacturing sector, except at the high end of the value-added chain. Employment is growing, however, in other parts of the tradable sector — most prominently, finance, computer design and engineering, and top management at multinational enterprises. Like the top end of the manufacturing chain, these expanding industries and positions generally employ highly educated people, and they are the areas in which the U.S. economy continues to have a comparative advantage and can successfully compete in the global economy.

In other words, the employment structure of the U.S. economy has been shifting away from the tradable sector, except for the upper end of the value-added chain, and toward the nontradable sector. This is a problem, because the nontradable sector is likely to generate fewer jobs than is expected of it in the future.

Moreover, the range of employment opportunities available in the tradable sector is declining, which is limiting choices for U.S. workers in the middle-income bracket.

It would be unwise to assume that under present circumstances, employment in the government and health care in the United States will continue to grow as much as it had been growing before the recent economic crisis.

If anything, it is remarkable that the U.S. economy did not have much of an employment problem until the recent economic crisis. If the nontradable sector continues to lose its capacity to absorb labour, as it has in recent years, and the tradable sector does not become an employment engine, the United States should brace itself for a long period of high unemployment.

For What It's Worth

One way to measure the size of a company, industry, or economy is to determine its output. But a better way is to determine its added value — namely, the difference between the value of its outputs, that is, the goods and services it produces, and the costs of its inputs, such as the raw materials and energy it consumes. (Value added comes from the capital and labour that turn the inputs into outputs.) Goods and services themselves are often purchased as intermediate inputs by other companies or industries, legal services purchased by a corporation being one example. The value added produced by all the industries in all the sectors of an economy adds up to that country's GDP.

Unlike employment, value added in the tradable and nontradable parts of the U.S. economy has increased at a similar rate since 1990. In the nontradable sector, which experienced rapid employment growth, this means that value added grew slightly faster than employment: value added per employee increased modestly, by an annual average of 0.7 percent since 1990. On the tradable side of the U.S. economy, where employment levels barely increased, both value added overall and value added per employee rose very swiftly as the U.S. tradable sector moved up the value-added chain and grew in sync with the global economy. Whereas in the nontradable sector, value added per employee grew from $72,000 to over $80,000 between 1990 and 2008, in the tradable sector it grew from $79,000 to $120,000 — in other words, it grew by just about 12 percent in the nontradable sector but by close to 52 percent in the tradable sector.

Most striking are the trends within the tradable sector. Value added rose across that sector, including in finance, where employment increased, and in manufacturing industries, where employment mostly declined.

In fact, at the upper end of the manufacturing chain, value added increased so much that it outweighed the losses at the lower end caused by the movement of economic activity from the United States to other countries.

Value added represents income for someone. For employed people, it means personal income; for shareholders and other owners of capital, profit or returns on investment; for the government, tax revenues. Generally, the incomes of workers are closely correlated with value added per employee (this is not the case in the mining industry and utilities, however, where value added per employee is much higher than wages because these activities are very capital intensive and most value added is a return on capital).

Since value added in the nontradable part of the U.S. economy did not rise much, neither did average incomes in that sector. In the tradable sector, on the other hand, incomes rose rapidly along with value added per employee thanks both to rising productivity gains in some industries and the movement of lower-income jobs to other countries.

And since most new jobs were created in the nontradable part of the economy, in which wages grew little, the distribution of income in the U.S. economy became more uneven.

The overall picture is clear: employment opportunities and incomes are high, and rising, for the highly educated people at the upper end of the tradable sector of the U.S. economy, but they are diminishing at the lower end. And there is every reason to believe that these trends will continue.

As emerging economies continue to move up the value-added chain — and they must in order to keep growing — the tradable sectors of advanced economies will require less labour and the more labour-intensive tasks will shift to emerging economies.

Highly educated U.S. workers are already gravitating toward the high-value-added parts of the U.S. economy, particularly in the tradable sector. As labour economists have noted, the return on education is rising. The highly educated, and only them, are enjoying more job opportunities and higher incomes.

Competition for highly educated workers in the tradable sector spills over to the nontradable sector, raising incomes in the high-value-added part of that sector as well.

But with fewer jobs in the lower-value-added part of the tradable sector, competition for similar jobs in the nontradable sector is increasing. This, in turn, further depresses income growth in the lower-value-added part of the nontradable sector.

Thus, the evolving structure of the global economy has diverse effects on different groups of people in the United States. Opportunities are expanding for the highly educated throughout the economy: they are expanding in the tradable sector because the global economy is growing and in the nontradable sector because that job market must remain competitive with the tradable sector. But opportunities are shrinking for the less well educated.

Faced with an undesirable economic outcome, economists tend to assume that its cause is a market failure. Market failures come in many forms, from inefficiencies caused by information gaps to the unpriced impacts of externalities such as the environment.

But the effects on the U.S. economy of the global economy's structural evolution is not a market failure: it is not an economically inefficient outcome. (If anything, the global economy is generally becoming more efficient.) But it is nonetheless a cause for concern in that it is creating a distributional problem in the advanced economies. Not everyone is gaining in those countries, and some may be losing.

Although everyone does benefit from lower-priced goods and services, people also care greatly about the chance to be productively employed and the quality of their work. Declining employment opportunities feel real and immediate; the rise in real incomes brought by lower prices does not.

For example, according to recent surveys, a substantial number of Americans believe that their children will have fewer opportunities than they have had. The slow recovery from the recent economic crisis may be affecting these perceptions, which means that they might dissipate as the situation improves and growth returns. But the long-term structural evolution of the U.S. and global economies suggests that distributional issues will remain. These must be taken seriously.

Making it Work

Analysts have been quick to point out that not all the structural changes under way in the U.S. economy should be attributed to greater openness in the global economy.

Some important changes in employment patterns and income distribution are the result of labour-saving information technology and the automation of transactions. Automation has undoubtedly cut jobs in the information- and transaction-intensive parts of value-added chains throughout the U.S. economy, in both the tradable and the nontradable sectors. But if that were the only trend, why would employment decline so much more in manufacturing than in other industries?

One answer might be that information processing and automation occupy a more significant fraction of the value-added chain in manufacturing. But this is not true. Information-processing technology, for example, has eliminated jobs throughout the U.S. economy, including in finance, retail, and the government — all areas in which employment has grown.

The structural trends affecting the U.S. economy cannot be explained by changes in technology alone. To think otherwise tends to yield the misleading conclusions that technology, not the global economy, is the principal cause of the United States' employment challenge and that the most important forces operating on the structure of the U.S. economy are internal, not external. In fact, all these factors are relevant, with some more significant in some sectors of the economy than in others.

If giving technology as the preferred explanation for the U.S. economy's distributional problems is a way to ignore the structural changes of the global economy, invoking multinational companies (MNCs) as the preferred explanation is a way to overstate their impact. MNCs are said to underpay and otherwise exploit poor people in developing countries, exporting jobs that should have stayed in the United States.

MNCs do, indeed, play a central role in managing the evolution of the global economy. They are the principal architects of global supply chains, and they move the production of goods and services around the world in response to supply-chain and market opportunities that are constantly changing. MNCs have generated growth and jobs in developing countries, and by moving to those countries some lower-value-added parts of their supply chains, they have increased growth and competitiveness in advanced economies such as the United States. A June 2010 report by the McKinsey Global Institute estimated that U.S.-based MNCs accounted for 31 percent of GDP growth in the United States since 1990.

With ample labour available in various skill and educational categories throughout the tradable sector globally, companies have little incentive to invest in technologies that save on labour or otherwise increase the competitiveness of the labour-intensive value-added activities in advanced economies.

In short, companies' private interest (profit) and the public's interest (employment) do not align perfectly. These conditions might not last: if growth continues to be high in emerging economies, in two or three decades there will be less cheap labour available there. But two or three decades is a long time.

In the meantime, even though public and private interests are not perfectly aligned today, they are not perfectly opposed either. Relatively modest shifts at the margin could bring them back in sync. Given the enormous size of the global labour force, the dial would not need to be moved very much to restore employment growth in the tradable sector of the U.S. economy.

Specifically, the right combination of productivity-enhancing technology and competitive wage levels could keep some manufacturing industries, or at least some value-added pieces of their production chains, in the United States and other advanced countries.

But accomplishing this will require more than a decision from the market; it must also involve labour, business, and governments. Germany, for one, has managed to retain its advanced manufacturing activities in industrial machinery by removing rigidities in the labour market and making a conscious effort to privilege employment over rapid rises in incomes.

Wages may have increased only modestly in Germany over the past decade, but income inequality is markedly flatter there than in the United States, where it is higher than in most other industrial countries and rising steadily.

Conditioning access to the domestic market on domestic production is a form of protectionism and a way to try to limit the movement out of the country of jobs and of value-added components in the supply chain. This is more common than might be supposed.

It exists in the aerospace industry; and in the 1970s and 1980s, in the car industry, quotas on Japanese imports to the United States led to an expansion of the manufacture of Japanese cars in the United States. However, if the large economies — such as China, the European Union, Japan, or the United States — pursue protectionist measures on a broad front, the global economy will be undermined.

Yet that may be exactly what happens if employment challenges such as the ones affecting the United States are not tackled differently. With pressure on government budgets at all levels, rapidly rising health-care costs, a fragile housing market, the postcrisis effort to curb excess consumption and boost savings, and the risk of a second economic downturn, it is highly unlikely that net employment in the nontradable sector of the U.S. economy will continue to grow as rapidly as it has been.

The drop in domestic consumption in the United States has left the country with a shortage of aggregate demand. More public-sector investment would help, but the fiscal consolidation currently under way may make expanding government investment difficult. Meanwhile, because private-sector investment responds to demand and currently there is a shortfall in demand caused by the economic crisis and increased savings by households, such investment will not return until domestic consumption or exports increase.

Therefore, the United States will need to focus on increasing job growth in the tradable sector. Some growth will naturally come from the high-value-added part of that sector. The question is whether there will be enough growth and whether the educational attainment of U.S. workers will keep pace with rising job requirements at that level. There are reasons to be skeptical.

The Big Tradeoff

It is a common view that the market will solve the disparities in employment and incomes once the economic crisis recedes and growth is restored. Warren Buffet and other very smart, experienced, and influential opinion-makers say so clearly. But as this analysis suggests, they may not be right. And as long as their view dominates U.S. public policy and opinion, it will be difficult to address the issues related to structural change and employment in the United States in a systematic way. What is needed instead of benign neglect is, first, an agreement that restoring rewarding employment opportunities for a full spectrum of Americans should be a fundamental goal. With that objective as a starting point, it will then be necessary to develop ways to increase both the competitiveness and the inclusiveness of the U.S. economy. This is largely uncharted territory: distributional issues are difficult to solve because they require correcting outcomes on the global market without doing too much damage to its efficiency and openness. But admitting that not all the answers are known is a good place to begin.

With considerable uncertainty about the efficacy of various policy options, a multistakeholder, multipronged approach to addressing these distributional problems is best. The relevant knowledge about promising new technologies and market opportunities is dispersed among business, the government, labour, and universities, and it needs to be assembled and turned into initiatives. President Barack Obama has already appointed a commission, led by Jeffrey Immelt, the CEO of General Electric, to focus on competitiveness and employment issues in the U.S. economy. This is an important step forward. But it will be hugely difficult to invest in human capital, technology, and infrastructure as much as is necessary at a time of fiscal distress and declining government employment. And yet restoring opportunities for future generations requires making sacrifices in the present.

Given the structural changes under way in the U.S. economy — especially the growing premium on highly educated workers at the top end of the value-added chain — education should be boosted. As many people as possible should be able to compete in that part of the economy. But if this goal is clear, the ways to achieve it are less so. Improving the performance of the educational system has been a priority for some years, yet the results are in doubt.

For example, the Organization for Economic Cooperation and Development administers a set of standardized tests, the Programme for International Student Assessment, across more than 60 countries, advanced and developing, to measure the cognitive skills of teenage students. The United States ranks close to the average in reading and science and well behind most countries in math. The problems in the quality and effectiveness of parts of the U.S. educational system have been recognized for some time. Numerous attempts to improve matters, including administering national standardized tests and providing merit-based compensation, have thus far yielded inconclusive results. And the problem extends beyond the school system. A lack of commitment to education in families and in communities makes the entire field of education seem unattractive, demoralizing dedicated teachers and turning off talented students from teaching.

That, in turn, reduces the incentives of communities to value the primacy of education. To break this pattern, it will be necessary to shift communities' — and the country's — values about education through moral leadership, at both the community and the national levels. Creating attractive employment opportunities conditional on educational success is another important incentive. One comes full circle, in other words: increased educational effectiveness is needed for the United States to be competitive, and the promise of rewarding employment is a necessary incentive for committing to improving education.

As important as education is, it cannot be the whole solution; the United States will not educate its way out of its problems. Both the federal and state governments must pursue complementary lines of attack. They should invest in infrastructure, which would create jobs in the short term and raise the return on private-sector investment in the medium to longer term.

They should also invest in technologies that could expand employment opportunities in the tradable sector of the U.S. economy at income levels other than the very top. The private sector will have to help guide these investments because it has much of the relevant knowledge about where these opportunities might lie. But this effort will also require the participation of the public sector.

The U.S. government already invests heavily in science and technology but not with job creation as its primary focus; that has generally been viewed only as a beneficial side effect. It is time to devote public funding to developing infrastructure and the technological base of the U.S. economy with the specific goal of restoring competitiveness and expanding employment in the tradable sector.

The tax structure also needs to be reformed. It should be simplified and reconfigured to promote competitiveness, investment, and employment. And both loopholes and distorting incentives should be eliminated. For example, corporate tax rates and tax rates on investment returns should be lowered in order to make the United

States more attractive for business and investment. MNCs with earnings outside the United States currently have a strong incentive to keep their earnings abroad and reinvest them abroad because earnings are taxed both where they are earned and also in the United States if they are repatriated.

Lower tax rates would mean a loss in revenue for the U.S. government, but that could be replaced by taxes on consumption, which would have the added benefit of helping shift the composition of demand from domestic to foreign — a necessary move if the United States wants to avoid high unemployment and an unsustainable current account deficit.

But even these measures may not be sufficient. Globalization has redefined the competition for employment and incomes in the United States. Tradeoffs will have to be made between the two. Germany clearly chose to protect employment in the industries of its tradable sector that came under competitive threat. Now, U.S. policymakers must choose, too.

Some will argue that global market forces should simply be allowed to operate without interference. Tampering with market outcomes, the argument goes, risks distorting incentives and reducing efficiency and innovation.

But this is not the only approach, nor is it the best one. The distribution of income across many advanced economies (and major emerging economies) differs markedly. For example, the ratio of the average income of the top 20 percent of the population to the average income of the bottom 20 percent is four to one in Germany and eight to one in the United States. Many other advanced countries have flatter income distributions than the United States, suggesting that tradeoffs between market forces and equity are possible. The U.S. government needs to face up to them.

Experimenting the Way Forward

The massive changes in the global economy since World War II have had overwhelmingly positive effects. Hundreds of millions of people in the developing world have escaped poverty, and more will in the future. The global economy will continue to grow — probably at least threefold over the next 30 years. One person's gain is not necessarily another's loss; global growth is not even close to a zero-sum game. But globalization hurts some subgroups within some countries, including the advanced economies.

The Role of Vocational Education and Training Curricula in Economic Development

Globalization has become one of the crucial topics of discussion and concern in recent times, since it has a decisive impact upon our lives. Therefore, if we are to compete on the global stage and meet the globalization challenges successfully we need to make significant improvements in terms of maximizing the effectiveness of the vocational education and training instruction based on specific design of curricula.

It is widely accepted that we live in a world where knowledge and technologies are renewed at an accelerating pace. To respond to the resulting updated requirements of economic trends and goals, our educational planning has to be shifted to new forms of instructional content and delivery.

Consequently, globalization and the new emerging economic and social order demand new policies and strategies to educational processes. To this effect, the educational and training reforms have to be based on the market needs assessment identified by appropriate market research.

The problem statements consisted of three major types of questions: (a) Will school alone achieve the goals of competencies-based education? (causal) (b) To what extent should formal education prepare people to work? (relationship) and (c) To what extent should vocational education and training respond to work? (impact).

Skills and the Knowledge Economy Across South Asia

Globalization and the knowledge economy pose numerous challenges as well as opportunities for developing countries, including those in the South Asia Region (SAR). Expanding trade and globalization of production and foreign capital make continuous learning over the work-life an imperative, as skills acquired in schools and in the workplace become obsolete more quickly and new and more complex skills are needed to respond to accelerating technological change.

Global flows of goods, services and know-how also create pressures for economies to restructure, as some industries decline and new opportunities arise in others; these forces, in turn, create demand for re-skilling of those made redundant and for skills-upgrading and training in new skills for others employed in new industries.

How educational and training systems respond to these challenges will have far reaching implications for economic growth and competitiveness of countries in the SAR, and for income growth, employment, job creation, and poverty reduction.

Policymakers in many SAR countries are currently grappling with the challenges of reforming their education and training systems. There is a broader debate going on whether to vocationalise secondary education to better prepare school graduates for the new skill challenges of the workplace and, given the magnitude of demands on the public education and training systems, on what the role of the private sector should be in education and training provision.

While globalization has increased economic growth in some countries, it has also demanded heightened competitiveness. Production systems based on new technologies that enable greater productivity and flexibility as well as workers with updated skills and more independent initiative are required if industries are to survive in this climate. Thus, with the demand for greater productivity, new technologies are radiating into almost every industrial sector, including the traditional labour-intensive industries. Rapid technological change makes skills obsolete very quickly and demands higher levels of initiative and more frequent retraining. This changing technological scenario may also require workers to change jobs several times during their working lives.

The basic challenge of the globalized economy is therefore the requirement to adjust and compete in a rapidly changing environment. Central to the effort to compete in the twenty-first century is the preparation of a productive, flexible workforce. Every country will be obliged to enable its citizens to acquire the skills necessary to survive and to improve their quality of life because the demands of the workplace are likely to leave people without skills unemployed and unemployable.

Yet there are large numbers of school leavers worldwide who are unlikely to obtain formal employment and who are even more in need of these survival skills. Inadequate opportunities for formal employment are now becoming a reality in most countries, developed as well as developing. The realization is growing that individuals will have to be prepared for a range of employment options, including self-employment. Many may have to hold down two or more jobs simultaneously in order to maintain a reasonable quality of life.

TVE is the component of education most directly concerned with the acquisition of the knowledge and skills required by workers in most manufacturing and service industries. Although TVE may not create jobs, it can provide people with the skills required to give them better opportunities for self-employment, wage employment, re-employment and even informal sector initiatives. TVE needs to strengthen basic cognitive learning to give students and trainees more flexibility to meet the changing requirements of the workplace.

It must also help them develop the competence to move on to higher learning. Newly emerging high technology jobs often require job seekers to have immediate 'plug-and-play' skills, cross-disciplinary knowledge, better communication and interpersonal skills, and the ability to work in teams. Other attributes such as motivation, creativity, self-adjustment, commitment, attention to detail and a sense of responsibility are critical to success and must take equal priority to functional skills in TVE. Initial training must also equip people with fundamental knowledge that will enable them to retrain themselves in mid-career for a change of trade or profession.

Bibliography

Anthony Landale: *Gower Handbook of Training and Development*, Gower Publishing, Ltd., UK, 1999.

Aron, L. Y., & Zweig, J. M.: *Educational Alternatives for Vulnerable Youth: Student Needs, Program Types, and Research Directions*, Urban Institute, Washington, DC, 2008.

Babbie, E.R.: *The Practice of Social Research,* Belmont, CA: Wadsworth, 1995.

Brick, Jean: *Academic Culture: A Student's Guide to Studying at University*, National Centre for English Language Teaching and Research, Sydney, N.S.W, 2006.

Camp, W.G.: *Professional Development of Teachers of Vocational Education*, University of California at Berkeley, Berkeley, CA, 1988.

Chism, N. V. N.: *Faculty as Teachers: Taking stock of What We Know*, National Center on Postsecondary Teaching, Learning, and Assessment, State College, PA, 1994.

Dent, K.S.: *Informal Agencies of Education: Proceedings of the 1977 Annual Conference of the History of Education Society of Great Britain*, Leicester, History of Education Society, 1979.

Elliott, J. : *Action Research for Educational Change*, Milton Keynes, Open University, 1991.

Finch, C.R., Reneau, C.E., Faulkner, S.L. Gregson, J.A., Hernandez- Gantes, V.M., & Linkous, G.A.: *Case Studies in Vocational Education Administration: Leadership in Action,* National Center for Research in Vocational Education, Berkeley, CA, 1992.

Gibbons, S., & Telhaj, S.: *Mobility and School Disruption,* Centre for the Economics of Education, London, 2007.

Heath-Camp, B., & Camp, W.G.: *Professional Development of Beginning Vocational Teachers: Implementation System,* University of California at Berkeley, Berkeley, CA, 1992.

Kolb, D.A.: *Experiential Learning: Experience as the Source of Learning and Development*, Prentice Hall, New Jersey, 1984.

Lee, V. E., & Burkam, D. T.: *Inequality at the Starting gate: Social background Differences in Achievement as Children begin School*, Economic Policy Institute, Washington, DC, 2002.

Marcinkiewicz, H., & Doyle, Terrence, D.: *New Faculty Professional Development: Planning an Ideal Program*, New Forums Press, 2004.

Mayer, R. E.: *Learning and Instruction,* Pearson Education, Inc., New Jersey, 2008.

Nurullah, S. and J.P. Naik: *A Students History of Education in India,* New Delhi, Macmillan, 1974.

Paris, K.A.: *A Leadership Model for Planning and Implementing Change for School-to-work Transition,* Center on Education and Work, University of Wisconsin-Madison, Madison, WI, 1994.

Rumberger, R. W., Larson, K. A., Ream, R. K., &. Palardy, G. J.: *The Educational Consequence of Mobility for California Students and Schools,* Policy Analysis of California Education, Berkeley, CA, 1999.

Sorcinelli, M. D., Austin, A., Eddy, P. & Beach, A.: *Creating the Future of Faculty Development: Learning from the Past, Understanding the Present,* Anker Publishing Company, Bolton MA, 2005.

Thrupp, J. & Willmott. : *Educational Management in Managerialist Times: Beyond the Textual Apologists*, Maidenhead, UK, 2003.

Williams G. : *Paying for Education beyond Eighteen: An Examination of Issues and Options,* Council for I0ndustry in Higher Education, London, 1996.

Wilkerson, L., & Lewis, K. G.: *A Guide to Faculty Development: Practical Advice, Examples, and Resources,* Anker Publishing, Bolton, MA, 2002.

Index

❑❑❑